THE BṚHAD-DEVATĀ

THE
BṚHAD-DEVATĀ

attributed to

ŚAUNAKA

A SUMMARY OF THE DEITIES AND MYTHS OF THE ṚGVEDA

CRITICALLY EDITED IN THE ORIGINAL SANSKRIT WITH AN INTRODUCTION AND SEVEN APPENDICES, AND TRANSLATED INTO ENGLISH WITH CRITICAL AND ILLUSTRATIVE NOTES

by

ARTHUR ANTHONY MACDONELL

Boden Professor of Sanskrit in the University of Oxford and Fellow of Balliol College

PART I

INTRODUCTION AND TEXT
AND APPENDICS

MOTILAL BANARSIDASS PUBLISHING HOUSE SINCE 1903

MOTILAL BANARSIDASS
PUBLISHING HOUSE • DELHI

Email: naraina@mlbd.in • Website: www.mlbd.in

@mlbdofficial

*3rd Reprint : Delhi, **2023***
First Published Cambridge, 1904

ISBN: 978-93-5760-113-9 (Hardcover set)
ISBN: 978-93-5760-095-8 (Paperback set)

Printed & Published by
Rajendra P Jain *for*
Motilal Banarsidass Publishing House
A-44, Naraina Industrial Area, Phase I,
New Delhi–110 028 (INDIA)
Email: naraina@mlbd.in Website: www.mlbd.in
Tel.: (+91-11)4751 1592
Showroom:
4637/20, F-2, Hari Sadan, First Floor, Ansari Road, Daryaganj
Delhi–110 002 (Opp. Fire Station) ***Tel.*** : (+91-11)4559 7999

TO

PROFESSOR ERNST LEUMANN

OF THE UNIVERSITY OF STRASSBURG

IN GRATEFUL RECOLLECTION OF HIS MANY

FRIENDLY SERVICES TO ME IN CONNEXION

WITH MY SANSKRIT STUDIES

I DEDICATE THIS

WORK

CONTENTS

INTRODUCTION

1. How I came to edit the Bṛhaddevatā.

AMONG the secondary works of Vedic literature, the Bṛhaddevatā has always attracted a considerable share of interest on the part of Vedic scholars. When Roth, in 1846, published his treatise, Zur Litteratur und Geschichte des Weda, he knew the work only from the quotations occurring in the commentaries of Ṣaḍguruśiṣya and Sāyaṇa, which were then, of course, accessible in manuscript only. He remarks, however (p. 49), that copies would in all probability yet be found in India. Not long after this a MS. (b) of the Bṛhaddevatā was actually acquired, along with the Chambers collection of Sanskrit MSS., by the Royal Library at Berlin. Adalbert Kuhn made it the basis of his account of the Bṛhaddevatā published in the first volume (pp. 101–120) of Indische Studien (1850). Kuhn transcribed this MS., subsequently adding collations from another MS. (h), which Haug procured at Poona in 1865, and which is now in the Royal Library at Munich. As he found these two MSS. insufficient for the purpose, Kuhn was unable to carry out his intention of publishing an edition of the Bṛhaddevatā.

Meanwhile Max Müller had obtained from India, in the sixties, three modern copies by the aid of Drs. Bühler and Bhāu Dāji. He, too, seems at one time to have contemplated editing the Bṛhaddevatā; for among his papers I found a transcript, in his own hand, coming down to the tenth Varga of the second Adhyāya[1]. But the inadequacy of his MS. material doubtless deterred him from proceeding any further.

Later on, Dr. Thibaut, while resident in Oxford as Max Müller's assistant, made extensive collations with a view to bringing out a critical edition of the Bṛhaddevatā. But he, too, relinquished the project, being convinced that a text constituted from the MS. material at his disposal, would prove too conjectural in its character.

[1] See Wickremasinghe's Catalogue of the Max Müller Sanskrit MSS. in the Journal of the Royal Asiatic Society, 1902, p. 641, no. 57.

In 1886 Professor Lanman contemplated the work of editing the Bṛhaddevatā; but the difficulty of obtaining access to some of the indispensable MSS., together with the pressure of other work, obliged him to desist from the enterprise. He then asked me to undertake the task of editing the text critically, together with a translation and various appendices, for the Harvard Oriental Series. I gladly accepted the offer, as I had already collated a number of passages in the work for my edition of Ṣaḍguruśiṣya[1], as well as for an article published in the Journal of the Royal Asiatic Society[2], and was, moreover, generally familiar with the auxiliary literature of the Ṛg-veda. Prof. Lanman accordingly handed over to me in 1897 his material, comprising Kuhn's collations and notes, together with a modern MS. (k) which Kuhn had obtained from India.

2. Rājendralāla Mitra's edition.

While Professor Lanman was still contemplating doing the work himself, the late Dr. Rājendralāla Mitra began, in 1889, to bring out, in the Bibliotheca Indica, his edition of the Bṛhaddevatā, the last fasciculus of which appeared in 1892. Soon after I had set to work on the text, I mentioned to Prof. Bühler, in the course of conversation, the task on which I was engaged, and I well remember his asking whether I really thought it worth while to edit the work afresh. Indeed, a cursory examination of Mitra's edition, with its array of critical notes, might easily lead one to suppose that little remained for a second editor to do, at least in regard to the constitution of the text. Such a supposition would, however, be very erroneous. Mitra's edition is in reality entirely inadequate and altogether untrustworthy as a basis for further research. Its value I estimate at less than that of a single good MS.; for it is full of defects from which such a MS. would be free. Besides a large number of misprints, it contains many impossible readings taken from incorrect MSS., omissions of lines, repetitions of lines, insertions of undoubtedly spurious lines, and lacunae. Thus, for example, in the second Adhyāya (p. 56) seven ślokas (128–134) are repeated, without word or comment, in promiscuous order, from among the preceding thirty ślokas; and in the fifth Adhyāya (p. 148) there is a lacuna of fifteen ślokas[3] due to pure carelessness, for there is no sign of any such lacuna in any of the nine MSS. I have examined. Mitra's edition is, moreover, eclectic on no recog-

[1] Kātyāyana's Sarvānukramaṇī, with extracts from Ṣaḍguruśiṣya's commentary; Anecdota Oxoniensia, Oxford, 1886.

[2] Volume for 1894, pp. 11–29: 'Two Legends from the Bṛhaddevatā.'

[3] Bṛhaddevatā v. 112–126 in my text.

nizable principle; for the reading chosen is not only constantly opposed to the predominant evidence of the MSS., but is frequently by no means the best *a priori*. Based mainly on one MS (or two which are practically identical), it shows haphazard selections and additions from MSS. of another recension. I have estimated that the edition contains one error of some kind on the average for every śloka, making a total of about 1200. I may refer the reader to p. 85 as a specimen, where a passage of three ślokas (93–95), as a comparison with my text (iii. 95–97) will show, contains twelve mistakes, and is consequently quite unintelligible.

Since Mitra gives no information whatever about the MS. material he used, his critical notes are hardly of any value as far as his own edition is concerned. They have, nevertheless, proved quite useful to me in the light of the MSS. which have been at my disposal. Judging by his notes, I infer that Mitra employed seven MSS. in the constitution of his text. These MSS. were sold after his death. Mahāmahopādhyāya Haraprasāda S'āstrī very kindly took much trouble in tracing them for me to their present owner; but my strenuous efforts to obtain access to them by purchase or loan have proved absolutely futile.

3. General account of the MSS. and their relationship.

For the purposes of my edition nine MSS. have been directly available. Eight of these fall into two well-defined groups, representing a shorter and a longer recension of the Bṛhaddevatā. The former group I have designated A, the latter B (suggestive of the Berlin and Bodleian codices which belong to it). The ninth MS. belongs, as will be seen, in a sense to both groups. To these nine may be added the seven which were used by Mitra. It is quite certain from his critical notes, in the light of the material accessible to me, that four of his MSS. belong to the A, and three to the B group. Thus the evidence of altogether sixteen MSS. has been available, directly or indirectly, in the constitution of my text. Of this total, eight belong to A. This group has **two subdivisions**: the first (A^1) comprising the Haug MS. (h), two of Max Müller's (m^2, m^3), Bhāu Dāji's (d), and Rājendralāla's No. 3 (r^3: called by him *ga*); the second (A^2) comprising Rājendralāla's Nos. 1, 4, 6 ($r^1r^4r^6$ = *ka gha ca*). The latter three are practically identical, for their readings are almost invariably the same, and often agree in opposition to the readings of all the other MSS. of both families. The readings of A^2 are on the whole inferior to those of A^1, being often clearly alterations of the original text; yet it is in some cases apparent that A^2 has preserved the correct reading as compared with all the other MSS. of both recensions. It is on A^2 that Mitra mainly relied in constituting his text[1]. It is to be noted that A^2 has some affinities with b, one of the MSS. of the B group.

Another MS. (m^1), which was procured by Max Müller from Bhāu Dāji in 1861, also belongs to A in that part of the text which is common to both recensions; here its readings nearly always agree with the subdivision A^1. This MS. occupies a very peculiar position, for it also contains all the additional matter of the longer recension represented by the B group. The fact that when the same line occurs in different forms in the two recensions, both forms are often (e.g. v. 13; vi. 15) found in this MS., shows that it had a composite origin: it must have been copied from a MS. of the A group, while the passages there wanting were added from a MS. of the B group.

I may here observe that the MSS. of the A group (including m^1) are much more correct than those of the B group.

B, comprising seven or (if m^1 be included) eight MSS., contains four subdivisions:—

1. b. The Chambers codex of the Berlin Library, which, though very incorrect, is occasionally the only MS. which has preserved the true reading.

2. f. The FitzEdward Hall MS. in the Bodleian Library, which though also very incorrect, is of importance in constituting that part of the text which is peculiar to the B recension. Closely connected with this MS. are three others, viz. one in the Cambridge University Library (c), Kuhn's (k), and Rājendralāla's No. 2 (r^2 = *kha*).

3. r^5 and r^7, two of Mitra's MSS. (= *ṅa* and *pustakāntaram*). They occupy together a somewhat independent position in the B group, as on the one hand they have a few additional ślokas not occurring in the remaining MSS., and on the other they alone sometimes preserve the correct reading.

4. m^1. This is the Max Müller MS. which belongs in part to both recensions. It is much more correct than any of the regular B MSS.; its readings diverge considerably from theirs and are often better. It has proved of great value to me; for without its aid I should have been unable to emend satisfactorily some of the corrupt passages in the longer recension (e.g. iii. 95–97; vii. 128, 129).

Six of these MSS. have a more or less independent value, viz. h, r^1, m^1, b, f, r^5 as each of them, in several cases, is the only one which furnishes the correct reading.

[1] It is evident that Mitra places the whole passage ii. 69–127 (pp. 53–56) in parentheses, because it is wanting in r^1 r^4 (see his footnote, p. 53), while the fragments contained in i. 28–134 (p. 56) are doubtless derived from the latter MSS.

The relationship of all the MSS. may be made clear by the following diagram:

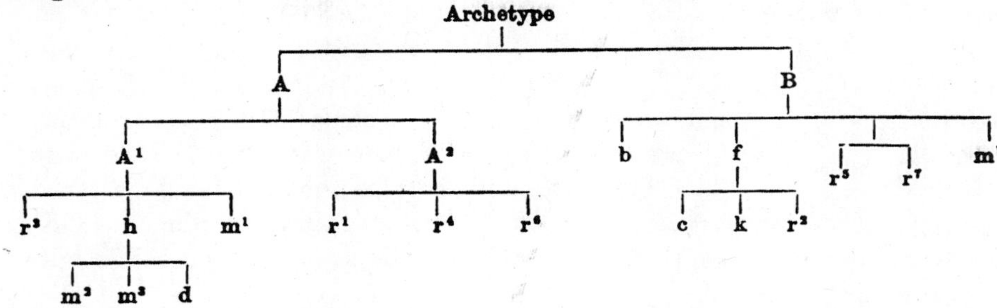

4. Detailed account of the Bṛhaddevatā MSS.

The A Group. 1. The most important MS. in this group, and the least incorrect of all the Bṛhaddevatā MSS. I have used, is **h** (= Haug), No. 43 of the Haug collection in the Royal Library at Munich. It consists of seventy-three leaves of paper, and is clearly written. Though very fairly correct on the whole, it contains a good many mistakes and corruptions in detail. It bears the name 'M. Haug,' and the date 'Poona, 11 März 1865.' On the title-page is written: *atha bṛhaddevatānukramaṇīprārambhaḥ.* Above and below this title, the page is covered with writing which consists chiefly of quotations from the Bṛhaddevatā itself in regard to the Vaiśvadeva hymns, beginning: *atha vaiśvadevasūkte devatāvicāraḥ: bhinne sūkte vaded eva* (i. 20), &c., and ending *aṣṭame ṣaṣṭhānte ca.* It concludes (fol. 73^b): *iti bṛhaddevatāyām aṣṭamo 'dhyāyaḥ.* In another hand is added: *śake* 1767 (= A. D. 1845) *viśvāvasunāmasaṃvatsare phālgunakṛṣṇatṛtīyāyāṃ candre* [the next four letters are obliterated with yellow pigment, then a strip of white paper, followed by one of blue, is pasted on, covering almost two-thirds of the line] *svārthaṃ paropakārārthaṃ ca śrīdurgācaraṇe 'rpitam.* Below this follow several lines beginning: *amoghanandanaśikṣāyāṃ: lakṣaṇasya virodhe 'pi,* and ending: *śaunakakārikāyām uktam.*

2. **m^2**. This is a modern copy, which belonged to Max Müller, and is now in the University Library at Tokyo. On the outside are written in red pencil the words: 'Sent me by Bühler (present).' It ends: 149 ॥ *Iti bṛhaddevatāyām aṣṭamo 'dhyāyaḥ śake* 1767 (= A. D. 1845) *viśvāvasunāmasaṃvatsare phālgunakṛṣṇatṛtīyāyāṃ candre dātaretyupahvayamaṇirāmabhaṭṭāṅgajagaṅgādhareṇa saṃpāditaṃ svārthaṃ paropakārārthaṃ ca.* Then follows *amoghanandanaśikṣāyām . . . śaunakakārikāyām uktam,* just as in h. This is again followed by an exact reproduction of the contents of the title-page of h: *atha vaiśvadevasūkte,* &c., down to *aṣṭame ṣaṣṭhānte ca.* There can be no doubt that this is a faithful copy of h. Like that MS. the ślokas

are numbered continuously from the beginning, the total, 1049, being the same as in h. Some further details are given in Wickremasinghe's Catalogue of the Max Müller Sanskrit MSS. in the JRAS., 1902, p. 640, no. 56.

3. m³. Another modern copy, which belonged to Max Müller, now at Tokyo. On the outside is written in Max Müller's hand: 'Sent by Dr. Bühler, Sept., 1866. A copy m. o. of the same MS. from which my other MS. (b) [= m²], likewise sent by Dr. Bühler, was taken.' It is dated *śake* 1788 (= A. D. 1866). The last page contains the additional matter at the conclusion of h, *amoghanandanaśikṣāyām*, &c., exactly reproduced. This, too, is undoubtedly a copy of h. Further details are given by Wickremasinghe, p. 640, no. 55.

4. d. A modern undated MS. of forty-two leaves, which formerly belonged to Bhāu Dāji, and is now in the Library of the Royal Asiatic Society, Bombay. When I wrote to Bombay for the loan of it, I had great hopes that it would prove to be the original of m¹. But a brief inspection, on its arrival, unfortunately showed that this too is a faithful copy of h. The title-page is blank, but fol. 1ᵇ reproduces the contents of the title-page of h: *atha vaiśvadevasūkte*, &c., and the additional matter at the end of h is likewise exactly copied *amoghanandanaśikṣāyām*, &c. It differs from h only in the numbering of the ślokas from the fourth Adhyāya onwards, where h goes wrong. h, and these three copies, as well as m¹, all agree in the mistake of describing the seventh Adhyāya as the sixth.

5. r³. This MS. of Mitra's, described by him as *ga*, is very closely allied to h, almost invariably agreeing with the readings of that MS., when the latter differs from all the rest (cp. the various readings of v. 11). It is therefore probably either the original or a copy of h; but an inspection would be necessary to decide the question of priority between the two. It may be identical with the MS. of the Bṛhaddevatā stated in one of the Bombay catalogues to have been sent on loan to Calcutta. It appears to be complete, as it is quoted by Mitra from the beginning to the end of his edition.

6, 7, 8. r¹, r⁴, r⁶. These are the MSS. of Mitra, respectively designated by him as *ka*, *gha*, and *ca*. Mitra's critical notes show that they are practically identical in their readings. The first two, being referred to from the beginning of the edition, appear to be nearly complete; the last six vargas of the introduction are, however, wanting in them (ii. 97–127, pp. 53–56). The third, r⁶, is incomplete, the whole of the introduction, or nearly two Adhyāyas, being omitted; it does not begin to be quoted till ii. 137 (p. 57). These three MSS. omit all the ślokas wanting in h, besides a good many more, while they contain the additional matter found in h. Their readings frequently agree in opposition to all the other MSS.[1] Either r^1 or r^4 was probably the original of the other two, and may have been the only MS. which, according to a letter of his to Max Müller, dated Dec. 3, 1873, Mitra at that time possessed. He there says: 'Of the Bṛhaddevatā I have an only MS. extending to eight chapters. It is tolerably correct, but apparently corrupt.' On the relation of these three MSS. the following anecdote may possibly throw some light. According to a rule of the series, no text may be edited in the Bibliotheca Indica unless based on at least three independent MSS. A certain Calcutta scholar was once anxious to edit a text of which he unfortunately had only one MS. This, however, did not prove an insuperable difficulty: he set his Pandits to work, 'and then there were three.'

The readings of these three MSS. are on the whole inferior to those of h and r^3, but in a few cases they alone have undoubtedly preserved the correct form of the text as compared with all the remaining MSS. (cp. i. 57; i. 75; i. 126; ii. 129)[2].

9. m^1. This is a modern MS. which formerly belonged to Max Müller and is now in the University Library at Tokyo. It is dated *śake* 1783 (= A. D. 1861), being a copy made from a MS. which belonged to Bhāu Dāji, but the whereabouts of which I have been unable to trace. It is the copy referred to by Bhāu Dāji in a letter to Max Müller, dated Bombay, March 12, 1862, in which he says he is forwarding a copy of S'aunaka's Bṛhaddevatā from a MS. in his collection. This copy has the peculiarity of representing both groups of MSS. On the one hand, in that part of the text which is common to both groups, it agrees in its readings with A, in particular with h and r^3 (A^1), and in this part may therefore be accounted an A MS. On the other hand, it contains all the additional matter of the B group, and to this extent belongs to that group also. Owing to its independence and comparative correctness, it has proved more valuable to me than any of the other B MSS. I would have given much to trace the source from which it is derived. It shows a special affinity to h in two points. In the first place, the end of the seventh Adhyāya is here wrongly described (as also in the copies m^2, m^3, d) with the words *iti bṛhaddevatāyām ṣaṣṭho 'dhyāyaḥ*. Secondly, this MS., like h, numbers the ślokas consecutively, the final figure, however (owing to the additional matter in B), being 1281, while in h it is 1049.

The B Group. 1. **b.** A MS. belonging to the Royal Library at

[1] Thus in Bṛhaddevatā i. 11 all the B MSS., as well as h r^3 m^1, read *'bhidhīyate*, while r^1 r^4 have *pradṛśyate* (cp. also the various readings in i. 18; ii. 158; iv. 16, &c.).

[2] Instances of a certain affinity between these MSS. and b of the B group are to be found; cp. for instance the various readings under i. 124, 126, 127.

Berlin (Chambers 197); consisting of ninety-six leaves. It is well preserved and clearly written, but is very incorrect. It begins: *śrīgaṇeśāya namaḥ. mantradṛgbhyo namaskṛtvā*, &c.; and ends: *viṃśati jyotir uttamam viṃśati jyotir uttamam iti* ॥ 28 ॥ *yāskāya namaḥ* ॥ *oṃ yāskāya namaḥ* ॥ *iti bṛhaddevatāyām aṣṭamo 'dhyāyaḥ samāptaḥ* ॥ *iti bṛhaddevatā samāptāḥ* ॥ *saṃvat* 1711 (= A.D. 1654) *varṣe vaiśāṣaśuklaṣaṣṭhyāṃ budhe likhitam idaṃ* ॥ [1] It occupies a somewhat independent position among the B MSS., showing some affinity with A^2.

2. f. A MS. in the Bodleian Library [2], presented by the late Dr. FitzEdward Hall. It is not dated, but has the appearance of being from 250 to 300 years old. It is written in a somewhat illegible hand, and is very incorrect. It is, nevertheless, in some cases, the only MS. which preserves the right reading. It is the original from which, probably, all the following three MSS. were copied.

3. c. A copy of FitzEdward Hall's Bodleian MS. (f) made at Calcutta in 1862 and presented to the Cambridge University Library by the late Prof. Cowell in 1875. I examined this MS. at Cambridge, but as it is admittedly a copy of f, I have given no collations from it.

4. k. This is a modern copy, which belonged to the late Adalbert Kuhn, now the property of Prof. E. Kuhn of Munich, and lent to me by him through Prof. Lanman for the purposes of this edition. On the fly-leaf is written 'A. Kuhn, 1865.' It is dated *saṃvat* 1921 (= A.D. 1864). Written in Devanāgarī on bluish paper, it consists of fifty leaves, with eighteen lines to the page, which, as in European books, is longer than it is broad. This MS. is very inaccurate, agreeing closely in errors and omissions with f. It contains many additional mistakes owing to the somewhat illegible writing of the latter MS. My critical notes prove, I think conclusively, that it is a copy of f. It must have been written before that MS. left India.

5. r^2. A MS. of Mitra's (= *kha*), which his critical notes show to agree so closely with f, that I have little doubt it is another copy made from FitzEdward Hall's MS. before it left India.

6, 7. r^5, r^7. These two MSS. of Mitra's, designated by him as *ṅa* and *pustakāntaram* respectively, agree very closely. They occupy a somewhat independent position in the B group, as they alone occasionally preserve the correct reading (e.g. *carūṇām* in iv. 29). In a few cases they also have additional ślokas not found in any of the other MSS. A correspondent, writing from Calcutta in 1898, informed me that one

[1] Described more fully in Weber's Catalogue of Sanskrit MSS., Berlin, 1853, p. 10, No. 47.

[2] Described more fully in Winternitz and Keith's forthcoming Catalogue of the Additional Sanskrit MSS. in the Bodleian Library, p. 21.

of Mitra's Bṛhaddevatā MSS. had belonged to his 'travelling Pandit,' but had been sold after Mitra's death along with the rest. This was perhaps r^7, the description of which as 'another MS.,' *pustakāntaram*, would thus be explained.

8. m^1. This MS., which partly belongs to the B group, has already been described as No. 9 of group A.

5. The Nītimañjarī MSS.

As the Nītimañjarī[1] quotes very largely—to the extent of about 180 ślokas[2]—from the Bṛhaddevatā, I considered it advisable to collate all the MSS. of that work accessible to me. Mr. A. B. Keith very kindly undertook to constitute a text of these passages from four MSS.[3] (a b c d), which text I designate by n in the critical notes. To these four were afterwards added three other MSS. (g h m), from which Mr. Keith furnished me with supplementary collations. When I give various readings from the Nītimañjarī, I indicate the particular MS. in parentheses; thus 'n (m),' 'n (b),' &c. I now append a brief account of these Nītimañjarī MSS. based on Mr. Keith's notes.

1. a. Prof. Kielhorn's MS., now in the University Library at Göttingen, is a copy (made in 1869) of a codex written in 1778 A.D. It contains all the eight Aṣṭakas complete.

2. b. India Office Library, No. 1649, dating from about 1750, contains the first four Aṣṭakas only.

3. c. India Office Library, No. 966, dating from about 1650, contains Aṣṭakas 3–5 (3 being in a different hand).

4. d. India Office Library, No. 966, date about 1650; contains Aṣṭakas 2, 5, 6, 7, all in one hand. Aṣṭakas 2 and 6 are fragmentary.

5. g. This and the following MS. have the appearance of being a single codex, but are in reality two fragmentary MSS. They belong to the Government Sanskrit College, Benares, having been sent by Mr. Ralph Griffith to Max Müller, among whose papers they were found after his death. g contains Aṣṭakas i–v. 13, its date being probably about 1600 A.D.

6. h. Contains Aṣṭakas ii. 9–viii, and is dated *saṃvat* 1684 (= A.D. 1627).

7. m. This MS. belonged to Max Müller, and is now in the Tokyo

[1] On this work see Kielhorn, Indian Antiquary, v. 116; Göttinger Nachrichten, 1891, p. 181 f.; Peterson, Second Report, 1883–4, p. 8; A. B. Keith, JRAS., 1900, pp. 127–136; Sieg, Sagenstoffe des Ṛgveda, Stuttgart, 1902, pp. 37–41.

[2] See Appendix v, p. 134 f.

[3] Of these Mr. Keith gives a short account in the JRAS., 1900, p. 127.

University Library. With the exception of a few small lacunae it is complete. It is dated *śake* 1786 (= A.D. 1864). It is described in Wickremasinghe's Catalogue of the Max Müller Sanskrit MSS., p. 642, no. 61.

According to Mr. Keith these seven MSS. fall into two groups: A, comprising a, b, m; and B, comprising c, d, g, h. A represents the more modern group, and shows a somewhat simplified text. Of this group m is perhaps the best. In the B group, g and h correspond on the whole, and have a general resemblance to c and d. The extract of the Ulwar MS. given by Peterson agrees with g (beginning) and h (end).

In the quoted Bṛhaddevatā passages, the Nītimañjarī MSS. follow the text of the longer recension (B) in nearly all decisive passages; but the quotations seem to have been very carelessly copied.

6. Two recensions of the Bṛhaddevatā.

An examination of these two main groups of MSS. shows that B (or the longer recension) contains 133 ślokas not to be found in A, while A has 18 not to be found in B. The question here arises, what is the relation of these two groups or recensions? A few years ago I read the Bṛhaddevatā critically with three of my advanced pupils (one of whom was Mr. A. B. Keith), in order to teach them how to collate MSS. and to constitute a correct text from them. At that time I formed the opinion that the shorter recension was the original one, as the extensions in B produced the general impression of superfluous matter. Continued study has, however, convinced me that the additions of the longer recension belonged, on the whole, to the original text, and that A is an abridgement [1].

This conclusion rests chiefly on two arguments. In the first place, the text of the Sarvānukramaṇī is not only based throughout on the Bṛhaddevatā as one of its main sources, but actually contains, although itself a Sūtra work, a large number of metrical passages from the Bṛhaddevatā embedded in its text: several of these passages are taken from the additional matter peculiar to B [2].

The second argument is founded on the length of the vargas into which each Adhyāya is divided. The normal number of ślokas in a varga is five [3]. The fifty-eight vargas of the first two Adhyāyas (in which the text of

[1] My text of the Bṛhaddevatā contains 1224 ślokas, of which 1073 are common to both recensions; A has 1091, B 1206. The original form of the text may have contained nearly 1200.

[2] The evidence for this will be found collected in Appendix vi, Relation of the Bṛhaddevatā to other Texts, pp. 147–153.

[3] This is derived from the division of the text of the Ṛg-veda, where the normal number of the stanzas contained in each varga is five, as far as the length of the hymn will admit of it.

A has no omissions) contain 289 ślokas, or one śloka less than 5 × 58 (= 290). These two Adhyāyas contain no vargas with fewer than four ślokas, and only four as short as that. The omissions in the text of A do not begin to appear till the middle of the third Adhyāya (iii. 62). We find that four ślokas are here omitted (85^{cd}–89^{ab}) at the end of the seventeenth and the beginning of the eighteenth varga, and two more in the nineteenth (95^{cd}–97^{ab}); yet the end of the nineteenth varga is indicated by the figure 19 after the same śloka [1] in A as in B. In other words, though the three vargas in A contain only nine ślokas, or an average of three for each, the old number 19 remains at the end of the third varga in A as well as B. The same thing occurs over and over again in the A MSS.

The conclusion that A is an abridgement of the original text is corroborated by another feature in the numbering of the A MSS. It is only the A group that, in addition to numbering the vargas, also numbers the ślokas continuously from the beginning of the book to the end. This seems almost certainly due to the fact that, by the omission of certain passages, the number of the varga (if occurring within such passages) also disappeared, and that the figures indicating the end of the vargas thus became intermittent in the shorter recension. Consequently a copyist would, I think, naturally come to adopt the additional method of numbering the ślokas of the whole work consecutively. It is obvious that this method of enumeration affords many opportunities of error. As a matter of fact, h shows frequent mistakes in this part of its numbering. Hence the figures of the final śloka, 1049, in h, as well as 1231 in m¹, do not correspond to the actual total of ślokas contained in those two codices.

7. Critical principles followed in constituting the Text.

In view of the existence of these two recensions, what method, it may be asked, have I adopted in constituting the text? Having arrived at the conclusion that the longer recension represents on the whole the original extent of the Bṛhaddevatā, I have admitted the additional matter of B to the text, with the exception of a few occasional ślokas or half-ślokas, which are clearly spurious, and which have therefore been relegated to the critical notes. Every one of the additional lines of B has, however, been indicated, both in text and translation, by a B prefixed to it. Similarly, the comparatively few ślokas which are peculiar to A are indicated by that letter. Hence the reader can see at a glance what lines are peculiar to either recension. I may here add that the text of the

[1] That is, in h d m² m³ as well as m¹. Mitra does not indicate the vargas in his edition; but it is to be assumed that his A MSS. agree with h in this respect as in others.

Sarvānukramaṇī proves some at least of the additional matter in A to have belonged to the original text of the Bṛhaddevatā [1].

But what method have I followed with regard to that part of the text which is common to both recensions, viz. six-sevenths of the whole work (or 1073 out of 1224 ślokas)? Now in this common portion of the text the divergence of the two recensions does not in the vast majority of cases go beyond a word or two in the line, A having as a rule the correct reading, while B has a corruption. Sometimes, however, the divergence cannot be accounted for by the same original reading; for while in these instances the matter is usually identical, the wording of part, or of all of the line, is entirely different [2]. In this latter case I have, owing to the much greater correctness of the A MSS., followed the principle of adopting, when other things are equal, the readings of A. I have been confirmed in this by an examination of Ṣaḍguruśiṣya, who, in his commentary on the Sarvānukramaṇī, quotes about fifty ślokas from the Bṛhaddevatā [3]. I find that he predominantly agrees with the readings of A, though he frequently quotes passages which are only to be found in B. From this I conclude that the readings of the B recension, as known to Ṣaḍguruśiṣya [4], have, in the parts which the two recensions have in common, on the whole been better preserved [5] by A.

It has, however, not by any means been my aim to supply here the text of the A recension pure and simple. I have endeavoured to constitute, by means of all the evidence that can be brought to bear on it, a text approximating as nearly as possible to the original form of the Bṛhaddevatā.

8. External evidence bearing on the text of the Bṛhaddevatā.

I doubt whether, with the exception of the Vedic Saṃhitās, there is any other work of Indian literature upon the text of which so much evidence outside its own MS. material can be concentrated. From the point of view of textual criticism the task of editing the Bṛhaddevatā has therefore proved

[1] See Appendix vi and note on Bṛhaddevatā viii. 137.

[2] The number of cases, in the common text, in which the divergence of wording extends more or less to the whole line, amounts, I think, to hardly twenty. There is no instance in the first Adhyāya, in which the two recensions can hardly be distinguished (there being also no omissions).

[3] Cp. especially the critical notes on v. 50–78. For a list of these quotations see Appendix v, pp. 134, 135.

[4] Ṣaḍguruśiṣya once quotes a passage (v. 64–67) which does not even occur in all the MSS. of the B family.

[5] Sāyaṇa, who quotes nearly as much (see Appendix v) of the Bṛhaddevatā as Ṣaḍguruśiṣya does, on the whole follows B, though he occasionally agrees with A. His relation to the recensions is not very clear, as he sometimes has a different reading when A and B are identical. This may have been due to quoting from memory. I have already mentioned that the Nītimañjarī follows B.

one of extraordinary interest. This external evidence has enabled me, in many cases, to decide on the correct reading, which, judged by the MS. evidcnce alone, would have remained conjectural. It has, at the same time, shown that B has occasionally preserved the original reading, even if in a corrupt form. It has further enabled me to emend with certainty some passages which are corrupt in the MSS. of both recensions [1]. It has in particular enabled me to restore several passages occurring in B only, which, without this aid, would have been desperate.

But in what does this outside evidence consist? In the first place, about one-fifth of the whole Bṛhaddevatā is quoted by Ṣaḍguruśiṣya, Sāyaṇa, and the author of the Nītimañjarī taken together.

In the second place, its text bears an intimate relation to that of the Naighaṇṭuka, the Nirukta, the Sarvānukramaṇī, the Ārṣānukramaṇī, the Anuvākānukramaṇī, and the Ṛgvidhāna; owing to the very nature of the work its connexion with the text of the Ṛg-veda is necessarily very close; the Maitrāyaṇī Saṃhitā, the Kauṣītaki and the Aitareya Brāhmaṇas occasionally throw light on it; and several of its legends are historically linked with those of the Mahābhārata.

9. Intimate relationship to the Nirukta and the Sarvānukramaṇī.

By far the most important relationship among all these works is, however, that which the Bṛhaddevatā bears to the Nirukta and the Sarvānukramaṇī. For it is historically wedged in between these two works in such a way that while it borrows largely from the former, it is borrowed from still more largely by the latter. There are many passages in which the exact words of the Nirukta are repeated, and others in which the diction is only so far modified as is required by the exigencies of metre. The wording of the Sarvānukramaṇī, in all that concerns the deities of the Ṛg-veda, is based on that of the Bṛhaddevatā throughout; and though the Sarvānukramaṇī is a Sūtra work, there are found embedded in its text fifteen anuṣṭubh pādas of the Bṛhaddevatā unaltered, besides about seventy-five others which are only slightly modified, by the omission of a particle, the transposition of a word, or the substitution of another word. There are, moreover, about ten passages which are clearly based in each case on a half-śloka of the Bṛhaddevatā. There is, finally, at least one clear instance of a whole śloka of the Bṛhaddevatā having been adapted by the author of the Sarvānukramaṇī [2]. In other words, what amounts to at least thirty

[1] Examples of such are: *rauśamaḥ* (v. 34), *satpatiḥ* (iii. 70), *antaḥparidhi* (vii. 98), *aindrāgnī* (vii. 119), *anupānīyāḥ* (v. 110), *ṛbīse* (v. 84), *viśvā* (v. 144). See the notes on these passages.

[2] All the evidence for this will be found collected in Appendix vi, pp. 147–153.

ślokas of the text of the Bṛhaddevatā can be unmistakeably traced in the Sarvānukramaṇī. This takes no account of the identity of diction which occurs at every step in the Sarvānukramaṇī, but cannot be shown to have a metrical source. Hence the high value of the Sarvānukramaṇī as a check on the readings of the Bṛhaddevatā is obvious.

With regard to the relationship of the Bṛhaddevatā to the other cognate works attributed to S'aunaka, I may here add that it has a half-śloka and the greater part of the following pāda in common with the Anuvākānukramaṇī. With the Ārṣānukramaṇī it shares three and a half ślokas, and with the Ṛgvidhāna two and a half ślokas. There are besides a number of other passages in which its wording is very similar to that of the two latter works. All this borrowed or common matter will be found collected in parallel columns in Appendix vi, 'Relation of the Bṛhaddevatā to other texts,' pp. 136–154.

10. Date and authorship of the Bṛhaddevatā.

What evidence does the relationship of the Bṛhaddevatā to other texts furnish towards determining the question of its date? An examination of the parallel material supplied in Appendix vi can leave no doubt whatever in regard, at least, to the relative date of the Bṛhaddevatā. From that material it results with certainty that the Bṛhaddevatā, while posterior to the Nirukta, is anterior to the Sarvānukramaṇī. This conclusion at the same time takes us a considerable way towards an approximate estimate of the actual date of our text. It must thus be later than 500 B.C., but earlier than the time of Kātyāyana. Owing to the concise character of their style, both the Sarvānukramaṇī and the S'rauta Sūtra of the White Yajur-veda probably belong to the later Sūtra period. Both works were composed by a Kātyāyana. The Vājasaneyi Anukramaṇī, which has nearly the whole of its introduction in common with that of the Sarvānukramaṇī[1], is also the work of a Kātyāyana. All this points to the author of these works being the same Kātyāyana, who, because the diction of the Sarvānukramaṇī shows several Vedic peculiarities and forms not sanctioned by Pāṇini's grammar[2], could hardly be identical with Pāṇini's commentator of that name. Hence it seems likely that the Sarvānukramaṇī, as a later but still probably pre-Pāṇinean Sūtra, dates from not later than the middle of the fourth century B.C.[3] The Bṛhaddevatā, its chief source, could, therefore,

[1] See my edition of the Sarvānukramaṇī, p. viii, bottom.

[2] Op. cit., p. viii, middle.

[3] This opinion has already been stated by me in my edition of the Sarvānukramaṇī, p. viii, and I see no reason to depart from it. But I do not think that its author can be identical with the grammarian Kātyāyana.

hardly be placed later than 400 B.C. Though ślokas have undoubtedly been added here and there and some modifications of diction have probably crept in, the authenticity of the text as a whole is better guaranteed than that of perhaps any other ancillary Vedic work, by the fragments of it which are found embedded, from beginning to end, in the Sarvānukramaṇī [1], itself a text which has been handed down with peculiar care. The early character of the Bṛhaddevatā is further indicated by its mythological standpoint, which is that of the Vedic triad Agni, Indra, and Sūrya; Indra, moreover, is the predominant deity. The comparatively large proportion (one-fourth) of narrative which it contains, in illustration of the hymns of the Ṛg-veda, is thus the earliest collection of epic matter which we possess, dating as it does from a period when the Mahābhārata could only have been in an embryonic state [2]. The fact of its containing this additional epic matter, points to its being somewhat later in date than the Devatānukramaṇī, which though not extant is known from ten quotations in Ṣaḍguruśiṣya [3] and was doubtless an index of deities only. There seems no reason to doubt the tradition which attributes this and the other short Anukramaṇīs to S'aunaka.

But is the ascription to him of the Bṛhaddevatā also probable? There can be little doubt that the Devatānukramaṇī, as the simpler of the two, was also the earlier. It is in itself unlikely that the same author should have reproduced this work in another form with exactly the same object, viz. to give a serial account of the deities of the Ṛg-veda. This assumption is borne out by the internal evidence of the Bṛhaddevatā itself. The writer several times speaks of himself in the first person [4]. On the other hand, S'aunaka is mentioned [5] fifteen times [6] by name, generally with other authorities, especially Yāska, when different views are stated. Indeed, the impression is once or twice conveyed, that S'aunaka's view was not shared by the writer. In any case, the author could not possibly have meant himself when speaking of the 'Ācārya Śaunaka' (ii. 136;

[1] I have shown in an article on the Ārṣānukramaṇī, Festgruss an R. von Roth (Stuttgart, 1893), p. 112, that the Sarvānukramaṇī contains metrical fragments from that work also; and it is clear that the Sarvānukramaṇī borrows from it throughout.

[2] In the longer recension, the Bṛhaddevatā has one śloka (v. 144) in common with the present text of the Mahābhārata. One half-śloka (viii. 98^cd^) has also a closely parallel form in the Bhagavadgītā. All points in which the narrative matter of our text is akin to the Great Epic deserve careful investigation.

[3] Cp. my edition of the Sarvānukramaṇī, pp. vi and 206.

[4] Bṛhaddevatā i. 1; ii. 146; iv. 32 (B); vii. 84 &c.

[5] The verb is in a past tense, *āha*, *uvāca*, *mene*, *abravīt*, excepting in two passages in which his opinion is stated with that of Yāska and Gālava (*manyante*), or that of Yāska and Śākaṭāyana (*manyate*).

[6] See the references in Appendix ii, p. 115, under 'Śaunaka.'

vi. 9), or of 'S'aunaka and other Ācāryas' (v. 39), or the 'Ācāryas S'aunaka, Yāska, Gālava' (vii. 38). My conclusion, therefore, is that the writer was not S'aunaka himself, but a teacher of his school, who was not separated from him by any great length of time.

11. Emendations.

The text, as it has been fixed by me, contains about 107 emendations[1]. As might be expected from the corrupt character of its MSS., no fewer than thirty-nine of these corrections had to be made in the passages peculiar to the B recension; while only one (and that a very slight one) occurs in the eighteen ślokas peculiar to A. Over a hundred emendations seem at first sight a formidable number, one to the page on the average. The correction is, however, generally very slight. In the first place, the emendations are, with only three exceptions, concerned with single isolated words, not with whole passages. In the second place, over seventy of the corrections are concerned with a single letter. Twenty-four affect two letters or one syllable, and eight are concerned with three letters or two syllables in a word. About seven of these cases consist of the omission, addition, or transposition of single syllables, chiefly for metrical reasons[2]. There is one case in which three successive words have been corrected (vii. 137), and only one in which the emendation affects the whole pāda (viii. 84^b). One pāda has been left blank (vi. 7^c). Only one of the emendations (vii. 114) can, I think, be said to be palaeographically improbable; while more than a dozen of them are rendered absolutely certain by external evidence. Wherever even a single letter has been added, omitted, or altered, without the authority of any of the MSS. of the Bṛhaddevatā itself, I have inserted an asterisk in the text; and the reasons for the emendations are always discussed in the critical notes. Where I have only corrected faulty spelling, as *tattva* for *tatva*, *sattra* for *satra*, *buddhvā* for *budhvā*, I have not added an asterisk; but in cases like *kṛttam* for *kṛtam* (iii. 23) I have done so. The asterisk has as far as possible been placed above the emended syllable. When I had first finished constituting the text, the number of passages in which I was doubtful as to the reading or the sense, was considerable. Continued study

[1] More than one-fourth (28) of these are found in the fifth Adhyāya; only three altogether in the first; and eight each in the second, third, and fourth. Thus three-quarters of the emendations occur in the second half of the text.

[2] Only one line (i. 119^{cd}) has been transposed against all the MSS.; while the position occupied by another line (viii. 108^{ab}) and of two ślokas (viii. 84, 85) has the support of one MS. only (m^1). I have in a few cases transposed or emended the figures which number the vargas. In the former case the asterisk is to the left, in the latter at the top.

in the light of all the external evidence I could bring to bear, has, however, now reduced these passages to hardly more than half a dozen.

I have, perhaps, been over cautious in the matter of conjectural emendation. If so, it is, I think, the effect of an experience I had at the age of twenty. When a student at the University of Göttingen, I was one day reading an English author, borrowed from the lending library, in the Tauchnitz edition. Here occurred the expression 'milch cow,' which was corrected on the margin to 'milk-cow,' written in a German hand. The lesson conveyed by this correction I have never forgotten. My hand has often been stayed by the reflexion, 'Is this a milk-cow emendation?'

Apart, however, from the question of emendations, it is quite impossible, even though I have always carefully weighed the evidence, that I should in every case have selected the best reading supplied by the MSS. at my disposal. I have, therefore, endeavoured everywhere to furnish the material which will render the correction of any errors I may have left as easy as possible.

12. Arrangement of translation and notes.

Besides the use in the text of asterisks to mark emendations, and of symbols to indicate divergences of recension, a peculiar feature of the present edition is the placing of the critical and illustrative notes, immediately after the translation of each śloka in the second volume. In this way the reader can have under his eye, at the same moment, the text on the one hand, and all the material for its interpretation on the other.

As regards the critical notes, I have very commonly added the readings of MSS. which have practically no independent value, partly to remove doubt as to the independent readings, and partly as evidence of the relationship of the various MSS. In a very few cases the readings of these secondary MSS. appear alone, because I sometimes found, after having returned the primary MS., that I had not specially noted its reading, and so became doubtful, even after careful collation, whether its reading after all agreed with that of the rest. I always remember what a German friend said to me many years ago in regard to assuming that a MS. has a particular reading unless a special statement to the contrary is made: 'ich traue Ihnen nicht!'—When the MSS. of a whole group agree (as to which there is occasionally some doubt, since Mitra does not always note the readings of his MSS.), I simply indicate this by A or B. These symbols, however, never include m^1. In the case of emendations or doubtful readings I state my reasons pretty fully, it being so much easier to refute an error when this is done. As to the illustrative notes,

I have not aimed at supplying an elaborate commentary, but only at giving enough to explain the text and facilitate its use as a trustworthy basis for further research. As the translation is for the use of scholars only, it is meant to be a close one in which every word is accounted for. I have endeavoured to make it as clear and serviceable as possible by the employment of parenthetical additions. Wherever I have been doubtful in difficult passages as to the interpretation, I have stated this in a note, leaving it to others to improve upon what I have been able to supply.

13. Irregularities in the text of the Bṛhaddevatā.

Metre. The Bṛhaddevatā is composed for the most part in the anuṣṭubh metre; but, like the other versified works attributed to Śaunaka, it contains an admixture of triṣṭubh stanzas, forty-three of which occur in different parts of the work.

It is to be noted that about 120 instances of hiatus are found between the first and second pāda of anuṣṭubh lines, or about one case in every ten ślokas. Thus even initial *a* must sometimes be read after *e* and *o* (e. g. ii. 129; iv. 3: but i. 54). The vowels are here for the most part run together in the MSS., and have to be separated in order to restore the metre, as in the case of the Vedic Saṃhitās. Occasionally some of the MSS. remove the hiatus by the insertion of a particle. In such cases I have always preferred the reading with the hiatus. Owing to this loose connexion between the pādas, I have separated the two halves of the line throughout the text (even in i. 30, 115).

There are several instances of anuṣṭubh pādas, when they form the first half of the line, consisting of nine syllables [1]. In these cases the line always begins with two short syllables. There is one instance of the second pāda containing seven syllables only, but this is accounted for by the line consisting of a pratīka of the Ṛg-veda, which has to be read with vyūha [2]. Triṣṭubh pādas not infrequently have one syllable too many [3], while others sometimes end iambically. This irregularity is doubtless due to the fact that jagatī pādas occasionally interchange with triṣṭubh verses.

Grammar. With regard to euphonic combination [4], the Bṛhaddevatā very usually does not contract a final *a* or *ā* with a following *ṛ* [5]; the hiatus is not avoided even in the case of *i* [6]. On the other hand, irre-

[1] BD. ii. 25; iv. 102; viii. 68, 70; and one or two other instances as various readings.

[2] *Ṛjram ukṣaṇyāyane*: RV. viii. 25. 22.

[3] e.g. iii. 126, 127; viii. 99.

[4] I have followed the regular practice of the MSS. in dropping visarga before a sibilant plus a hard consonant.

[5] e.g. *atha ṛtus*, ii. 13; hence *vai ṛcaḥ*, i. 18.

[6] *Naipātikāni ṛgbhāñji*, ii. 78.

gular contraction after the dropping of Visarga is somewhat frequent, especially in the case of pratīkas[1]. In two instances *a* is elided after the dual *e*: *dṛśyete 'lpāḥ* (i. 8) and *dve 'numateḥ* (iv. 88). Sandhi is further applied to a Pragṛhya in *vaidadaśvy ṛṣī* (v. 62; also 89). The irregularities in regard to nouns, pronouns, and verbs are not inconsiderable. The weak base is used in the feminine participle *ārohati* (vii. 130). The base *sudāsa* is once used instead of *sudās* (vi. 34). Adjectives derived from compounds, especially from Devatā-dvandvas, are often irregularly formed: *viśvabhaiṣajya* (viii. 50), *trisāṃvatsarika* (v. 97); *aindrā-soma* (vi. 27), *somā-pauṣṇa* (iv. 91), and others as in the Sarvānukramaṇī[2]. The nom. plur. of *patnī* appears as *patnayaḥ* (ii. 8, 9, 12; iii. 92) and *patnīḥ* (viii. 128) beside the regular *patnyaḥ*. *Prathamasyām* (beside *dvitīyasyām*) occurs once (viii. 95). The form *caturbhiḥ* is frequently used instead of *catasṛbhiḥ*, sometimes even in direct association with a feminine noun[3]. *Enam* appears to be once used for *enad* (i. 73). *Mantra* is once used as a neuter (viii. 129)[4]. The neuter *haras* appears once (v. 19) as a masculine. In the verb, unaugmented forms occur several times: *sīdat* (iv. 113), *barhayat* (iv. 69), *bodhayat* (iv. 115), *śāmayat* (iv. 53). *Anuśāsati* once stands for the 3rd sing. present (vii. 37); the present base of *bandh* is twice *badhya* (v. 134; vi. 14); *apāhanat* stands for *apāhan* (iv. 114), *mocire* for *mumucire* (vi. 15), *asuṣvapat* for *asūṣupat* (vi. 13). The form *mathyati* has a passive sense (iii. 62). Compound gerunds sometimes take *-tvā*: *namaskṛtvā* (i. 1), *saṃgṛhītvā* (ii. 47), *ā-nītvā* (v. 18); while *-ya* is once used in the simple gerund *śāntvya* (iv. 3). With regard to syntax, the nominative is a few times used for the accusative: *hetavaḥ* for *hetūn* (i. 28); *pañcāśat* for *pañcāśatam* (vi. 54); *bhrātaraḥ* for *bhrātṝn* (iv. 32); and the accusative with *iti* instead of the nominative occurs several times. The order of the words is frequently disregarded, especially in the case of *iti*[5]. This irregularity goes altogether too far in two or three cases[6], making the passage either unintelligible without external evidence, or positively misleading.

Vocabulary. With regard to vocabulary, the vowel of a few words appears shortened under the influence of the metre: *sikată* (vii. 79), *āśīḥ* (v. 170), *Năbhāka* (vii. 128). To the same cause are due the peculiar formations *uruvāsinī* (ii. 59) = *urvaśī*, and *vāriṣākapa* (ii. 69) = *vārṣākapa*. *Bṛhataspati* is meant (ii. 3) for an etymological explanation of *bṛhaspati*.

[1] *Jātavedātha*, ii. 30; *tisroktāḥ*, vi. 136; *vidvāṃsarṣigatām*, vii. 112; *samiddhāpryaḥ*, iv. 62; *daṇḍeti*, i. 50; *iḷeti*, iii. 138; *tīvrendravāyubhyām*, iii. 94; *payasvatyuttarā*, vii. 10. There are besides a few irregular contractions of pratīkas of a different kind: *vitatādiḥ* (*vitatau*), i. 57; *rakṣohaṇādi*, vii. 142.

[2] See my edition, p. x, top.

[3] See Index of Words, under *catur*.

[4] Probably also in ii. 132.

[5] v. 46; vi. 91; vii. 12, 46, 111.

[6] See i. 115; ii. 13[a]; iii. 92.

A fair number of Vedic words are used, such as *kṛntatra* (ii. 60), *ṛbīsa* (v. 84), *āṣṭrī* (viii. 68), *kāru* (ii. 22), *kīrin* (iii. 96), *kṛpaṇyu* (ii. 27), *tamasvatī* (iii. 10), *vādhūya* (vii. 134), *vīḍvaṅga* (iii. 147), *vṛktabarhis* (i. 65), *śyāvī* (iii. 8), *sūna* (=*sūnā*: iv. 29); *viśva* (ii. 134), *śukra* (vi. 144); *kathā* as an adverb (ii. 98); the verb *ribh*, 'to praise' (iii. 96). The use of such words, however, is not always an independent one, as they sometimes occur in passages which are only adaptations of the statements of the Ṛg-veda[1]. The Bṛhaddevatā also contains a few words which have not been noted elsewhere: *kuntya*, *pratipūrvaka*, *prāüga* (adj.), *yājamāna* (adj.), *nānānīya*, *śaṃnomitrīyā*; *vi-śokaya*, 'to console' (vii. 36), has been borrowed by the Sarvānukramaṇī (x. 33).

14. Summary of the contents of the Bṛhaddevatā.

The contents of the eight Adhyāyas of the Bṛhaddevatā do not correspond in any way to the eight Aṣṭakas of the Ṛg-veda. Thus the enumeration of the deities of the hymns does not begin till near the end of the second Adhyāya (ii. 126). Each Adhyāya contains about thirty vargas of generally five ślokas. The division into Adhyāyas and vargas is quite mechanical, as it often cuts into the middle of a discussion or a story (e. g. the end of vi, or the seventh varga of viii).

The Bṛhaddevatā begins with a long introduction embracing the whole of the first Adhyāya, and twenty-five vargas of the second. This introduction consists mainly of a classification and enumeration of the Vedic deities, in connexion with Prajāpati as representing them collectively, and with the Vedic triad of Fire, Indra or Vāyu, and Sun, as representing respectively the gods of the three worlds. Seven vargas at the end of the introduction contain an interesting grammatical discussion, closely related to the Nirukta, and dealing with particles, prepositions, nouns, pronouns, compounds, and the analysis of words, together with a criticism of Yāska's errors in dividing words[2].

The main body of the work, commencing with the twenty-sixth varga of the second Adhyāya, is, for the most part, concerned with stating the deities, in their successive order, for the hymns and stanzas of the Ṛg-veda. It is, however, by no means a mere index of deities, such as the Devatānukramaṇī doubtless was. On the contrary, it contains a considerable amount of other matter, notably about forty legends, meant to explain the circumstances under which the hymns they are connected

[1] With the above irregularities, cp. those collected from the Ṛgvidhāna by Meyer in his edition, pp. viii–xi.

[2] This grammatical part of the Introduction has been printed by me, with translation and notes, in the Album-Kern, pp. 333–340.

with, were composed[1]. About 300 ślokas, or approximately one-fourth of the whole work, are devoted to these legends. This is the most important, as well as the most interesting portion of the book, for it comprises the oldest systematic collection of legends which we possess in Sanskrit. Narrated in an epic style, they are historically connected with a number of stories told in the Mahābhārata. This historical connexion deserves to be carefully examined. Dr. Sieg, in the first part of his meritorious work, 'Die Sagenstoffe des Ṛg-veda und die indische Itihāsatradition[2],' has done this in the case of some legends. I cannot, however, in the present state of our knowledge, agree with him in supposing that the Bṛhaddevatā has borrowed from the Mahābhārata. He thinks that the story of Devāpi Ārṣṭiṣeṇa[3] is a clear example of such borrowing. In my opinion, the evidence is all the other way The single fact that Devāpi's patronymic, Ārṣṭiṣeṇa, has, in the Mahābhārata, become an independent name designating another person, but mentioned along with Devāpi, is a clear indication of the posteriority of the Mahābhārata form of the story; a differentiation of this kind being a not infrequent phenomenon in mythological development. In the Mahābhārata, moreover, a third brother appears, and the name S'aṃtanu has become S'āṃtanu. It is, besides, impossible on general grounds that a Vedic work which is undoubtedly earlier than the Sarvānukramaṇī, and not much later than Yāska, should have borrowed from the Mahābhārata, which must have assumed the form known to us so many centuries later. The possibility even of interpolation appears to me, as regards the legend in question, to be entirely precluded by the internal evidence of the Bṛhaddevatā[4].

Our text further contains other matters connected with the deities of the Ṛg-veda, such as an enumeration of Rishis[5], of female seers[6], of the steeds of the various gods[7], a detailed account of the Āprī hymns[8], and a full discussion of the character of the Vaiśvadeva hymns[9]. The concluding nine vargas state the gods presiding over various kinds of ritual verses and over the different tones, with some remarks about knowing the deities of the Veda. Important and interesting is the statement, occurring in the Anuvākānukramaṇī also, as to a different sequence of the groups of hymns in the first Maṇḍala[10]. The statements of the

[1] A list of these is given in Appendix iv, pp. 132, 133.

[2] Pp. 150; Stuttgart, 1902.

[3] Bṛhaddevatā vii. 155–viii. 9.

[4] Cp. my review of Sieg's work in the Deutsche Litteraturzeitung, Sept. 19, 1903, columns 2302–4; and my History of Sanskrit Literature (London, 1900), p. 287.

[5] ii. 129–131; iii. 55–57.

[6] ii. 82–84 = Ārṣānukramaṇī x. 100–102.

[7] iv. 140–142.

[8] ii. 158–iii. 32.

[9] ii. 132–134; iii. 41–52.

[10] iii. 125; see note [a].

Bṛhaddevatā about the khilas, or supplementary hymns, are curious. Both of these subjects have been ably discussed by Prof. Oldenberg in his Prolegomena[1] with reference to the evidence then available.

15. The khilas of the Ṛg-veda in the Bṛhaddevatā.

With regard to the khilas, a more trustworthy text than Mitra's, and the discovery of new evidence, enable us now to speak with greater precision on many points. Thus we can now say with certainty that the Bṛhaddevatā knows nothing of four khilas which Meyer, in his preface to the Ṛgvidhāna (p. xxvi), supposes to be referred to in the corrupt MS. (b) of the Bṛhaddevatā which he used.

The relation of our text to the khilas is peculiar in two ways. In the first place, the Sarvānukramaṇī, which is so largely based on the Bṛhaddevatā, makes no mention of the thirty-seven khilas[2] to which the Bṛhaddevatā refers. It only notices the group of khilas in the eighth Maṇḍala[3], besides referring to the existence, after Ṛg-veda i. 99, of a group of hymns by Kaśyapa[4].

In the second place, of the twenty-five khilas printed in Aufrecht's[5], and of the thirty-two in Max Müller's edition of the Ṛg-veda[6], the Bṛhaddevatā refers to only seven[7], while, on the other hand, it mentions thirty other khilas not in Aufrecht.

Of the total of thirty-seven khilas, eleven occur after Ṛg-veda i. 73, seven are found at the end of the fifth Maṇḍala, one after vi. 44 (B), the remaining eighteen being scattered through the latter half of the tenth Maṇḍala[8]. Of the thirty not in Aufrecht, about twenty have been known

[1] Die Hymnen des Ṛg-veda, Band 1, Metrische und textgeschichtliche Prolegomena, Berlin, 1888; see chapter v: Die Ṣâkala-und die Vâshkala-Ṣâkhâ.

[2] These may be found in their respective places by consulting Appendix iii, Index of Deities, part i, pp. 116 ff.; and the corresponding pratīkas in Appendix i, part i, pp. 105 ff.

[3] One of these (58) is not mentioned in any MS. of Sarvānukramaṇī, two of them (57, 58) are not mentioned in the Bṛhaddevatā, while the whole group is ignored in the Ārṣānukramaṇī.

[4] This reference is based on Bṛhaddevatā iii. 130: see note [a].

[5] Second ed., vol. ii, pp. 672-688.

[6] Second ed., vol. iv, pp. 519-541; see introductory remarks there.

[7] Aufrecht's vii, viii (*v.r.*), xviii, xx (M.M. xxvii), xxii, xxiii, xxv.

[8] Two after x. 84, one after 85, two after 103, three after 128, one after 137, two after 151, one after 162, one after 166, one after 184, four after 191. In these thirty-seven khilas we probably have the additional matter of the Bāṣkala recension which the Bṛhaddevatā follows (cp. iii. 125 and Anuvākānukramaṇī 21). They probably constitute eight groups corresponding to the eight hymns which the Bāṣkalas are stated to have in excess of the S'ākalas (Anuv. Anuk., 36). Thus the eleven Sauparṇa khilas would form one (cp. Weber, Literature, p. 313, bottom) and *saṃjñānam* and the two following would form another of fifteen stanzas (cp. Oldenberg, Prolegomena, p. 495, bottom).

to exist from the mention of their pratīkas or some general reference in other Vedic works, but of the rest not a trace has been found till now.

It was a most fortunate circumstance that when I read a paper at the Hamburg Congress of Orientalists, in September 1902, on my forthcoming edition of the Bṛhaddevatā, I said a good deal about the khilas which are referred to in that work. As a result of these remarks, I heard, in March last, from my friend Prof. E. Leumann, of Strassburg, telling me that he had in his possession a transcript made by the late Dr. H. Wenzel of a collection of khilas found in a MS. of the Ṛg-veda which was purchased in Kashmir by the late Prof. Bühler [1]. I gladly availed myself of his kind offer to lend me this transcript; and by great good fortune Dr. Wenzel's note-book arrived in time for me to utilize, in my translation and notes, the material which it contained in regard to every khila mentioned in the text of the Bṛhaddevatā. It has proved of the utmost service, since it has saved me from several mistakes, besides giving certainty in various passages where all would otherwise have been conjecture. In addition to the information I have supplied in the notes regarding the thirty-seven khilas mentioned in the text, it is here only possible to give a brief account of the collection as a whole. Now that the text is accessible it will be interesting to investigate how many of the eighty-nine [2] hymns contained in it are referred to in Vedic works. The Bṛhaddevatā alone quotes more than three-eighths of the whole number. There are indications that the text has been well preserved. Thus the initial pādas of the first four stanzas of the khila *brahma jajñānam* quoted in the Aitareya Brāhmaṇa (i. 19. 1–4) are found practically without any variation of reading and in the same order in the Kashmir collection.

The khilas are here arranged in five Adhyāyas, which are subdivided into vargas. Each Adhyāya has prefixed to it a regular Anukramaṇī, giving the pratīka, the Rishi, the deity, and the metre of the following group of hymns. The position of the khila is indicated by the appended pratīka of the hymn of the Ṛg-veda which immediately follows. The first Adhyāya contains twelve khilas, the first corresponding to Aufrecht's no. i, from which it differs in the initial pāda only. Then come the eleven Sauparṇa hymns, of which, as they have been the subject of a good deal of speculation [3], I give the beginnings, along with the number of stanzas contained in each: 1. *śaśvan nāsatyā* (14); 2. *pra dhārayantu madhunaḥ* (7); 3. *jyotiṣman-*

[1] See his 'Detailed Report,' Bombay, 1877, Appendix i, No. 5, and some account of the MS., p. 35 f.

[2] I am not yet certain as to the exact number, being still doubtful in a few cases as to whether what seems one khila may not really be two.

[3] Cp. Meyer, Ṛgvidhāna, p. xxiv; Oldenberg, Prolegomena, p. 508; Weber, History of Indian Literature, English Translation, 2nd ed., p. 313 f.

taṃ ketumantaṃ tricakram (10); 4. *kṛśas tvaṃ bhuvanasya te* (11); 5. *imāni vāṃ bhāgadheyāni sisrataḥ* (7); 6. *ayaṃ somas susomo adribudhnaḥ* (6); 7. *yadā yuñjāthe maghavānam āśum* (3); 8. *yaṃ gachathas sutapā devavantam* (6); 9. *ayaṃ somo devayāvān sumedhāḥ* (4); 10. *idaṃ devā bhāgadheyaṃ* (8); 11. *āśvinā vahataṃ pīvarīḥ* (8). This makes an aggregate of eighty-four stanzas.

The second Adhyāya contains seventeen hymns, eleven of which are printed in Aufrecht's edition (ii–xii). The six others which follow the S'rīsūkta are described in the notes on Bṛhaddevatā v. 91, 92. The thirteenth (*cakṣuḥ*) and the fifteenth (*svapnaḥ*) each consist of a single stanza only, while the corresponding khilas in Aufrecht (viii and x) have two and eight additional stanzas respectively.

The third Adhyāya contains twenty-two hymns, the last being that of Nakula (*brahma jajñānam*). Of these only five[1] appear in Aufrecht, and one besides in Max Müller[2]. Two of the latter are much shorter than in Aufrecht or Max Müller. The tenth, beginning *pāvamānīḥ*, in which there is a lacuna after the middle of the third stanza, has six stanzas according to the Anukramaṇī; while in Aufrecht this khila has no fewer than twenty. The seventeenth (*dhruvā*)[3], which consists of a single stanza, forms the conclusion of a khila of six stanzas in Aufrecht. Aufrecht's xvi, consisting of one stanza, is not to be found in the collection.

The fourth Adhyāya consists of fourteen khilas, most of which are quoted by the Bṛhaddevatā and all of which are described in the notes[4]. Six of them are found in Aufrecht[5], one of these, however (*ā rātri*), having only four stanzas to Aufrecht's fourteen.

The fifth Adhyāya comprises at least twenty-three khilas, of which, however, only the first four are noticed in the Bṛhaddevatā[6]. The last in Aufrecht is one of these (*saṃjñānam*). The fifth, of eleven stanzas, beginning *agnir deveddhaḥ* and characterized in the Anukramaṇī as *yajūṃṣi*, is mentioned in the Aitareya Brāhmaṇa. The eighteenth, with eighteen stanzas, beginning *etā aśvāḥ* (= AV. xx. 129. 1), is in the Anukramaṇī ascribed to Aitaśa. The nineteenth, of six stanzas, beginning *vitatau kiraṇau* (= AV. xx. 133. 1–6), is referred to in the Bṛhaddevatā (i. 57) as an example of 'enigma.' It is quite possible that several of the stanzas which seem to be quoted in the Bṛhaddevatā from other Vedas, may really be meant to refer to khilas of the Ṛg-veda.

With the exception of a few small lacunae, which could probably be

[1] xiii, xiv, xv, xvii, xviii.

[2] That beginning *ilaiva* (no. xviii).

[3] This khila seems to be treated by the Bṛhaddevatā as the last stanza of RV. x. 85. Cp. vii. 137, note [b]; Oldenberg, Prolegomena, p. 507, bottom.

[4] See notes on viii. 44, 45, 51, 58, 59, 69, 93.

[5] Corresponding to his xix, xx. 1, xx. 2–12, xxii, xxiii, xxiv.

[6] See notes on viii. 93, 94, 100.

filled up in most cases from corresponding stanzas in the later Vedas, the text of the khilas is complete, and as far as I have been able tō examine it yet, seems to be very fairly correct. Hence there seems reason to believe that a satisfactory edition of the text of these khilas could be produced from the Kashmir MS.

16. Appendices.

In order to make this edition as useful as possible, I have added seven appendices to the text. The first (pp. 105–114) contains an alphabetical list of all the Vedic pratīkas occurring in the Bṛhaddevatā. Besides Ṛg-vedic stanzas there occur here only pratīkas of the khilas and of a few verses from other Saṃhitās, mainly the Taittirīya. A few pratīkas represent only the first member of a word or compound (*ambi-*, *sam-*, *aghora-*). In a very few cases the pratīka is slightly altered for metrical reasons, chiefly by the dropping of visarga (e.g. *kaṅkata*, *tīvrā*, *daṇḍā*) and subsequent contraction with *iti*.

The second appendix furnishes a list of the authorities quoted by the Bṛhaddevatā. It will be observed that the only ones frequently mentioned are Yāska (eighteen times), S'aunaka (fifteen times), S'ākaṭāyana (eight times), the Aitareya Brāhmaṇa (eight times), S'ākapūṇi (seven times), and Gālava (five times). It is somewhat remarkable that the Aitareya is mentioned, with only one exception, in passages peculiar to B, while S'ākaṭāyana and S'ākapūṇi never appear in such passages, and Yāska only two or three times. The references to S'aunaka are, on the other hand, almost equally divided between B and the common text.

The third appendix (pp. 116–131) furnishes an Anukramaṇī of the deities as stated by the Bṛhaddevatā, with the deviations of the Sarvānukramaṇī added in the footnotes. These variations, which consist mainly of omissions of details on the part of the Sarvānukramaṇī, are otherwise surprisingly few and unimportant. They are doubtless due to modified statements in other authorities, principally, no doubt, the Devatānukramaṇī which we do not possess, but which Ṣaḍguruśiṣya often quotes. This commentator, in fact, sometimes expressly notes that the Sarvānukramaṇī follows the combined statements of the two Anukramaṇīs.

The fourth appendix (pp. 132, 133) gives an alphabetical list, with cross references, of the stories related in the Bṛhaddevatā.

The fifth (pp. 134, 135) contains a list of passages following the order of occurrence in the Bṛhaddevatā, which are quoted elsewhere, chiefly in Saḍguruśiṣya, Sāyaṇa, and the Nītimañjarī.

The sixth (pp. 136–154) is of critical importance as furnishing, in parallel columns, the evidence for the relationship of the Bṛhaddevatā to eight other texts, notably the Nirukta and the Sarvānukramaṇī.

The last and longest appendix (pp. 155–198) is a very full index of the words and names occurring in the Bṛhaddevatā. I have excluded from it all words occurring in pratīkas (Appendix i), in the list of authorities (Appendix ii), and the names of constantly recurring deities and the corresponding derivative adjectives (such as *agni*, *āgneya*), as these may all be found by consulting Appendix iii. Thus, *agni* and *āgneya* are omitted when occurring after the end of the introduction (ii. 125), unless there is some special reason for specifying them. Words of any importance found in various readings are also given and indicated as such (e.g. *āntra*). I have found this index extremely useful to myself, not only for the purposes of the translation, but for the final revision of the text. The help afforded by the possibility of constantly comparing cognate passages has been very considerable, and has often led to certainty in regard to the correct reading or sense, when I should otherwise have remained in doubt, or perhaps altogether in the dark. Indeed, I doubt whether a difficult Sanskrit text can ever be satisfactorily edited without an index of the entire work made *before* the editor sends his first sheet to press. This is one of the reasons why I have long had a strong objection to the wretched method of bringing out texts in fasciculi. It has, as far as I can see, absolutely nothing in its favour. The editor probably begins to bring out his text before he knows it thoroughly, and the final fasciculus, if it ever sees the light, probably has, or ought to have, a long list of corrigenda in consequence. Meanwhile the work remains practically useless to scholars, while its interpretation is rendered additionally difficult by its hidden errors. Much loss of time is also entailed; for while, for instance, the whole of the present work of about 560 pages has taken less than a year to pass through the press, experience shows that four fasciculi of, say, 100 pages spread themselves over some six years in the process of publication. I am also convinced that it is the duty of every competent and careful editor, not only to refrain from this futile form of publication, but to extract as much material as possible from his text while engaged in editing it. As he must, necessarily, be more familiar with his text than any one else is likely to make himself, research is sure to be more rapidly advanced by the adoption of this method.

17. Acknowledgment of obligations.

There now remains to me only the pleasant duty of thanking all those who have in any way assisted in the production of the present work. One or more valuable notes, which I have utilized in one form or another,

I owe to Prof. Lanman, Prof. Kielhorn, C. I. E., D. Litt. (Oxon.), Prof. J. Eggeling, Prof. Aufrecht [1], Prof. Hanns Oertel, and Dr. E. Sieg.

To my friend Prof. Ernst Kuhn I must express my gratitude for his kindness in placing at my disposal his eminent father's material, which considerably lightened my labours, especially in their initial stage.

Prof. Leumann has placed not only myself, but all other Vedic scholars, under an obligation by lending me Dr. Wenzel's transcript of the Kashmir Khila collection. The information extracted from it will, I believe, render the present work more useful in furthering Vedic studies than anything else which it supplies.

Mr. A. B. Keith has read proofs of the whole text and translation with great care and insight, and I have benefited by his many sagacious suggestions in regard to both parts of the work. This is the third book of mine in which he has rendered me these valuable services within the course of four years. Mr. J. C. Pembrey, Hon. M.A. (Oxon.), the Oriental Reader at the Clarendon Press, has as usual gone far beyond what his duty required in the care he has bestowed on correcting the final proofs of this book. The advantage accruing to the present work from the minute attention of a man who has fifty-seven years' experience in reading Sanskrit proofs behind him, can hardly be over-estimated.

To Prof. Lanman's unrivalled skill in editorship I am indebted for many improvements in the arrangement of matter and details of typography, which will render this book more useful to scholars than it would otherwise have been. I must also thank him sincerely for having given me the opportunity of editing the Bṛhaddevatā, a task from which I have derived more enjoyment than from any other work I have yet taken in hand.

A. A. MACDONELL.

OXFORD, *July* 27, 1904.

[1] I am very glad that the extraordinarily extensive and valuable collectanea of this veteran scholar, consisting largely of indexes and glossaries to Vedic and other works, have been acquired by the India Office Library and will soon be available for the use of scholars.

॥ अथ शौनकीयबृहद्देवताप्रारम्भः ॥

मन्त्रदृग्भ्यो नमस्कृत्वा समाम्नायानुपूर्वशः ।
सूक्तर्गर्धर्चपादानाम् ऋग्भ्यो वक्ष्यामि दैवतम् ॥१॥
वेदितव्यं दैवतं हि मन्त्रे मन्त्रे प्रयत्नतः ।
दैवतज्ञो हि मन्त्राणां तदर्थमवगच्छति ॥२॥
तद्धितांस्तदभिप्रायान् ऋषीणां मन्त्रदृष्टिषु ।
विज्ञापयति विज्ञानं कर्माणि विविधानि च ॥३॥
न हि कश्चिदविज्ञाय याथातथ्येन दैवतम् ।
लौक्यानां वैदिकानां वा कर्मणां फलमश्नुते ॥४॥
प्रथमो भजते त्वासां वर्गोऽग्निमिह दैवतम् ।
द्वितीयो वायुमिन्द्रं वा तृतीयः सूर्यमेव च ॥५॥
अर्थमिच्छन्नृषिर्देवं यं यमाहायमस्त्विति ।
प्राधान्येन स्तुवन्भक्त्या मन्त्रस्तद्देव एव सः ॥६॥ १॥
स्तुतिस्तु नाम्ना रूपेण कर्मणा बान्धवेन च ।
स्वर्गायुर्धनपुत्राद्यैर् अर्थैराशीस्तु कथ्यते ॥७॥
स्तुत्याशिषौ तु यास्वृक्षु दृश्येतेऽल्पास्तु ता इह ।
ताभ्यश्चाल्पतरास्ताः स्युः स्वर्गो याभिस्तु याच्यते ॥८॥
स्तुवन्तं वेद सर्वोऽयम् अर्थयत्येष मामिति ।
स्तौतीत्यर्थे ब्रुवन्तं च सार्थं मामेष पश्यति ॥९॥
स्तुवद्भिर्वा ब्रुवद्भिर्वा ऋषिभिस्तत्त्वदर्शिभिः ।
भवत्युभयमेवोक्तम् उभयं ह्यर्थतः समम् ॥१०॥

प्रत्यक्षं देवतानाम यस्मिन्मन्त्रेऽभिधीयते ।
तामेव देवतां विद्यान् मन्त्रे लक्षणसंपदा ॥११॥ २॥
तस्मात्तु देवतां नाम्ना मन्त्रे मन्त्रे प्रयोगवित् ।
बहुत्वमभिधानानां च प्रयत्नेनोपलक्षयेत् ॥१२॥
संपूर्णमृषिवाक्यं तु सूक्तमित्यभिधीयते ।
दृश्यन्ते देवता यस्मिन्न् एकस्मिन् बहुषु द्वयोः ॥१३॥
देवतार्षार्थछन्दस्तो वैविध्यं च प्रजायते ।
ऋषिसूक्तं तु यावन्ति सूक्तान्येकस्य वै स्तुतिः ॥१४॥
श्रूयन्ते तानि सर्वाणि ऋषेः सूक्तं हि तस्य तत् ।
यावदर्थसमाप्तिः स्याद् अर्थसूक्तं वदन्ति तत् ॥१५॥
समानछन्दसो याः स्युस् तच्छन्दःसूक्तमुच्यते ।
वैविध्यमेवं सूक्तानाम् इह विद्याद्यथातथम् ॥१६॥ ३॥
देवतानामधेयानि मन्त्रेषु त्रिविधानि तु ।
सूक्तभाञ्ज्यथर्ग्भाञ्जि तथा नैपातिकानि तु ॥१७॥
सूक्तभाञ्जि भजन्ते वै सूक्तान्यृग्भाञ्जि वै ऋचः ।
मन्त्रेऽन्यदैवतेऽन्यानि निगद्यन्तेऽत्र कानिचित् ॥१८॥
सालोक्यात्साहचर्याद्वा तानि नैपातिकानि तु ।
तस्माद्बहुप्रकारेऽपि सूक्ते स्यात्सूक्तभागिनी ॥१९॥
देवता तद्यथा सूक्तम् अविशेष्यं प्रतीयते ।
भिन्ने सूक्ते वदेदेव देवतामिह लिङ्गतः ॥२०॥
तत्र तत्र यथावच्च मन्त्रान्कर्मसु योजयेत् ।
देवतायाः परिज्ञानात् तद्धि कर्म समृध्यते ॥२१॥ ४॥
आद्यन्तयोस्तु सूक्तानां प्रसङ्गपरिकीर्तनात् ।
स्तोतृभिर्देवता नाम्ना उपेक्षेतेह मन्त्रवित् ॥२२॥
तत्खल्वाहुः कतिभ्यस्तु कर्मभ्यो नाम जायते ।

सत्त्वानां वैदिकानां वा यच्चान्यदिह किंचन ॥२३॥
नवभ्य इति नैरुक्ताः पुराणाः कवयश्च ये ।
मधुकः श्वेतकेतुश्च गालवश्चैव मन्वते ॥२४॥
निवासात्कर्मणो रूपान् मङ्गलाद्वाच आशिषः ।
यदृच्छयोपवसनात् तथामुष्यायणाच्च यत् ॥२५॥
चतुर्भ्य इति तच्चाहुर् यास्कगार्ग्यरथीतराः ।
आशिषोऽथार्थवैरूप्याद् वाचः कर्मण एव च ॥२६॥ ५॥
सर्वाण्येतानि नामानि कर्मतस्त्वाह शौनकः ।
आशी रूपं च वाच्यं च सर्वं भवति कर्मतः ॥२७॥
यदृच्छयोपवसनात् तथामुष्यायणाच्च यत् ।
तथा तदपि कर्मैव तच्छृणुध्वं च हतवः ॥२८॥
प्रजाः कर्मसमुत्था हि कर्मतः सत्त्वसंगतिः ।
क्वचित्संजायते सत्त्व निवासात्तत्प्रजायते ॥२९॥
यादृच्छिकं तु नामाभि धीयते यत्र कुत्रचित् ।
औपम्यादपि तद्विद्याद् भावस्यैवेह कस्यचित् ॥३०॥
नाकर्मकोऽस्ति भावो हि न नामास्ति निरर्थकम् ।
नान्यत्र भावान्नामानि तस्मात्सर्वाणि कर्मतः ॥३१॥ ६॥
मङ्गलात्क्रियते यत्र नामोपवसनाच्च यत् ।
भवत्येव तु सा ह्याशीः स्वस्त्यादेर्मङ्गलादिह ॥३२॥
अपि कुत्सितनामायम् इह जीवेत्कथं चिरम् ।
इति क्रियन्ते नामानि भूतानां विदितान्यपि ॥३३॥
मन्त्रा नानाप्रकाराः स्युर् दृष्टा ये मन्त्रदर्शिभिः ।
स्तुत्या चैव विभूत्या च प्रभावाद्देवतात्मनः ॥३४॥
स्तुतिः प्रशंसा निन्दा च संशयः परिदेवना ।
स्पृहाशीः कत्थना याच्ञा प्रश्नः प्रैषः प्रवल्हिका ॥३५॥

नियोगश्चानुयोगश्च श्लाघा विलपितं च यत् ।
आचिख्यासाथ संलापः पवित्राख्यानमेव च ॥३६॥ ७॥
आहनस्या नमस्कारः प्रति*राँधस्तथैव च ।
संकल्पश्च प्रलापश्च प्रतिवाक्यं तथैव च ॥३७॥
प्रतिषेधोपदेशौ च प्रमादापह्नवौ च ह ।
उपप्रैषश्च यः प्रोक्तः संज्वरो यश्च विस्मयः ॥३८॥
आक्रोशोऽभिष्टवश्चैव क्षेपः शापस्तथैव च ।
उपसर्गो निपातश्च नाम चाख्यातमित्यपि ॥३९॥
भूतं भव्यं भविष्यं च पुमान् स्त्री च नपुंसकम् ।
एवंप्रकृतयो मन्त्राः सर्ववेदेषु सर्वशः ॥४०॥
वाक्यार्थदर्शनार्थीया ऋचोऽर्धर्चाः पदानि च ।
ब्राह्मणे चाथ कल्पे च निगद्यन्तेऽत्र कानिचित् ॥४१॥ ८॥
शब्देनोच्चरितेनेह येन द्रव्यं प्रतीयते ।
तदक्षरविधौ युक्तं नामेत्याहुर्मनीषिणः ॥४२॥
अष्टौ यत्र प्रयुज्यन्ते नानार्थेषु विभक्तयः ।
तन्नाम कवयः प्राहुर् भेदे वचनलिङ्गयोः ॥४३॥
क्रियासु बह्वीष्वभिसंश्रितो यः पूर्वापरीभूत इहैक एव ।
क्रियाभिनिर्वृत्तिवशेन सिद्ध आख्यातशब्देन तमर्थमाहुः ॥४४॥
क्रियाभिनिर्वृत्तिवशोपजातः कृदन्तशब्दाभिहितो यदा स्यात् ।
संख्याविभक्त्यव्ययलिङ्गयुक्तो भावस्तदा द्रव्यमिवोपलक्ष्यः ॥४५॥ ९॥
यथा नानाविधैः शब्दैर् अपश्यन्नृषयः पुरा ।
विविधानीह वाक्यानि तान्यनुक्रमतः शृणु ॥४६॥
रूपादिभि स्तुतिः प्रोक्ता आशीः स्वर्गादिभिस्तथा ।
यानि वाक्यान्यतोऽन्यानि तान्यपि स्युरनेकधा ॥४७॥
मन्त्रे प्रशंसा भोजस्य चित्र इत् सोभरे स्तुतिः ।

आक्रोशार्थास्तु दृश्यन्ते माता चेत्यभिमेथति ॥४८॥
ऋङ् मोघमन्नं निन्दा च शापो यो मेत्यृगेव तु ।
याञ्चा यदिन्द्र चिचेति क्षेपोऽभीदमिति त्वृचि ॥४९॥
आशीस्तु वात आ वातु दण्डेति परिदेवना ।
प्रश्नश्च प्रतिवाक्यं च पृच्छामि त्वेत्यृचौ पृथक् ॥५०॥ १०॥
संशयोऽधः स्विदासीच्च कत्थना स्यादहं मनुः ।
इमं नो यज्ञमित्यस्यां नियोगः पाद उच्यते ॥५१॥
इह ब्रवीत्वनुयोगः संलाप ऋगुपोप मे ।
प्रतिषेधोपदेशौ तु अक्षैर्मेत्यक्षसंस्तुतौ ॥५२॥
आख्यानं तु हये जाये विलापः स्यान्नदस्य मा ।
अवीरामात्मनः श्लाघा सुदेव इति तु स्पृहा ॥५३॥
नमस्कारः शुनःशेपे नमस्ते अस्तु विद्युते ।
संकल्पयन्निदं तुल्योऽहं स्यामिति यदुच्यते ॥५४॥
संकल्पस्तु यदिन्द्राहं प्रलापस्त्वैतशस्य यः ।
महानग्न्याहनस्या स्यात् प्रतिराधो भुगित्यपि ॥५५॥ ११॥
प्रमादस्त्वेष हन्ताहं न स स्व इत्यपह्नवः ।
इन्द्राकुत्सेत्युपप्रैषो न विजानामि संज्वरः ॥५६॥
होता यक्षदिति प्रैषः को अद्येति तु विस्मयः ।
जामयेऽपह्नवो नैषा विततादिः प्रवल्हिका ॥५७॥
न मृत्युरासीदित्येताम् आचिख्यासां प्रचक्षते ।
अभिशापोऽप्रजाः सन्तु भद्रमाशीस्तु गोतमे ॥५८॥
बह्व्येवंप्रकारं तु शक्यं द्रष्टुमितीदृशम् ।
वक्तुं प्रयोगतश्चैषाम् ऋक्सूक्तार्धर्चसंश्रितम् ॥५९॥
एते तु मन्त्रवाक्यार्था देवतां सूक्तभागिनीम् ।
संश्रयन्ते यथान्यायं स्तुतिस्त्वत्रानुमानिकी ॥६०॥ १२॥

भवद्भूतस्य भव्यस्य जङ्गमस्थावरस्य च ।
अस्यैके सूर्यमेवैकं प्रभवं प्रलयं विदुः ॥ ६१ ॥
असतश्च सतश्चैव योनिरेषा प्रजापतिः ।
यदक्षरं च वाच्यं च यथैतद्ब्रह्म शाश्वतम् ॥ ६२ ॥
कृत्वैष हि त्रिधात्मानम् एषु लोकेषु तिष्ठति ।
देवान्यथायथं सर्वान् निवेश्य स्वेषु रश्मिषु ॥ ६३ ॥
एतद्भूतेषु लोकेषु अग्निभूतं स्थितं त्रिधा ।
ऋषयो गीर्भिरर्चन्ति व्यञ्जितं नामभिस्त्रिभिः ॥ ६४ ॥
तिष्ठत्येष हि भूतानां जठरे जठरे ज्वलन् ।
त्रिस्थानं चैनमर्चन्ति होत्रायां वृक्तबर्हिषः ॥ ६५ ॥ १३ ॥
इहैष पवमानोऽग्निर् मध्यमोऽग्निर्वनस्पतिः ।
अमुष्मिन्नेव विप्रैस्तु लोकेऽग्निः शुचिरुच्यते ॥ ६६ ॥
इहाग्निभूतस्त्वृषिभिर् लोके स्तुतिभिरीडितः ।
जातवेदा स्तुतो मध्ये स्तुतो वैश्वानरो दिवि ॥ ६७ ॥
रसान् रश्मिभिरादाय वायुनायं गतः सह ।
वर्षत्येष च यल्लोके तेनेन्द्र इति स स्मृतः ॥ ६८ ॥
अग्निरस्मिन्नथेन्द्रस्तु मध्यतो वायुरेव च ।
सूर्यो दिवीति विज्ञेयास् तिस्र एवेह देवताः ॥ ६९ ॥
एतासामेव माहात्म्यान् नामान्यत्वं विधीयते ।
तत्तत्स्थानविभागेन तत्र तत्रेह दृश्यते ॥ ७० ॥ १४ ॥
तासामियं विभूतिर्हि नामानि यदनेकशः ।
आहुस्तासां तु मन्त्रेषु कवयोऽन्योन्ययोनिताम् ॥ ७१ ॥
यथास्थानं प्रदिष्टास्ता नामान्यत्वेन देवताः ।
तद्भक्तास्तत्प्रधानाश्च केचिदेवं वदन्ति ताः ॥ ७२ ॥
पृथक्पुरस्ताद्ये तूक्ता लोकादिपतयस्त्रयः ।

तेषामात्मैव तत्सर्वं यद्यद्भक्तिः प्रकीर्त्यते ॥७३॥
तेजस्त्वेवायुधं प्राहुर् वाहनं चैव यस्य यत् ।
इमामैन्द्रीं च दिव्यां च वाचमेवं पृथक् स्तुताम् ॥७४॥
बहुदेवता स्तुतयो द्विवत्संस्तुतयश्च याः ।
प्राधान्यमेव सर्वासु पतीनामेव तास्वपि ॥७५॥ १५॥
स्थानं नामानि भक्तीश्च देवताया स्तुतौ स्तुतौ ।
संपादयन्नुपेक्षेत यां कांचिदिह संपदम् ॥७६॥
अग्निभक्तिस्तुतान्सर्वान् अग्नावेव समापयेत् ।
यदिन्द्रभक्ति तच्चेन्द्रे सूर्ये सूर्यानुगं च यत् ॥७७॥
निरुप्यते हविर्यस्यै सूक्तं च भजते च या ।
सैव तत्र प्रधानं स्यान् न निपातेन या स्तुता ॥७८॥
इति त्रयाणामेतेषाम् उक्तः सामासिको विधिः ।
समासेनैवमुक्तस्तु विस्तरेण त्वनुक्रमः ॥७९॥
अवश्यं वेदितव्यो हि नाम्नां सर्वस्य विस्तरः ।
न हि नामान्यविज्ञाय मन्त्राः शक्या हि वेदितुम् ॥८०॥ १६॥
सत्त्वान्यमूर्तान्यपि च देवतावन्महर्षयः ।
तुष्टुवुर्ऋषयः शक्त्या तासु तासु स्तुतिष्विह ॥८१॥
यैस्त्वग्निरिन्द्रः सोमश्च वायुः सूर्यो बृहस्पतिः ।
चन्द्रोऽथ विष्णुः पर्जन्यः पूषा चाप्यृभवोऽश्विनौ ॥८२॥
रोदसी मरुतो देवाः पृथिव्यापः प्रजापतिः ।
देवौ च मित्रावरुणौ पृथक् सह च तावुभौ ॥८३॥
विश्वे च देवाः सविता त्वष्टा वै रूपकृन्मतः ।
अश्वोऽन्नमृत्विजो वज्रो ग्रावाणो रथसंयुताः ॥८४॥
स्तुताः पृथक् पृथक् स्वैः स्वैः सूक्तैर्ऋग्भिश्च नामभिः ।
स्तुतौ स्तुतौ प्रवक्ष्यामि तानि तेषामनुक्रमात् ॥८५॥ १७॥

व्यवस्येन्मन्त्रमाग्नेयं लिङ्गैरग्नेश्च लक्षितम् ।
हविष्पङ्क्तिप्रधानैश्च नामाह्वानैश्च केवलैः ॥८६॥
ऐन्द्रस्तु मन्त्रो वायव्यैर् लिङ्गैरैन्द्रैश्च लक्ष्यते ।
नामधेयैश्च वज्रस्य बलकृत्या बलेन च ॥८७॥
सौर्यस्तु लिङ्गैः सूर्यस्य गुणैः सर्वैश्च तैजसैः ।
नामधेयैश्च चन्द्रस्य सूक्तं च भजतेऽत्र यैः ॥८८॥
एतासां देवतानां तु नामधेयानुकीर्तनैः ।
यस्य यस्येह यावन्ति न व्यवस्यन्त्यतोऽन्यथा ॥८९॥
अयं प्रयोगस्त्वेतेषां ज्योतिषां त्रिषु वर्तताम् ।
लोकेषु मन्त्रविद्विद्वान् प्रयोगे नावसीदति ॥९०॥ १८॥
नीयतेऽयं नृभिर्यस्मान् नयत्यस्मादसौ च तम् ।
तेनेमौ चक्रतुः कर्म सनामानौ पृथक् पृथक् ॥९१॥
यद्विद्यते हि जातः सञ् जातैर्यश्चात्र विद्यते ।
तेनेमौ तुल्यनामानौ उभौ लोकौ समाप्नुतः ॥९२॥
विसृजन्नयमेतेषां भ्राजते व्योम्नि मध्यमः ।
निपातमात्रे कथ्यन्ते तथाग्नेयानि कानिचित् ॥९३॥
अर्चिर्भिः केश्ययं त्वग्निर् विद्युद्भिश्चैव मध्यमः ।
असौ तु रश्मिभिः केशी तेनैनानाह केशिनः ॥९४॥
एतेषां तु पृथक्त्वेन त्रयाणां केशिनामिह ।
संलक्ष्यन्ते प्रक्रियासु त्रयः केशिन इत्यृचि ॥९५॥ १९॥
न चैवैषां प्रसूतिर्वा विभूतिस्थानजन्म वा ।
निर्वक्तुं शक्यमेतैर्हि कृत्स्नं व्याप्तमिदं जगत् ॥९६॥
वैश्वानरं श्रितो ह्यग्निर् अग्निं वैश्वानरः श्रितः ।
अनयोर्जातवेदास्तु तथैते जातवेदसी ॥९७॥
सालोक्याच्चैकजातत्वाद् व्याप्तिमत्त्वात्तु तेजसः ।

तस्य तस्येह देवत्वं दृश्यन्ते च पृथक् स्तुताः ॥९८॥
यत्त्वाग्नेयमिति ब्रूमः सूक्तभाक् तत्र पार्थिवः ।
जातवेदस्यमित्युक्ते सूक्तेऽस्मिन्मध्यमः स्मृतः ॥९९॥
वैश्वानरीयमिति तु यत्र ब्रूमोऽथ वा क्वचित् ।
सूर्यः सूक्तस्य भाक् तत्र ज्ञेयो वैश्वानरस्तुतौ ॥१००॥ २०॥
सूर्यप्रसूतावग्नी तु दृष्टौ पार्थिवमध्यमौ ।
एतेषामेव लोकानां त्रयाणामध्वरेऽध्वरे ॥१०१॥
रोहात्प्रत्यवरोहेण चिकीर्षन्नाग्निमारुतम् ।
शस्त्रं वैश्वानरीयेण सूक्तेन प्रतिपद्यते ॥१०२॥
ततस्तु मध्यमस्थाना देवतास्त्वनुशंसति ।
रुद्रं च मरुतश्चैव स्तोत्रियेऽग्निमिमं पुनः ॥१०३॥
यथैतदुक्तमेतेषां विभूतिस्थानसंभवम् ।
तथा च देवदेवस्य तत्र तत्रेह दृश्यते ॥१०४॥
यद्यच्च पृथिवीस्थानं पार्थिवं चाग्निमाश्रितम् ।
तत्सर्वमानुपूर्व्येण कथ्यमानं निबोधत ॥१०५॥ २१॥
जातवेदाः श्रितो ह्यग्निम् अग्निं वैश्वानरः श्रितः ।
द्रविणोदास्तथेध्मश्च श्रितश्चाग्निं तनूनपात् ॥१०६॥
नराशंसः श्रितश्चैनम् एनमेवाश्रितस्त्विळः ।
बर्हिर्द्वारश्च देव्योऽग्निम् एनमेव तु संश्रिताः ॥१०७॥
नक्तोषासा च दैव्यौ च होतारावेतदाश्रयौ ।
देव्यस्तिस्रः श्रिताश्चैनं त्वष्टा चैवैतदाश्रयः ॥१०८॥
श्रितो वनस्पतिश्चैनं स्वाहाकृतय एव च ।
अश्वश्च शकुनिश्चैव मण्डूकाश्चैतदाश्रयाः ॥१०९॥
ग्रावाणश्चैनमक्षाश्च नराशंसस्तथा रथः ।
दुन्दुभिश्चेषुधिश्चैनं हस्तघ्नोऽभीशवो धनुः ॥११०॥ २२॥

ज्या चैतदाश्रितेषुश्च श्रिता सम्माजनी च या ।
वृषभो द्रुघणश्चैनम् एनं पितुरुलूखलम् ॥१११॥
नद्यश्चैवैनमापश्च सर्वा ओषधयश्च ह ।
राय्यप्वामाय्यरण्यानी श्रद्धेळा पृथिवी तथा ॥११२॥
भजेते चैनमेवार्त्नी द्वन्द्वभूते च रोदसी ।
मुसलोलूखले चैनं हविर्धाने च ये स्मृते ॥११३॥
जोष्ट्री चोर्जाहुती चैनं शुतुद्र्या च विपाट् सह ।
यौ च देवौ शुनासीरौ तौ चाग्नी चैतदाश्रयौ ॥११४॥
लोकोऽयं यत्र वै प्रातः सवनं क्रियते मखे ।
वसन्तशरदौ चर्तू स्तोमोऽनुष्टुबथो त्रिवृत् ॥११५॥ २३॥
गायत्री चैकविंशश्च यत्र साम रथंतरम् ।
साध्याः साम च वैराजम् आप्याश्च वसुभिः सह ॥११६॥
इन्द्रेण च मरुद्भिश्च सोमेन वरुणेन च ।
पर्जन्येनर्तुभिश्चैव विष्णुना चास्य संस्तवः ॥११७॥
अस्यैवाग्नेस्तु पूष्णा च साम्राज्यं वरुणेन च ।
देवतामर्थतत्त्वज्ञो मन्त्रैः संयोजयेद्धविः ॥११८॥
असंस्तुतस्यापि सतो हविरेकं निरुप्यते ।
देवतावाहनं चैव वहनं हविषां तथा ॥११९॥
कर्म दृष्टे च यत्किंचिद् विषये परिवर्तते ।
इत्युक्तोऽयं गणः सर्वः पृथिव्यग्न्याश्रयो महान् ॥१२०॥ २४॥
यश्चेन्द्रो मध्यमस्थानो गणः सोऽयमतः परः ।
विमानानि च दिव्यानि गणश्चाप्सरसां तथा ॥१२१॥
इन्द्राश्रयस्तु पर्जन्यो रुद्रो वायुर्बृहस्पतिः ।
वरुणः कश्च मृत्युश्च देवश्च ब्रह्मणस्पतिः ॥१२२॥
मन्युश्च विश्वकर्मा च मित्रः क्षेत्रपतिर्यमः ।

ताक्ष्र्यो वास्तोष्पतिश्चैव सरस्वांश्चैवमत्र ह ॥१२३॥
अपांनपाद्दधिक्राश्च सुपर्णोऽथ पुरूरवाः ।
ऋतोऽसुनीतिर्वेनश्च तस्यैतस्याश्रयेऽदितिः ॥१२४॥
त्वष्टा च सविता चैव वातो वाचस्पतिस्तथा ।
धाता प्रजापतिश्चैव अथर्वाणश्च ये स्मृताः ॥१२५॥
श्येनश्चैवैवमग्निश्च तथेळा चैव या स्मृता ।
विधातेन्दुरहिर्बुध्न्यः सोमोऽहिरथ चन्द्रमाः ॥१२६॥ २५॥
विश्वानरश्च वै देवो रुद्राणां संस्तुतो गणः ।
मरुतोऽङ्गिरसश्चैव पितरश्च*र्भुभिः सह ॥१२७॥
राका वाक् सरमाख्याश्च भृगवोऽघ्या सरस्वती ।
यम्युर्वशी सिनीवाली पथ्या स्वस्तिरुषाः कुहूः ॥१२८॥
पृथिव्यनुमतिर्धेनुः सीता लाक्षा तथैव गौः ।
गौरी च रोदसी चैव इन्द्राण्याश्चैष वै पतिः ॥१२९॥
छन्दस्त्रिष्टुप् च पङ्क्तिश्च लोकानां मध्यमश्च यः ।
एतेष्वेवाश्रयो विद्यात् सवनं मध्यमं च यत् ॥१३०॥
ऋतू च ग्रीष्महेमन्तौ यच्च सामोच्यते बृहत् ।
शक्करीषु च यद्गीतं नाम्ना तत्साम शाक्करम् ॥१३१॥
नाम्ना तत्साम शाक्करम् ॥ २६॥

॥ इति बृहद्देवतायां प्रथमोऽध्यायः ॥

आह चैवास्य द्वौ स्तोमाव् आग्नेयौ शाकटायनः ।
यश्च पञ्चदशो नाम्ना संख्यया त्रिणवश्च यः ॥१॥
संस्तुतश्चैव पूष्णा च विष्णुना वरुणेन च ।
सोमवाय्वग्निकुत्सैश्च ब्रह्मणस्पतिनैव च ॥२॥
बृहतस्पतिना चैव नाम्ना यश्चापि पर्वतः ।
कासुचित्केचिदित्याहुर् निपाता स्तुतिषु स्तुताः ॥३॥
मित्रश्च श्रूयते देवो वरुणेन सहासकृत् ।
रुद्रेण सोमः पूष्णा च पुनः पूषा च वायुना ॥४॥
वातेनैव च पर्जन्यो लक्ष्यतेऽन्यत्र वै क्वचित् ।
ऋक्ष्वर्धर्चेषु पादेषु सूक्तेष्वेषु तु कृत्स्नशः ॥५॥
रसादानं तु कर्मास्य वृत्रस्य च निबर्हणम् ।
स्तुतेः प्रभुत्वं सर्वस्य बलस्य निखिला कृतिः ॥६॥ १॥
इत्यैन्द्रो मध्यमस्थानो गणः सम्यगुदाहृतः ।
यः परस्तु गणः सौर्यो द्युस्थानस्तं निबोधत ॥७॥
तस्य मुख्यतमौ देवाव् अश्विनौ सूर्यगाश्रितौ ।
वृषाकपायी सूर्योषाः सूर्यस्यैव तु पत्नयः ॥८॥
अमुतोऽर्वाङ् निवर्तन्ते प्रतिलोमास्तदाश्रयाः ।
पुरोदयात्तामुषसं सूर्यां मध्यंदिने स्थिते ॥९॥
वृषाकपायीं* सूर्यस्य तामेवाहुस्तु निम्रुचि ।
तस्याश्रये सरण्यूश्च भगः पूषा वृषाकपिः ॥१०॥
यमो वैश्वानरो विष्णुर् वरुणश्चैकपादजः ।
पृथिवी च समुद्रश्च देवाः सप्तर्षयश्च ये ॥११॥ २॥

आदित्याः केशिसाध्याश्च सविता वसुभिर्मनुः ।
दध्यङ्ङथर्वा विश्वे च वाजिनो देवपत्न्यः ॥१२॥
असौ तृतीयं सवनं लोकः साम च रैवतम् ।
वैरूपं चैव वर्षाश्च शिशिरोऽथ ऋतुस्तथा ॥१३॥
त्रयस्त्रिंशश्च य स्तोमः कृस्या सप्तदशश्च यः ।
छन्दश्च जगती नाम्ना तथातिछन्दसश्च याः ॥१४॥
पौरुषं चाहुरस्यैतत् सर्वमेव तु पौरुषम् ।
एतस्यैव तु विज्ञेया देवाः संस्तविकास्त्रयः ॥१५॥
चन्द्रमाश्चैव वायुश्च यं* च संवत्सरं विदुः ।
केचित्तु निर्वपन्त्यस्य सौर्यवैश्वानरं हविः ॥१६॥ 3॥
सौर्यवैश्वानरीयं हि तत्सूक्तमिव दृश्यते ।
ऋगर्धर्चोऽथवा पादो द्वृचो वा यदि वा तृचः ॥१७॥
अनेन तु प्रवादेन दृष्टा मूर्धन्वता स्तुतिः ।
सूर्यवैश्वानराग्नीनाम् ऐकात्म्यमिह दृश्यते ॥१८॥
हरणं तु रसस्यैतत् कर्मामुष्य च रश्मिभिः ।
येन नातिविजानन्ति सर्वभूतानि चक्षुषा ॥१९॥
विभागमिममेतेषां विभूतिस्थानसंभवम् ।
संयग्विजानन्मन्त्रेषु तं तु कर्मसु योजयेत् ॥२०॥
अध्यापयन्नधीयानो मन्त्रं चैवानुकीर्तयन् ।
स्थानं सालोक्यं सायुज्यम् एतेषामेव गच्छति ॥२१॥ ४॥
अग्नेस्तु यानि सूक्तानि पञ्च नामानि कारवः ।
षड्विंशतिस्तथेन्द्रस्य प्राहुः सूर्यस्य सप्त च ॥२२॥
तेषां पृथङ्निर्वचनम् एकैकस्येह कर्मजम् ।
उच्यमानं यथान्यायं शृणुध्वमखिलं मया ॥२३॥
जातो यदग्रे भूतानाम् अग्रणीरध्वरे च यत् ।

नाम्ना संनयते वाङ्गं स्तुतोऽग्निरिति सूरिभिः ॥२४॥
द्रविणं धनं बलं वापि प्रायच्छ्येन कर्मणा ।
तत्कर्म दृष्ट्वा कुत्सस्तु प्राहैनं द्रविणोदसम् ॥२५॥
अयं तनूनपादग्निर् असौ हि तननात्तनुः ।
ततस्तु मध्यमो जज्ञे स्थानेऽयं मध्यमात्ततः ॥२६॥ ५॥
अनन्तरां प्रजामाहुर् नपादिति कृपण्यवः ।
नपादमुष्य चैवायम् अग्निस्तेन तनूनपात् ॥२७॥
पृथक्त्वेन समासैस्तु यज्ञे यच्छस्यते नृभिः ।
स्तुवन्त्याप्रीषु तेनेमं नराशंसं तु कारवः ॥२८॥
पुनाति यदिदं विश्वम् एवाग्निः पार्थिवोऽथ च ।
वैश्वानरर्षिभिस्तेन पवमान इति स्तुतः ॥२९॥
भूतानि वेद यज्जातो जातवेदाश्च कथ्यते ।
यश्चैष जातविद्योऽभूद् वित्तं जातोऽधिवेत्ति वा ॥३०॥
विद्यते सर्वभूतैर्हि यद्वा जातः पुनः पुनः ।
तेनैष मध्यभागेन्द्रो जातवेदा इति स्तुतः ॥३१॥ ६॥
अणिष्ठ एष यत्तु त्रीन् व्याप्यैको व्योम्नि तिष्ठति ।
तेनैनमृषयोऽर्चन्तः कर्मणा वायुमब्रुवन् ॥३२॥
त्रीणीमान्यावृणोत्येको मूर्तेन तु रसेन यत् ।
तथैनं वरुणं शक्त्या स्तुतिष्वाहुः कृपण्यवः ॥३३॥
अरोदीदन्तरिक्षे यद् विद्युद्वृष्टिं ददन्नृणाम् ।
चतुर्भिर्ऋषिभिस्तेन रुद्र इत्यभिसंस्तुतः ॥३४॥
चतुर्विधानां भूतानां प्राणो भूत्वा व्यवस्थितः ।
ईष्टे चैवास्य सर्वस्य तेनेन्द्र इति स स्मृतः ॥३५॥
इरां दृणाति यत्काले मरुद्भिः सहितोऽम्बरे ।
रवेण महता युक्तस् तेनेन्द्रमृषयोऽब्रुवन् ॥३६॥ ७॥

यदिमां प्रार्जयत्येको रसेनाम्बरजेन गाम् ।
कालेऽभिरौर्वशश्चर्षी तेन पर्जन्यमाहतुः ॥३७॥
तर्पयत्येष यल्लोकाञ् जन्यो जनहितश्च यत् ।
परो जेता जनयिता यद्वामेयस्ततो जगौ ॥३८॥
बृहन्तौ पाति यल्लोकाव् एष द्वौ मध्यमोत्तमौ ।
बृहता कर्मणा तेन बृहस्पतिरितीळितः ॥३९॥
ब्रह्म वाग् ब्रह्म सत्यं च ब्रह्म सर्वमिदं जगत् ।
पातारं ब्रह्मणस्तेन शौनहोत्र स्तुवञ्जगौ ॥४०॥
अन्नं क्षितिभ्यो विदधद् यदृतुष्वविशन्क्षितौ ।
तेनैनमाह क्षेत्रस्य वामदेव स्तुवन्पतिम् ॥४१॥
मनसेमं तु यद्भूश्यं मध्यमं लोकमाश्रितम् ।
शंसात्सत्येन सत्ये वै स एष स्तुतवानृतम् ॥४२॥ ८॥
रवेणान्तारसैः क्षिप्रे स्थितो व्योम्न्येष मायया ।
ऋतस्य श्लोक इत्येष पुनश्चैनं ततोऽब्रवीत् ॥४३॥
वास्तु प्रयच्छंल्लोकस्य मध्यमः स तु पाति यत् ।
तेन वास्तोष्पतिं प्राह चतुर्भिरिममौर्वशः ॥४४॥
वाचा वेदा ह्यधीयन्ते वाचा छन्दांसि तत्र ह ।
अथो वाक् सर्वमेवेदं तेन वाचस्पति स्तुतः ॥४५॥
न कुतश्चन यद्धीनो वृत्वा तिष्ठति मध्यमः ।
राहूगण ऋषिस्तेन प्राहैनं गोतमोऽदितिम् ॥४६॥
प्रजाभ्यस्त्वेष यच्छर्म कमिच्छन्मनसा सुखम् ।
हिरण्यगर्भस्तेनैनम् ऋषिरर्चन्नुवाच कम् ॥४७॥
इह प्रजाः प्रयच्छन्स संगृहीत्वा प्रयाति च ।
ऋषिर्विवस्वतः पुत्रं तेनाहैनं यमो यमम् ॥४८॥ ९॥
मिषीकृत्य जना विश्वे यदिमं पर्युपासते ।

मित्र इत्याह तेनैनं विश्वामित्रः स्तुवन्स्वयम् ॥४९॥
निदाघमासातिगमे यदृतेनावति क्षितिम् ।
विश्वस्य जनयन्कर्म विश्वकर्मैष तेन सः ॥५०॥
सरांसि घृतवन्त्यस्य सन्ति लोकेषु यत्त्रिषु ।
सरस्वन्तमिति प्राह वाचं प्राहुः सरस्वतीम् ॥५१॥
प्राणभूतस्तु भूतेषु यद्वेनत्येषु तिष्ठति ।
तेनैनं वेनमाहर्षिर् वेनो नामेह भार्गवः ॥५२॥
ससृजे मासि मास्येनम् अभिमत्य तपोऽग्रजम्* ।
तेनैनं मन्युरित्याह मन्युरेव तु तापसः ॥५३॥ १०॥
यदन्तकाले भूतानाम् एक एव नयत्यसून् ।
तेनासुनीतिरुक्तोऽयं स्तुवता श्रुतबन्धुना ॥५४॥
निदाघमासातिगमे जन्म मध्ये भवत्यपाम् ।
नपात्मारमाह तेनैनम् ऋषिर्गृत्समद स्तुवन् ॥५५॥
अपामम्बरगर्भोघम् आदधत्सोऽष्टमासिकम् ।
यत्क्रन्दत्यसकृन्मध्ये दधिक्रास्तेन कथ्यते ॥५६॥
मासेन संभृतं गर्भं नवमेनाथ मासिकम् ।
स्वयं क्रन्दन्दधात्युर्व्यां धातेत्यृग्भिः स गीयते ॥५७॥
स्तीर्णेऽन्तरिक्षे क्षियति यद्वा तूर्णं क्षरत्यसौ ।
अरिष्टनेमिस्तार्क्ष्यर्षिस् तार्क्ष्यं तेनैवमुक्तवान् ॥५८॥ ११॥
रुवन्व्योम्न्युदयं याति कृन्तन्वाब्धिसृजन्नपः ।
पुरूरवसमाहैनं स्ववाक्येनोरुवासिनी ॥५९॥
यत्तु प्रच्यावयन्नेति घोषेण महता मृतम्* ।
तेनर्षिर्मृत्युमिमं सन्तं स्तौति मृत्युरिति स्वयम् ॥६०॥
नाम्ना संकुसुको नाम यमपुत्रो जघन्यजः ।
संवर्तयंस्तमः सूर्याद् उषसं च प्रवर्तयन् ॥६१॥

दिवाकरं प्रसौत्येकः सविता तेन कर्मणा ।
उदितो भासयंल्लोकान् इमांश्चैष स्वरश्मिभिः ।
स्वयं वसिष्ठस्तेनैनम् ऋषिराह स्तुवन्भगम् ॥६२॥ १२॥
पुष्यन् क्षितिं पोषयति प्रणुदन् रश्मिभिस्तमः ।
तेनैनमस्तौत्पूषेति भरद्वाजस्तु पञ्चभिः ॥६३॥
त्रीणि भान्ति रजांस्यस्य यत्पदानि तु तेजसा ।
तेन मेधातिथिः प्राह विष्णुमेनं त्रिविक्रमम् ॥६४॥
कृत्वा सायं पृथग्याति भूतेभ्यस्तमसोऽत्यये ।
प्रकाशं किरणैः कुर्वंस् तेनैनं केशिनं विदुः ॥६५॥
संप्रत्येकैकशस्त्वेनं यन्मन्यन्ते पृथङ्नराः ।
विश्वे विश्वानरस्तेन कर्मणा स्तुतिषु स्तुतः ॥६६॥
वृषैष कपिलो भूत्वा यन्नाकमधिरोहति ।
वृषाकपिरसौ तेन विश्वस्मादिन्द्र उत्तरः ।
रश्मिभिः कम्पयन्नेति वृषा वर्षिष्ठ एव सः ॥६७॥ १३॥
सायाह्नकाले भूतानि स्वापयन्नस्तमेति यत् ।
वृषाकपिरितो वा स्याद् इति मन्त्रेषु दृश्यते ॥६८॥
त्रिषु धन्वेति हीन्द्रेण प्रयुक्तो वारिषाकपे ।
विष्णातेर्विशतेर्वा स्याद् वेवेष्टेर्व्याप्तिकर्मणः ।
विष्णुर्निरुच्यते सूर्यः सर्वं सर्वान्तरश्च यः ॥६९॥
पञ्च षड्विंशतिश्चैव यानि नामानि सप्त च ।
सम्यगग्नीन्द्रसूर्याणां तान्युक्तानि यथाक्रमम् ॥७०॥
नैपातिकानां नाम्नां तु प्रागुक्तैर्नामलक्षणैः ।
संपन्नानां पृथक्त्वेन परिसंख्या न विद्यते ॥७१॥ १४॥
पार्थिवी मध्यमा दिव्या वागपि त्रिविधा तु या ।
तस्याः सूक्तानि नामानि यथास्थानं निबोधत ॥७२॥

कृत्स्नं तु भजते सूक्तम् एषा नद्य स्तुता भुवि ।
यदा चैनं भजन्त्यापो यदा चौषधयो यदा ॥७३॥
अरण्यानी च रात्री च श्रद्धा चोषाः सरस्वती ।
पृथिवी चैव नामैषा भूत्वाप्यृचं* भजन्ति च ॥७४॥
अग्नायी नामतोऽप्येषा भूत्वाग्नेयेषु केषुचित् ।
स्तुता निपातमात्रेण तत्र तत्रेह दृश्यते ॥७५॥
मध्ये सत्यदितिर्वाक् च भूत्वा चैषा सरस्वती ।
समग्रं भजते सूक्तं त्रिभिरेव तु नामभिः ॥७६॥ १५॥
एषैव दुर्गा भूत्वर्चं कृत्वा स्यात्सूक्तभागिनी ।
तन्नामानि यमीन्द्राणी सरमा रोमशोर्वशी ।
भवत्यग्न्या सिनीवाली राका चानुमतिः कुहूः ॥७७॥
गौर्धेनुर्देवपत्न्योऽघ्न्या पथ्या स्वस्तिश्च रोदसी ।
नैपातिकानि ऋग्भाञ्जि येषां नामानि कानिचित् ॥७८॥
यदा तु वाग्भवत्येषा सूर्यामुं लोकमाश्रिता ।
तथा सूक्तमुषा भूत्वा सूर्या च भजतेऽखिलम् ॥७९॥
वृषाकपाय्यृचं भूत्वा सरण्यूर्द्वे च ते ध्रुवम् ।
निपातमात्रं भजते द्युवच्च पृथिवी सती ॥८०॥
सूर्यामेव सतीमेतां गौरीं वाचं सरस्वतीम् ।
पश्यामो वैश्वदेवेषु निपातेनैव केवलाः ॥८१॥ १६॥
घोषा गोधा विश्ववारा अपालोपनिषन्निषत् ।
ब्रह्मजाया जुहूर्नाम अगस्त्यस्य स्वसादितिः ॥८२॥
इन्द्राणी चेन्द्रमाता च सरमा रोमशोर्वशी ।
लोपामुद्रा च नद्यश्च यमी नारी च शश्वती ॥८३॥
श्रीर्लाक्षा सार्पराज्ञी वाक् श्रद्धा मेधा च दक्षिणा ।
रात्री सूर्या च सावित्री ब्रह्मवादिन्य ईरिताः ॥८४॥

नवकः प्रथमस्त्वासां वर्गस्तुष्टाव देवताः ।
ऋषिभिर्देवताभिश्च समूदे मध्यमो गणः ॥८५॥
आत्मनो भाववृत्तानि जगौ वर्गस्तथोत्तमः ।
उत्तमस्य तु वर्गस्य य ऋषिः सैव देवता ॥८६॥ १७॥
आत्मानमस्तौद्वर्गस्तु देवतां यस्तथोत्तमः ।
तस्मादात्मस्तवेषु स्याद् य ऋषिः सैव देवता ॥८७॥
संवादेष्वाह वाक्यं यः स तु तस्मिन्भवेदृषिः ।
यस्तेनोच्येत वाक्येन देवता तत्र सा भवेत् ॥८८॥
उच्चावचेषु चार्थेषु निपाताः समुदाहृताः ।
कर्मोपसंग्रहार्थे च क्वचिच्चौपम्यकारणात् ॥८९॥
ऊनानां पूरणार्था वा पादानामपरे क्वचित् ।
मिताक्षरेषु ग्रन्थेषु पूरणार्थास्त्वनर्थकाः ॥९०॥
कमीमिद्विति विज्ञेया ये त्वनेकार्थकाश्च ते ।
इव न चिन्नु चत्वार उपमार्था भवन्ति ते ॥९१॥ १८॥
उपमार्थे नकारस्तु क्वचिदेव निपात्यते ।
मिताक्षरेषु ग्रन्थेषु प्रतिषेधे त्वनल्पशः ॥९२॥
इयन्त इति संख्यानं निपातानां न विद्यते ।
वशात्प्रकरणस्यैते निपात्यन्ते पदे पदे ॥९३॥
उपसर्गास्तु विज्ञेयाः क्रियायोगेन विंशतिः ।
विवेचयन्ति ते ह्यर्थं नामाख्यातविभक्तिषु ॥९४॥
अच्छ* श्रदन्तरित्येतान् आचार्यः शाकटायनः ।
उपसर्गान्* क्रियायोगान् मेने ते तु त्रयोऽधिकाः ॥९५॥
त्रीण्येव लोके लिङ्गानि पुमान् स्त्री च नपुंसकम् ।
नामसूक्तप्रयोगेषु वाच्यं प्रकरणं तथा ॥९६॥ १९॥
तेषां तु नामभिर्लिङ्गैर ग्रहणं सर्वनामभिः ।

कृताकृतस्य सदृशो गृहीतस्य पुनर्ग्रहः ॥९७॥
पादसूक्तर्चगर्धर्चनामान्यन्यानि यानि च ।
सर्वे नामानि चैवाहुर् अन्ये चैवं यथा कथा ॥९८॥
प्रधानमर्थः शब्दो हि तद्गुणायत्त इष्यते ।
तस्मान्नानान्वयोपायैः शब्दानर्थवशं नयेत् ॥९९॥
अतिरिक्तं पदं त्याज्यं हीनं वाक्ये निवेशयेत् ।
विप्रकृष्टं च संदध्याद् आनुपूर्वीं च कल्पयेत् ॥१००॥
लिङ्गं धातुं विभक्तिं च संनमेत्तत्र तत्र च ।
यद्यत्स्याच्छान्दसं मन्त्रे तत्तत्कुर्यात्तु लौकिकम् ॥१०१॥ २०॥
यावतामेव धातूनां लिङ्गं रूढिगतं भवेत् ।
अर्थश्चाप्यभिधेयः स्यात् तावद्भिर्गुणविग्रहः ॥१०२॥
धातूपसर्गावयवगुणशब्दं द्विधातुजम् ।
बह्वेकधातुजं वापि पदं निर्वाच्यलक्षणम् ॥१०३॥
धातुजं धातुजाज्जातं समस्तार्थजमेव वा ।
वाक्यजं व्यतिकीर्णं च निर्वाच्यं पञ्चधा पदम् ॥१०४॥
द्विगुर्द्वन्द्वोऽव्ययीभावः कर्मधारय एव च ।
पञ्चमस्तु बहुव्रीहिः षष्ठस्तत्पुरुषः स्मृतः ॥१०५॥
विग्रहान्निर्वचः कार्यं समासेष्वपि तद्धिते ।
प्रविभज्यैव निर्ब्रूयाद् दण्डार्हो दण्ड्य इत्यपि ॥१०६॥ २१॥
भार्या रूपवती चास्य रूपवद्भार्य इत्यपि ।
इन्द्रश्च सोमश्चेत्येवम् इन्द्रासोमौ निदर्शनम् ॥१०७॥
शब्दरूपं पदार्थश्च व्युत्पत्तिः प्रकृतिर्गुणः ।
सर्वमेतदनेकार्थं दशानवगमे गुणाः ॥१०८॥
सामान्यवाचिनः शब्दा विशेषे स्थापिताः क्वचित् ।
पलायने यथा वृत्तिः को नु मर्या इतीषते ॥१०९॥

विशेषवाचिनस्त्वन्ये सामान्ये स्थापिताः क्वचित् ।
हिमेनाग्निमिति मन्त्रे हिमशब्दो निदर्शनम् ॥११०॥
पदमेकं समादाय द्विधा कृत्वा निरुक्तवान् ।
पूरुषादःपदं यास्को वृक्षेवृक्ष इति त्वृचि ॥१११॥ २२॥
अनेकं सत्तथा चान्यद् एकमेव निरुक्तवान् ।
अरुणो मा सकृन्मन्त्रे मासकृद्विग्रहेण तु ॥११२॥
पदव्यवायेऽपि पदे एकीकृत्य निरुक्तवान् ।
गर्भे निधानमित्येते न जामय इति त्वृचि ॥११३॥
पदजातिरविज्ञाता त्वःपदेऽर्थः शितामनि ।
स्वरानवगमोऽधायि वने नेत्यृचि दर्शितः ॥११४॥
शुनःशेपं नराशंसं द्यावा नः पृथिवीति च ।
निरस्कृतेतिप्रभृतिष्व् अर्थादासीत्क्रमो यथा ॥११५॥
वर्णस्य वर्णयोर्लोपो बहूनां व्यञ्जनस्य च ।
अचाणीति कपिर्नाभा दनो यामीत्यघासु च ॥११६॥ २३॥
अर्थात्पदं स्वाभिधेयं पदाद्वाक्यार्थनिर्णयः ।
पदसंघातजं वाक्यं वर्णसंघातजं पदम् ॥११७॥
अर्थात्प्रकरणाल्लिङ्गाद् औचित्याद्देशकालतः ।
मन्त्रेष्वर्थविवेकः स्याद् इतरेष्विति च स्थितिः ॥११८॥
इति नानान्वयोपायैर् नैरुक्ते यो यतेत सः ।
जिज्ञासुर्ब्रह्मणो रूपम् अपि दुष्कृत्परं व्रजेत् ॥११९॥
यथेदमग्रे नैवासीद् असदप्यथवापि सत् ।
जज्ञे यथेदं सर्वं तद् भाववृत्तं वदन्ति तु ॥१२०॥
भावप्रधानमाख्यातं षड्विकारा भवन्ति ते ।
जन्मास्तित्वं परीणामो वृद्धिर्हानं विनाशनम् ॥१२१॥ २४॥
एतेषामेव षण्णां तु येऽन्ये भावविकारजाः ।

ते यथावाक्यमभ्यूह्याः सामर्थ्यान्मन्त्रवित्तमैः ॥१२२॥
देवानां च पितॄणां च नमस्कारैस्तथैव च ।
अथ व्यस्तं समस्तं वा शृणु व्याहृतिदैवतम् ॥१२३॥
व्याहृतीनां समस्तानां दैवतं तु प्रजापतिः ।
व्यस्तानामयमग्निश्च वायुः सूर्यश्च देवताः ॥१२४॥
वाग्देवत्योऽथवाप्यैन्द्रो यदि वा परमेष्ठिनः ।
ओंकारो वैश्वदेवो वा ब्राह्मो दैवः क एव वा ॥१२५॥ २५॥

RV. i. आग्नेयं प्रथमं सूक्तं मधुछन्दस आर्षकम् ।
ज्ञेयाः सर्वेऽन्यदेवत्यास् तृचाः सप्तात उत्तराः ॥१२६॥
वायव्यः प्रथमस्त्वेषाम् ऐन्द्रवायव उत्तरः ।
मैत्रावरुणोऽथाश्विनोऽथैन्द्रोऽतो वैश्वदेवकः ॥१२७॥
तन्नामा विश्वलिङ्गो वा गायत्रोऽन्यस्तु यस्तृचः ।
बहुदैवतमन्यत्तु वैश्वदेवेषु शस्यते ॥१२८॥
लुशे दुवस्यौ शार्याते गोतमेऽथ ऋजिश्वनि ।
अवत्सारे परुच्छेपे अत्रौ दीर्घतमस्यृषौ ॥१२९॥ २६॥
वसिष्ठे नाभानेदिष्ठे गये मेधातिथौ मनौ ।
कक्षीवति विहव्ये च बहुष्वन्येष्वथर्षिषु ॥१३०॥
अगस्त्ये बृहदुक्थे च विश्वामित्रे च गाथिनि ।
दृश्यन्ते विप्रवादाश्च तासु तासु स्तुतिष्विह ॥१३१॥
बह्वीनां संनिपातस्तु यस्मिन्मन्त्रे प्रदृश्यते ।
आचार्यौ यास्कशाण्डिल्यौ वैश्वदेवं तदाहतुः ॥१३२॥
पादं वा यदि वार्धर्चम् ऋचं वा सूक्तमेव वा ।
वैश्वदेवं वदेत्सर्वं यत्किंचिद्बहुदैवतम् ॥१३३॥
ऋषिभिर्देवताः सर्वा विश्वाभि स्तुतिभि स्तुताः ।
संज्ञा तु विश्वमित्येषा सर्वावाप्नी निपातिता ॥१३४॥ २७॥

सारस्वतस्तु सप्तम एताः प्रउगदेवताः ।
सरस्वतीति द्विविधम् ऋक्षु सर्वासु सा स्तुता ॥१३५॥
नदीवद्देवतावच्च तत्राचार्यस्तु शौनकः ।
नदीवन्निगमाः षट् ते सप्तमो नेत्युवाच ह ॥१३६॥
अम्बितमे च दृषद्वत्यां चित्र इच्च सरस्वती ।
इयं शुष्मेभिरित्येतं मेने यास्कस्तु सप्तमम् ॥१३७॥
पशोः सारस्वतस्यैतां याज्यां* मैत्रायणीयके ।
प्राधान्याद्धविषः पश्यन् वाच एवेतरोऽब्रवीत् ॥१३८॥
सुरूपकृत्नुमित्यैन्द्रं सप्त चान्यान्यतः परम् ।
षळादह स्वधामनु मारुत्योऽनन्तरा ऋचः ॥१३९॥ २८॥
एका वीळु चिदिन्द्राय मरुद्भिः सह गीयते ।
तस्या एकान्तरायास्तु अर्धर्चोऽन्यो द्विदेवतः ॥१४०॥
मरुद्गणप्रधानो हीत्थं चेन्द्रो विचिकित्सितः ।
मन्दू समानवर्चसा मन्दुना वा सवर्चसा ॥१४१॥
मन्दू इति प्रगृह्णन्ति येषामेव द्विदेवतः ।
एकदेवत्यमाम्नाय्यो विज्ञायाध्ययनात्पदम् ॥१४२॥
रोदसी देवपत्नीनाम् अथर्वाङ्गिरसे यथा ।
मरुद्गणप्रधानेयम् आचार्याणां स्तुतिर्मता ॥१४३॥
मरुद्गणप्रधानत्वाद् इन्द्रस्तु विचिकित्सितः ।
मरुद्गणं महेन्द्रस्य समांशं सकलं विदुः ॥१४४॥ २९॥
अग्निमित्यग्निदैवत्यं पादस्तत्र द्विदेवतः ।
निर्मथ्याहवनीयार्थाव् अग्निनाग्निः समिध्यते ॥१४५॥
द्वितीये द्वादशर्चे तु प्रत्यृचं यास्तु देवताः ।
स्तूयन्ते ह्यग्निना सार्धं तासां नामानि मे शृणु ॥१४६॥
प्रथमायां स्तुतस्त्विध्मो द्वितीयायां तनूनपात् ।

नराशंसस्तृतीयायां चतुर्थ्यां स्तूयते त्विळः ॥१४७॥
बर्हिरेव तु पञ्चम्यां द्वारो देव्यस्ततोऽन्यया ।
नक्तोषासा तु सप्तम्याम् अष्टम्यां संस्तुतौ सह ॥१४८॥
दैव्याविति तु होतारौ नवम्यामृचि संस्तुताः ।
तिस्रो देव्यो दशम्यां तु ज्ञेयस्त्वष्टैव तु स्तुतः ॥१४९॥ ३०॥
एकादश्यां तु सूक्तस्य स्तुतं विद्याद्वनस्पतिम् ।
द्वादश्यां तु स्तुता देवीर् विद्यात्स्वाहाकृतीरिति ॥१५०॥
सूक्तेऽस्मिन्प्रत्यृचं यास्तु देवताः परिकीर्तिताः ।
ता एव सर्वास्त्वाप्रीषु द्वितीया तु विकल्पते ॥१५१॥
प्रैषैः सहाप्रीसूक्तानि तान्येकादश सन्ति च ।
यजूंषि प्रैषसूक्तं वा दशैतानीतराणि तु ॥१५२॥
सौत्रामणानि तु त्रीणि प्राजापत्याश्वमेधिके ।
पुरुषस्य तु यन्मेधे यजुःष्वेव तु तानि षट् ॥१५३॥
अत्रैव प्रैषसूक्तं स्यान् न यजुःष्वाद्रियेत तत् ।
तेषां प्रैषगतं सूक्तं यत्तु दीर्घतमा जगौ ॥१५४॥ ३१॥
मेधातिथौ यदुक्तं च त्रीण्येवोभयवन्ति तु ।
ऋषौ गृत्समदे यत्तु वाध्र्यश्वे च यदुच्यते ॥१५५॥
नराशंसवदत्रेश्च ददर्श च यदौर्वशः ।
तनूनपादगस्त्यश्च जमदग्निश्च यज्जगौ ॥१५६॥
विश्वामित्र ऋषिर्यच्च जगौ वै काश्यपोऽसितः ।
मेधातिथेर्ऋचां यास्तु प्रोक्ता द्वादश देवताः ॥१५७॥
संपद्यन्ते यथाग्निं ताः संपदं तां निबोधत ।
इध्मो यः सर्वमेवाग्निर् अयं हीध्मः समिध्यते ।
ध्मातेर्वैतत्कृतं रूपं ध्मातो हीध्मः समिध्यते ॥१५८॥
ध्मातो हीध्मः समिध्यते ॥ ३२॥

॥ इति बृहद्देवतायां द्वितीयोऽध्यायः ॥

तनूनपादयं त्वेव नाम्ना यच्छत्यसौ तनुम् ।
नपादिति प्रजामाहुर् अमुतोऽस्य च संभवम् ॥१॥
नराशंसमिहैके तु अग्निमाहुरथेतरे ।
नराः शंसन्ति सर्वेऽस्मिन् आसीना इति वाध्वरे ॥२॥
एतमेवाहुरन्येऽग्निं नराशंसोऽध्वरे ह्ययम् ।
नरैः प्रशस्य आसीनैर् आहुश्चैवर्त्विजो नरः ॥३॥
इळस्त्वृषिकृतं रूपम् ईडेश्च स्तुतिकर्मणः ।
इळावांस्तेन वोक्तोऽग्निर् इडिना वर्द्धि*कर्मणा ॥४॥
बर्हिरेवायमग्निस्तु सर्वं हि परिबृंहितम् ।
अन्नेन यज्ञुतो वा सन् इध्मेन परिबृंहितः ॥५॥ १॥
द्वारस्तु देव्यो याः प्रोक्ता विश्वेषां तास्तु पत्नयः ।
अग्नायीमनुवर्तन्ते तथाग्नाय्यग्निमेव च ॥६॥
अग्नौ ध्रुवं स्थितास्तास्तु संस्तूयन्तेऽग्निना सह ।
प्राधान्यं तासु चैवाग्ने स्तुतिष्वेव हविःषु च ॥७॥
नक्तोषासौ च ये देव्याव् आग्नेय्यावेव ते स्मृते ।
श्याव्याग्नेयी हि कालस्य तस्यैवोषाः कलेव तु ॥८॥
तम उच्छत्युषा नक्तानक्तीमां हिमबिन्दुभिः ।
अपि वाव्यक्तवर्णेति नञ्पूर्वाञ्चेरिदं भवेत् ॥९॥
सा हि दोषा भवत्यादौ निशीथे सा तमस्वती ।
नाम्ना भवत्युषाश्चैव सैषा प्रागुदयाद्रवेः ॥१०॥ २॥
दैव्याविति तु होताराव् अग्नी पार्थिवमध्यमौ ।
दिव्यादग्नेर्हि जज्ञाते दैव्यौ तेनेह जन्मना ॥११॥

तिस्रस्तु देव्यो याः प्रोक्तास् त्रिस्थानैवेह सा तु वाक् ।
त्रिविधेनोच्यते नाम्ना ज्योतिःषु त्रिषु वर्तिनी ॥१२॥
अग्निमेवानुगेळा तु मध्यं प्राप्ता सरस्वती ।
अमुं स्थिताधि लोकं तु भारती भवति ह्यसौ ॥१३॥
सैषा तु त्रिविधा वाग्वै दिवि च व्योम्नि चेह च ।
व्यस्ता चैव समस्ता च भजत्यग्नीनिमानपि ॥१४॥
त्वष्टा तु यस्त्वयमेव पार्थिवोऽग्निरिति स्तुतिः ।
पार्थिवस्यास्य वर्चः स्युः कस्याप्पृक् चार्तवेषु च ॥१५॥　　३॥
त्विषितस्त्वक्षतेर्वा स्यात् तूर्णमश्नुत एव वा ।
कर्मसूत्त्वारणो वेति तेन नामैतदश्नुते ॥१६॥
यः सहस्रतमो रश्मी रवेश्चन्द्रमुपाश्रितः ।
सोऽपि त्वष्टारमेवाग्निं परं चेह च यन्मधु ॥१७॥
प्रादाद्ब्रह्मापि सुप्रीतः सुताय तदथर्वणः ।
स चाभवदृषिस्तेन ब्रह्मणा दीप्तिमत्तरः ॥१८॥
तमृषिं निषिषेधेन्द्रो मैवं वोचः क्वचिन्मधु ।
न हि प्रोक्ते मधुन्यस्मिञ् जीवन्तं त्वोत्सृजाम्यहम् ॥१९॥
तमृषिं त्वश्विनौ देवौ विविक्ते मध्वयाचताम् ।
स च ताभ्यां तदाचष्टे यदुवाच शचीपतिः ॥२०॥　　४॥
तमब्रूतां तु नासत्याव् आश्व्येन शिरसा भवान् ।
मध्वाशु ग्राहयत्वावां मेन्द्रस्त्व त्वा वधीत्ततः ॥२१॥
आश्व्येन शिरसा तौ तु दध्यङ्ङाह यदश्विनौ ।
तदस्येन्द्रोऽहरत्स्वं तन्* न्यधत्तामस्य यच्छिरः ॥२२॥
दधीचश्च शिरश्चाश्व्यं कृत्तं* वज्रेण वज्रिणा ।
पपात सरसो मध्ये पर्वते शर्यणावति ॥२३॥
तदश्वस्तु समुत्थाय भूतेभ्यो विविधान्वरान् ।

प्रादाय युगपर्यन्तं तास्वेवाप्सु निमज्जति ॥२४॥
त्वष्टा रूपविकर्ता च योऽसौ माध्यमिके गणे ।
स्तुतः स च निपातेन सूक्तं तस्य न विद्यते ॥२५॥ ५॥
वनस्पतिं तु यं प्राहुर् अयं सोऽग्निर्वनस्पतिः ।
अयं वनानां हि पतिः पाता पालयतीति वा ॥२६॥
अग्निर्गृत्समदेनायं वनस्पतिरितीक्षितः ।
मन्दस्वेत्यस्य सूक्तस्य षळृचस्य तृतीयया ॥२७॥
यूपवत्तरुवच्चैव स्तुतिर्यास्य प्रसङ्गजा ।
सर्वेणाञ्जन्तिसूक्तेन तृतीये सा तु मण्डले ॥२८॥
स्वाहाकृतयोऽनेकाश्च विदुषां मतयोऽभवन् ।
तत्सर्वं त्वयमेवाग्निर् भवतीति विनिश्चयः ॥२९॥
अयं हि कर्ता स्वाहानां कृतिस्तासामिहैकजा ।
अयं प्रसूतिर्भूतानां सर्वेषामयमव्ययः ॥३०॥ ६॥
तनूनपाद्द्वितीया च नराशंसवती च या ।
समस्येते प्रयोक्तृभ्ये त्रिष्वेवोभयवत्सु तु ॥३१॥
नराशंसवती वा स्याद् द्वितीया च प्रजार्थिनाम् ।
बलकामोऽन्नकामो वा भूतिमिच्छेदथापि यः ॥३२॥
आग्नेयं सूक्तमेभिर्यद् वैश्वदेवमिहोच्यते ।
तद्विश्वलिङ्गं गायत्रं वैश्वदेवेषु शस्यते ॥३३॥
इन्द्र सोमं पिबेतीदं यद्द्वादशकमार्तवम् ।
तस्मिन्सहर्तुना सप्त प्रत्यृचं स्तौति देवताः ॥३४॥
तथर्तुनेति षट्स्वृक्षु चतसृष्वृतुभिः सह ।
पुनर्द्वयोर्ऋतुनेति बहुत्वैकत्वलक्षिताः ॥३५॥ ७॥
ऋतवो देवताभिश्च निपातेनेह संस्तुताः ।
तथर्तुप्रैषसूक्ते च तथा गार्त्समदेऽपि च ॥३६॥

मुख्यया त्विन्द्रमेवास्तौन् मरुतस्तु द्वितीयया ।
तृतीयया तु त्वष्टारं चतुर्थ्या चाग्निमेव च ॥३७॥
पञ्चम्या तु पुनः शक्रं षष्ठ्या देवावृतावृधौ ।
सप्तम्याद्याभिरग्निं च चतुर्भिर्द्रविणोदसम् ॥३८॥
आदेशाद्दैवतं ज्ञेयम् ऋङ्मन्त्राणां न लिङ्गतः ।
न शक्यं लिङ्गतो ह्यासां ज्ञातुं तत्त्वेन दैवतम् ॥३९॥
एकादश्या तु नासत्यौ द्वादश्याग्निमिमं पुनः ।
पृथक्पृथक्स्तुतीदं तु सूक्तमाह रथीतरः ॥४०॥ ८॥
बहुदैवे द्विदैवे वा गुणैर्वा यत्र कर्मजैः ।
स्तूयते देवतैकैका विभक्तस्तुति तद्विदुः ॥४१॥
वैश्वदेवानि सूक्तानि त्रिविधानि भवन्ति तु ।
सूर्यसंस्तवसंयुक्तं विश्वलिङ्गं पृथक्स्तुति ॥४२॥
पृथक्स्तुतीति यत्प्रोक्तं तद्विद्याद्बहुदैवतम् ।
विश्वलिङ्गं तु तद्यत्र विश्वैः स्वैः कर्मजैर्गुणैः ॥४३॥
विश्वानुद्दिश्य यद्देवान् स्तौति सूर्यमनेकधा ।
देवानेवाभिसंस्तौति तं प्राहुः सूर्यसंस्तवम् ॥४४॥
न तु भागस्य सूक्तादौ सूक्तेष्वेवौषसेषु वा ।
न सावित्रे हुयामीति न सूर्यायां क्रतौ मखे ॥४५॥ ९॥
न चैवैवं प्रवादेषु मन्त्रेष्वन्येषु केषुचित् ।
न च यत्र सजोषेति पदं वा स्यात्सजूरिति ॥४६॥
यस्मिन्प्रसङ्गादपि तु बह्वीनां परिकीर्तनम् ।
वैश्वदेवं तदप्याह स्थविरो लामकायनः ॥४७॥
असंस्तुतं स्तुतं वापि प्रदिष्टं दैवतं क्वचित् ।
मन्त्रैस्तदृषयोऽर्चन्ति तां तु बुध्येत शास्त्रवित् ॥४८॥
आदौ हि मध्ये चान्ते च पृथक्त्वेषु च कर्तृभिः ।

कर्माण्यनपदिष्टानि प्रदिष्टान्यपि तु क्वचित् ॥४९॥
कर्मैव तावत्सावित्र्यां निविदि स्तौति कर्मणा ।
यद्धेनुः सप्तनड्वाहौ वोळ्हा दोग्ध्र्याशुरेव वा ॥५०॥ १०॥
भागे यत्स्तौति चाग्न्यादीन् मित्रादींश्चाश्वसंस्तुतौ ।
यदैभिरिति चैतस्मिन् वैश्वदेवेऽग्निमर्चति ॥५१॥
तदाहुरादावन्ते च प्रायशोऽन्या स्तुवन्नृचः ।
प्रतियोगात्प्रसङ्गाद्वा स्तौत्यन्यामपि देवताम् ॥५२॥
यस्यां वदत्यर्थवादान् सा ज्ञेया सूक्तभागिनी ।
यां तु स्तौति प्रसङ्गेन सा विज्ञेया निपातिनी ॥५३॥
चतुर्धा भण्यते तस्मिन् सूक्ते वा सूक्तभागिनी ।
यस्मिन्सर्वांस्तु राजर्षीन् ऋषीन्वापि स्तुवन्नृषिः ॥५४॥
मेधातिथिरगस्त्यस्तु बृहदुक्थो मनुर्गयः ।
ऋजिश्वा वसुकर्णश्च शार्यातो गोतमो लुशः ॥५५॥ ११॥
स्वस्त्यात्रेयः परुच्छेपः कक्षीवान् गाथिनौर्वशौ ।
नाभाकश्चैव निर्दिष्टो दुवस्युर्ममतासुतः ॥५६॥
विहव्यः कश्यप ऋषिर् अवत्सारश्च नाम यः ।
वामदेवो मधुच्छन्दाः पार्थो दक्षसुतादितिः ॥५७॥
जुहूर्गृत्समदश्चर्षिर् देवाः सप्तर्षयश्च ये ।
यमोऽग्निस्तापसः कुत्सः कुसीदी चित्र एव च ॥५८॥
बन्धुप्रभृतयश्चैव चत्वारो भ्रातरः पृथक् ।
विष्णुश्च नेजमेषश्च नाम्ना संवननश्च यः ॥५९॥
एते तु सर्व एवास्य विश्वैः स्वैः कर्मजैर्गुणैः ।
समस्तैरथ च व्यस्तैः पृथक्सूक्तेषु तुष्टुवुः ॥६०॥ १२॥
पार्थिवो द्रविणोदोऽग्निः पुरस्ताद्यस्तु कीर्तितः ।
तमाहुरिन्द्रं दातृत्वाद् एके तु बलवित्तयोः ॥६१॥

अयं हि द्रविणोदोऽग्निर् अयं दाता बलस्य हि ।
Bजायते च बलेनायं मथ्यत्यृषिभिरध्वरे ॥६२॥
Bहवींषि द्रविणं प्राहुर् हविषो यत्र जायते ।
Bदातारश्चर्त्विजस्तेषां द्रविणोदास्ततः स्वयम् ॥६३॥
Bऋषीणां पुत्र इत्येषां दृश्यते सहसो यहो ।
Bमध्यमाद्वा यतो जज्ञे तस्माद्वा द्राविणोदसः ॥६४॥
Aद्रविणोदोऽग्निरेवायं द्रविणोदास्तदोच्यते ।
Aआग्नेयेष्वेव दृश्यन्ते प्रवादा द्रविणोदसः ॥६५॥
ऐन्द्रस्य नवकस्येह यदैन्द्रावरुणं परम् ।
तस्योत्तरं च सोमानं स्तूयते ब्रह्मणस्पतिः ॥६६॥ १३॥
ऋग्भिः पञ्चभिराद्याभिस् तिसृभिः सदसस्पतिः ।
नराशंसोऽन्यया चर्चा सोमेन्द्रौ तु निपातितौ ॥६७॥
चतुर्थ्यां सोम इन्द्रश्च पञ्चम्यां दक्षिणाधिका ।
प्रसङ्गादृषिणा प्रोक्ताः संबन्धा स्थानलोकयोः ॥६८॥
प्राजापत्यं तथेन्द्रः स्याद् इति तस्येह नामनी ।
कथिते द्वे च षट् चान्यान्य् एषां चाद्यः प्रजापतिः ॥६९॥
Bशिष्टानि यानि नामानि तानि वक्ष्याम्यतः परम् ।
*सत्पतिः कश्च कामश्च सदसस्पतिरेव च ॥७०॥
इळस्पतिर्वाचस्पतिस् ततस्तु ब्रह्मणस्पतिः ।
तृतीयान्त्ये* तु सूक्तस्य प्रथमं पञ्चमं च यत् ॥७१॥ १४॥
चतुर्भिरितरैस्त्वेनं न सूक्तं नाप्यृगश्नुते ।
सर्वाण्येव तु सर्वासां देवतानां प्रजापतेः ॥७२॥
नामानि कथयन्त्येते सम्यग्भक्तिदिदृक्षवः ।
तदाहुर्नैतदेवं स्याद् अष्टानामेष हि स्मृतः ॥७३॥
तैरेव चास्य कल्पन्त ऋतवश्च हवींषि च ।

मरुद्भिर्मध्यमस्थानैर् अयमग्निस्तु पार्थिवः ॥७४॥
नवकेनेह सूक्तेन प्रति त्यमिति संस्तुतः ।
मरुतां साहचर्यात्तु सूक्तेऽस्मिन्नाग्निमारुते ॥७५॥
मन्यते मध्यमं चैव यास्कोऽग्निं न तु पार्थिवम् ।
स्यादयं पार्थिवस्त्वेव तथा रूपं हि दृश्यते ॥७६॥ १५॥
हूयसे पीतये चेति वैद्युते न तदस्ति हि ।
अथ स्यादभिधानस्य देवतायाः पृथक् पृथक् ॥७७॥
ऋचोऽर्धर्चस्य पादस्य कथं ज्ञायेत दैवतम् ।
यथा निविदि सावित्र्यां स्तूयते कर्म कर्मणा ॥७८॥
दोग्ध्री धेनुर्वोढानड्वान् आशुः सप्तिः पुरंधिया ।
यथा च शंनोमित्रीया वरुणः प्राविता भुवत् ॥७९॥
सूक्तप्रायेणैभिरग्ने परीक्ष्यास्तत्र देवताः ।
शब्दानां द्विपदादीनां द्विदैवबहुदैवतम् ॥८०॥
असंस्तुतं संस्तुतवत् प्रदिष्टं दैवतं क्वचित् ।
यत्र द्विदैवते मन्त्र एकवद्देवतोच्यते ॥८१॥
विभक्तस्तुति तद्विद्याद् बहुष्वबहुवच्च यत् ।
आशीर्वादेषु संज्ञासु कर्मसंस्थासु देवताः ।
बह्व्यो ह बहुवत्तत्र द्विपदे यत्र संस्तुते ॥८२॥ १६॥
सुधन्वन आङ्गिरसस्यासन्पुत्रास्त्रयः पुरा ।
ऋभुर्विभ्वा च वाजश्च शिष्यास्त्वष्टुश्च तेऽभवन् ॥८३॥
शिक्षयामास तांस्त्वष्टा त्वाष्ट्रं यत्कर्म किंचन ।
परिनिष्ठितकर्माणो विश्वे देवा उपाह्वयन् ॥८४॥
विश्वेषां ते ततश्चक्रुर् वाहनान्यायुधानि तु ।
B धेनुं सबर्दुघां चक्रुर् अमृतं सबरुच्यते ॥८५॥
B बृहस्पतेरथाश्विभ्यां रथं दिव्यं त्रिवन्धुरम् ।

B इन्द्राय च हरी देवप्रहितेनाग्निनापि यत् ॥ ८६॥
B एकं चमसमित्युक्ते ज्येष्ठ आहेत्यथो दिवि ।
B उक्त्वा ततश्चक्षुश्चमसान् यथोक्तं तेन हर्षिताः ॥ ८७॥ १७॥
B त्वष्टा च सविता चैव देवदेवः प्रजापतिः ।
B सर्वान्देवान् समामन्त्र्य अमृतत्वं ददुश्च ते ॥ ८८॥
B तेषामाद्यान्ययोर्नाम्ना दृश्यते बहुवत्स्तवः ।
तृतीयसवने तेषां तैस्तु भागः प्रकल्पितः ॥ ८९॥
अपिबत्सोममिन्द्रश्च तैस्तत्र सवने सह ।
तेषां स्तुतिरिदं सूक्तं त्वयमित्यष्टकं परम् ॥ ९०॥
इहेन्द्राग्नी स्तुतौ देवौ तृतीयस्यादिरश्विनौ ।
हिरण्यपाणिं सावित्र्यश् चतस्रश्चाप्यथोत्तराः ॥ ९१॥
एकाग्नेर्द्वे तु देवीनां द्वादश्यां देवपत्नयः ।
इन्द्राणी वरुणानी च अग्नायी च पृथक् स्तुताः ॥ ९२॥ १८॥
द्यावापृथिव्यौ द्वे च स्यात् स्योनेत्यृक् पार्थिवी स्मृता ।
देवानां वात इत्येषा सूक्तशेषस्तु वैष्णवः ॥ ९३॥
वायोस्तीव्रेन्द्रवायुभ्यां तृचो द्वाभ्यां ततः परम् ।
तृचो मित्रावरुणयोस् तथेन्द्राय मरुत्वते ॥ ९४॥
तृचो विश्वेषां देवानां पूष्ण आघृणये तृचः ।
B आसक्तो हि घृणिस्तस्य दध्नः पूर्णो दृती रथे ॥ ९५॥
B आघृणिस्तत्स्तुतः पूषा कीरिभी रिभ्यते ततः ।
B यथा हि मधुनः पूर्णो दृतिरर्ध्येंति चाश्विनौ ॥ ९६॥
B सा वर्तनिं मधुनेति दृतिरे*व च दृश्यते ।
अर्धाष्टमा अपां ज्ञेया अध्यर्धान्याग्निदेवता ॥ ९७॥ १९॥
कस्य नूनं तु काय्याद्या आग्नेय्यृक् सवितुस्तृचः ।
भगभक्तस्य भागी वा परं यच्चिद्ध वारुणम् ॥ ९८॥

वसिष्वा हीति चाग्नेये त्वृगग्नेर्मध्यमस्य तु ।
जराबोधेति विज्ञेया वैश्वदेव्युत्तमा नमः ॥९९॥
पराश्वतस्रो यत्रेति इन्द्रोलूखलयो स्तुतिः ।
मन्येते यास्ककात्थक्याव् इन्द्रस्येति तु भागुरिः ॥१००॥
यच्चिद्ध्युलूखलस्य द्वे द्वे परे मुसलस्य तु ।
चर्माधिषवणीयं वा सोमं वान्या प्रशंसति ॥१०१॥
ऐन्द्रं यच्चिद्धि सत्येति उत्तरं चाश्विनात्तृचात् ।
आश्विनादुत्तरः कस्त उषस्यस्तृच उत्तमः ॥१०२॥ २०॥
स्तूयमानः शश्वदिति प्रीतस्तु मनसा ददौ ।
शुनःशेपाय दिव्यं तु रथं सर्वं हिरण्मयम् ॥१०३॥
आग्नेयं यत्त्वमैन्द्रे च त्रिश्चिदित्याश्विनं ततः ।
ऋतेऽर्थवादं कर्मैतद् इन्द्रस्येति तु शंसति ॥१०४॥
पादोऽग्नये ह्वयामीति मैत्रावरुण उत्तरः ।
तृतीयो रात्रिसंस्तावः सूक्तं सावित्रमुच्यते ॥१०५॥
पञ्चैतानि जगौ दृष्ट्वा सूक्तान्याङ्गिरसो मुनिः ।
हिरण्यस्तूपतां प्राप्य सख्यं चेन्द्रेण शाश्वतम् ॥१०६॥
आग्नेयं प्रेति मरुतां* क्रीळं त्रीणि पराण्यतः ।
उत्तिष्ठ ब्राह्मणस्पत्यं यं रक्षन्ति त्रयस्तृचाः ॥१०७॥ २१॥
वरुणार्यममित्राणां मध्य आदित्यदैवतः ।
पौष्णं सं पूषन्षड्ढीध्र्यस् तृतीया न तु केवला ॥१०८॥
मित्रेण वरुणेनाथ विश्वैर्देवैश्च संस्तवः ।
Bउक्तमत्रर्षिणा पूर्वम् आदेशाद्दैवतं विना ॥१०९॥
Bज्ञातुं न शक्यते लिङ्गात् तथापि क्वचिदुच्यते ।
Bआदित्या वसवो रुद्रास् त्वमग्न इति संस्तुताः ॥११०॥
Bतिस्रः सौम्योऽग्न आग्नेये प्रगाथेनाश्विनौ स्तुतौ ।

B सहोषसा लिङ्गभाजा अयं सोमः सुदानवः ॥१११॥
अर्धर्चो देवदेवत्य एषो इत्याश्विने परे ।
B आदित्यं मन्यते यास्को हविषेति सह स्तुतम् ॥११२॥ २२॥
सहौषसे ततः सौर्यम् उदु त्यमिति संस्तुतः ।
शुभक्तिर्येन वरुणो रोगघ्नस्तृच उत्तमः ॥११३॥
रोगापनुत्तिराद्याभ्याम् उद्यन्नित्युत्तमे तृचे ।
अर्धर्चे तु द्विषद्द्वेषः ऐन्द्रः सव्यः शतर्चिषु ॥११४॥
स्वयमिन्द्रस्समं पुत्रम् इच्छतोऽङ्गिरसो मुनेः ।
वज्र्येव सव्यो भूत्वर्षेर् योगित्वात्पुत्रतां गतः ॥११५॥
प्रथमे मण्डले ज्ञेया ऋषयस्तु शतर्चिनः ।
क्षुद्रसूक्तमहासूक्ता अन्ये मध्येषु मध्यमाः ॥११६॥
नवकं जातवेदस्यं नू चिद् यत्तु वया इति ।
वैश्वानरीयं तत्सूक्तं वह्निमाग्नेयमुत्तरम् ॥११७॥ २३॥
ऐन्द्राण्यस्मै ततस्त्रीणि वृष्णे शर्धाय मारुतम् ।
आग्नेयानि तु पश्वेति नव शश्वद्धि वामिति ॥११८॥
दशाश्विनानीमानीति इन्द्रावरुणयो स्तुतिः ।
सौपर्णेयास्तु याः काश्चिन् निपातस्तुतिषु स्तुताः ॥११९॥
उपप्रयन्तः सूक्तानि आग्नेयान्युत्तराणि षट् ।
हिरण्यकेशो रजसस् तृचोऽग्नेर्मध्यमस्य तु ॥१२०॥
इत्थेति पञ्च त्विन्द्राणि यामित्यस्यां निपातिताः ।
दध्यङ् मनुरथर्वा च मारुतानि प्र ये ततः ॥१२१॥
चत्वार्या नो वैश्वदेवे द्वे देवानां स्तुतिर्मते ।
आ नो भद्राश्च देवानां भद्रं आवच्छतं पुनः ॥१२२॥ २४॥
मधु वातास्तृचे तस्मिन् परमं मध्वपीष्यते ।
अदितिर्द्यौरिति त्वस्यां विभूतिः कथितादितेः ॥१२३॥

त्वं सोम सौम्यमौषसम् एता उ त्यास्तृचोऽश्विनोः ।
अश्विनाग्नेः ससोमस्य अग्नीषोमाविति स्तुतिः ॥१२४॥
गोतमादौशिजः कुत्सः परुच्छेपादृषेः परः ।
कुत्साद्दीर्घतमाः शश्वत् ते द्वे एवमधीयते ॥१२५॥ २५॥

इमं कुत्स आङ्गिरसो ददर्श जातवेदस्यं जगाद षोळशर्चम् ।
A पूर्वो देवा इत्यृचो देवदेवास् त्रयः पादा उत्तमायास्ततोऽर्धम् ॥१२६॥
A तस्यैव वा यस्य तत्पूर्वसूक्तं मित्रादिभ्यो वाच षड्भ्यः प्रकृताभ्यः ।
अन्त्योऽर्धर्चस्तु वा षण्णां स्तुतानां पूर्वो देवाः पादैस्तु त्रिभि स्तुताः ॥१२७॥
भरद्वाजे गृत्समदे वसिष्ठे नोधस्यगस्त्ये विमदे नभाके ।
कुत्से नोदर्का बहुदैवतेषु तथा द्विदेवेषु समानधर्मिणः ॥१२८॥
द्वे विरूपे सूक्तमौषसायाग्नये स प्रत्नथेति द्रविणोदसेऽग्नये ।
वैश्वानरस्येति वैश्वानरीयम् अस्मात्पूर्वं शुचयेऽग्नये पुनः ॥१२९॥
B जातवेदस्यं सूक्तसहस्रमेक ऐन्द्रात्पूर्वं कश्यपार्षं वदन्ति ।
B जातवेदसे सूक्तमाद्यं तु तेषाम् एकभूयस्त्वं मन्यते शाकपूणिः ॥१३०॥

स यो वृषेन्द्राणि पञ्च वैश्वदेवानि चन्द्रमाः ।
त्रीण्यैन्द्राग्ने य इन्द्राग्नी ततमित्यार्भवे परे ॥१३१॥ २६॥

त्रितं गास्त्वनुगच्छन्तं क्रूराः सालावृकीसुताः ।
कूपे प्रक्षिप्य गाः सर्वास् तत एवापजह्रिरे ॥१३२॥
स तत्र सुषुवे सोमं मन्त्रविन्मन्त्रवित्तमः ।
देवांश्चावाहयत्सर्वांस् तच्छुश्राव बृहस्पतिः ॥१३३॥
B आगच्छतोऽथ तान्दृष्ट्वा क्व वसत्यस्य तत्त्वतः ।
B सर्वदृक्कं च वरुणस्यार्यम्णश्चेत्युपालभत् ॥१३४॥
B कूपेष्टकाभिर्भ्रेणितान्य् अङ्गान्येवाभवन्मम ।
B दृष्ट्वा सर्वानहं स्तौमि यद्यप्येको न पश्यति ॥१३५॥
बृहस्पतिप्रचोदिता विश्वेदेवगणास्त्रयः ।

जग्मुस्त्रितस्य तं यज्ञं भागांश्च जगृहुः सह ॥१३६॥ २७॥
बृहस्पतिस्त्रितस्यैतज् ज्ञानं विज्ञानमेव च ।
तृचेनान्त्येन सूक्तस्य जगादर्षिरसाविति ॥१३७॥
द्यावापृथिव्योरीळेति आग्नेयः पाद उत्तरः ।
आश्विनः सूक्तशेषः स्याद् इदं रात्र्युषसो स्तुतिः ॥१३८॥
इमा रौद्रं परं सौर्यं चित्रं पञ्चाश्विनान्यतः ।
नासत्याभ्यामिति त्वन्त्ये अन्त्या दुःस्वप्ननाशिनी ॥१३९॥
ऐन्द्रं कवैश्वदेवं च प्रोषसे पृथुरुत्तरे ।
ऋषिर्दानं च भाव्यस्य प्रातरित्यत्र शंसति ॥१४०॥
काक्षीवतं कदित्थेति यदैन्द्रमुपदिश्यते ।
परोक्षं वैश्वदेवं तत् प्रदिष्टं स्वरसामसु ॥१४१॥ २८॥
अधिगम्य गुरोर्विद्यां गच्छन्स्वनिलयं किल ।
कक्षीवानध्वनि श्रान्तः सुष्वापारण्यगोचरः ॥१४२॥
तं राजा स्वनयो नाम भावयव्यसुतो व्रजन् ।
क्रीडार्थं सानुगोऽपश्यत् सभार्यः सपुरोहितः ॥१४३॥
अथैनं रूपसंपन्नं दृष्ट्वा देवसुतोपमम् ।
कन्यादाने मतिं चक्रे वर्णगोत्राविरोधतः ॥१४४॥
संबोध्यैनं स पप्रच्छ वर्णगोत्रादिकं ततः ।
राजन्नाङ्गिरसोऽस्मीति कुमारः प्रत्युवाच तम् ॥१४५॥
पुत्रोऽहं दीर्घतमस औचथ्यस्य ऋषेर्नृप ।
अथास्मै स ददौ कन्या दशाभरणभूषिताः ॥१४६॥ २९॥
तावतश्च रथान्छ्यावान् वीड्वङ्गान्वै चतुर्युजः ।
वधूनां वाहनार्थाय धनकुप्यमजाविकम् ॥१४७॥
निष्काणां वृषभाणां च शतं शतमदात्पुनः ।
एतदुत्तरसूक्तेन शतमित्यादिनोदितम् ॥१४८॥

शतमश्वाञ्छतं निष्कान् रथान्दश वधूमतः।
चतुर्युजो गवां चैव सहस्रं षष्ट्युपाधिकम् ॥१४९॥
स्वनयाद्भावयव्याद्यः कक्षीवान्प्रत्यपद्यत।
प्रतिगृह्य च तुष्टाव प्रातः पित्रे शशंस च ॥१५०॥ ३०॥

A फलप्रदर्शनं तस्य क्रियते प्रायशस्त्विह।
A द्वितीयां तु पितापश्यत् सुगुरित्यादिकामृचम् ॥१५१॥
A काक्षीवतं* सर्वमिति भगवानाह शौनकः।
A एषा तु दैर्घतमसी सानुलिङ्गा कथं भवेत् ॥१५२॥
A उच्यते प्रातरित्युक्ते सूनोर्दानेन हर्षितः।
A राज्ञश्चाशिषमाहाथ सुगुरित्यादिना किल ॥१५३॥

कर्माणि याभिः कथितानि राज्ञां दानानि चोच्चावचमध्यमानि।
नाराशंसीरित्यृचस्ताः प्रतीयाद् याभि स्तुतिर्दाशतयीषु राज्ञाम्॥१५४॥
पञ्चामन्दान्भावयव्यस्य गीता जायापत्योः संप्रवादो द्वृचेन।
संप्रवादं रोमशयेन्द्रराज्ञोर् एते ऋचौ मन्यते शाकपूणिः ॥१५५॥
इन्द्रेण जायापत्योश्चेतिहासं द्वृचेऽस्मिन्मन्यते शाकटायनः।
प्रादात्सुतां रोमशां नाम नाम्ना बृहस्पतिर्भावयव्याय राज्ञे ॥१५६॥
बृहस्पतिर्भावयव्याय राज्ञे ॥ ३१॥

॥ इति बृहद्देवतायां तृतीयोऽध्यायः॥

ततस्तमर्थं हरिवान्विदित्वा प्रियं सखायं स्वनयं दिदृक्षुः ।
अभ्याजगामाशु शचीसहायः प्रीत्यार्चयत्तं विधिनैव राजा ॥१॥
अभ्याजगामाङ्गिरसी च तत्र हृष्टा तयोः सा चरणौ ववन्दे ।
इन्द्रः सखित्वादथ तामुवाच रोमाणि ते सन्ति न सन्ति राज्ञि ॥२॥
सा बालभावादथ तं जगाद उपोप मे शक्र परामृशेति ।
तां पूर्वया सान्त्व्य नृपः प्रहृष्टो अन्वव्रजत्साथ पतिं पतिव्रता ॥३॥
अथाग्नेये अग्निमित्युत्तरे यं पञ्चैन्द्राणि प्र तदैन्द्र्यृगत्र ।
युवं तमिन्द्रापर्वतौ सह स्तुतौ त्विन्द्रं मेन इह यास्कः प्रधानम् ॥४॥
ऋक्षु स्तुतः पर्वतवद्धि वज्रो द्विवत्स्तुतौ चेन्द्रमाहुः प्रधानम् ।
आ त्वा वायोर्नव पञ्चेन्द्रवाय्वोर् एका वायोरुत्तरं द्विप्रधानम् ॥५॥ १॥
तत्र पञ्च वरुणमित्रदेवा दिवादिभ्यः कथिताभ्यः परे द्वे ।
द्वे द्वे पदे संस्तुते रोदसी च देवाश्चार्धर्चेन विभक्तमन्यत् ॥६॥
मैत्रावरुणं सुषुमेति सूक्तं प्रप्र पौष्णं वैश्वदेवं तृतीयम् ।
अस्तु श्रौषड् वैश्वदेवं तृतीयं वैश्वदेवं स्याद्बहुदेवतेषु ॥७॥
बहुशस्तु वैश्वदेवेषु सन्त्यृचः पादार्धर्चा द्वैपदास्त्रैपदाश्च ।
द्विप्रधाना अपि चैकप्रधाना बहुप्रधाना अपि वैश्वदेवाः ॥८॥
वैश्वदेवी मैत्रावरुणी द्वितीया तिस्रोऽश्विभ्यां तत ऐन्द्री ततोऽग्नेः ।
मारुत्येका तत ऐन्द्राग्न्यनन्तरा बार्हस्पत्या चोत्तमा स्तौति देवान् ॥९॥
ऋषीनृषिर्वा स्तौति दध्यङ् ह मेऽस्याम् आत्मानं वा तेषु शंसन्स्वजन्म ।
तस्मादस्यां विप्रवदन्ति केचिद् इन्द्राग्नी तस्यां तु निपातभाजौ ॥१०॥ २॥

द्वावुचथ्यबृहस्पती ऋषिपुत्रौ बभूवतुः ।
आसीदुचथ्यभार्या तु ममता नाम भार्गवी ॥११॥

तां कनीयान्बृहस्पतिर् मैथुनायोपचक्रमे ।
शुक्रस्योत्सर्गकाले तु गर्भस्तं प्रत्यभाषत ॥१२॥
इहास्मि पूर्वसंभूतो न कार्यः शुक्रसंकरः ।
तच्छुक्रप्रतिषेधं तु न ममर्ष बृहस्पतिः ॥१३॥
स व्याजहार तं गर्भं तमस्ते दीर्घमस्त्विति ।
स च दीर्घतमा नाम बभूवर्षिरुचथ्यजः ॥१४॥
स जातोऽभ्यतपद्देवान् अकस्मादन्धतां गतः ।
ददुर्देवास्तु तन्नेत्रे ततोऽनन्धो बभूव सः ॥१५॥ ३॥
स वेदिषद इत्यस्तौच् चतुर्भिर्जातवेदसम् ।
समिद्ध आप्रियोऽन्त्यैन्द्री तमित्यग्नेः पराणि षट् ॥१६॥
स्तुतौ तु मित्रावरुणौ सूक्तैर्मित्रमिति त्रिभिः ।
मित्रं मैत्रीं वदत्येताम् आ धेनवश्च शंसति ॥१७॥
अदितिं वाथवाप्यग्निं तथा रूपं हि दृश्यते ।
अग्निं मेनेऽदितिं त्वेव कुत्से चेह च शौनकः ॥१८॥
ऋषिरत्र प्रसङ्गाद्वा दर्शनाद्वानुकीर्तयेत् ।
विष्णोर्नु कमिति त्रीणि वैष्णवानि पराण्यतः ॥१९॥
प्र वश्च तिसृभिर्ऋग्भिर् इन्द्राविष्णू सह स्तुतौ ।
गृहाणि वा वैष्णवानि ता वामित्यृचि काङ्क्षति ॥२०॥ ४॥
जीर्णं तु दीर्घतमसं खिन्नास्तत्परिचारिणः ।
दासा बद्ध्वा नदीतोये दृष्टिहीनमवादधुः ॥२१॥
तत्रैकस्त्रैतनो नाम शस्त्रेणैनमपाहनत् ।
शिरश्चांसावुरश्चैव स्वयमेव न्यकृन्तत ॥२२॥
B हत्वा दीर्घतमास्तं तु पापेन महता वृतम् ।
B आत्माङ्गान्यनुदच्चैव तत्रोदोन्मोहितो भृशम् ॥२३॥
अङ्गदेशसमीपे तु तं नद्यः समुदक्षिपन्* ।

B अङ्गराजगृहे युक्ताम् उशिजं पुत्रकाम्यया ॥२४॥
B राज्ञा च प्रहितां दासीं भक्तां मत्वा महातपाः ।
जनयामास चोत्थाय कक्षीवत्प्रमुखानृषीन् ॥२५॥ ५॥
तुष्टाव चैव सूक्ताभ्याम् अबोधीत्यश्विनावृषिः ।
प्रेति द्यावापृथिव्यौ तु पराभ्यामेतदुत्तरम् ॥२६॥
किमार्भवं परे मा नो मेध्यस्याश्वस्य संस्तवः ।
ईर्मान्तास इति त्वस्यां नीयमानं प्रशंसति ॥२७॥
स्वयूथ्यास्तस्य चैवात्र बहवः संस्तुता हयाः ।
नियुक्ताश्चानियुक्ताश्च प्रसङ्गादनुकीर्तिताः ॥२८॥
संज्ञप्तवदसंज्ञप्तं भविष्यं चाह भूतवत् ।
तस्य मांसस्य सूनस्य चरूणां हविषस्तथा ॥२९॥
वासोऽधिवाससोश्चात्र यद्विशस्यं च कीर्तितम् ।
गात्रस्य शूलस्थूणानां स्वधितेश्च प्रकीर्तनम् ॥३०॥ ६॥
छागस्य कीर्तनं चात्र इन्द्रापूष्णोः सह स्तुतिः ।
सूक्तं यदस्यवामीयं वैश्वदेवं तदुच्यते ॥३१॥
प्रवादा विविधास्तत्र देवानां चात्र कीर्तनम् ।
B सूक्तेऽस्यर्चि परोक्षोक्ता वक्ष्यामि *भ्रातरस्त्रयः ॥३२॥
अग्निस्तु वामः पलितो वायुर्भ्राता तु मध्यमः ।
घृतपृष्ठस्तृतीयोऽत्र सप्त वै रश्मय स्तुताः ॥३३॥
परास्तु कथयन्त्यग्निं यथा वर्षति पाति च ।
अहोरात्रान्दिनान्मासान् ऋतूंश्च परिवर्तिनः ॥३४॥
पञ्चधा च त्रिधा चैव षोढा द्वादशधैव च ।
संवत्सरं चक्रवच्च पराभिः कीर्तयत्यृषिः ॥३५॥ ७॥
क्षेत्रज्ञानं च धेनुं च गौरीं वाचं सरस्वतीम् ।
धर्मं पूर्वयुगीयं च साध्यान्देवगणांस्तथा ॥३६॥

विविधानि च कर्माणि अग्निवायुविवस्वताम् ।
विभूतिमग्नेर्वायोश्च जगति स्यात्तु* जङ्गमे ॥३७॥
हरणं रश्मिभिर्वारो विसर्गं पुनरेव च ।
कर्मानुकीर्तनं चात्र पर्जन्याग्निविवस्वताम् ॥३८॥
मातापुत्रौ तु वाक्प्राणौ माता वागितरः सुतः ।
सरस्वन्तमिति प्राणो वाचं प्राहुः सरस्वतीम् ॥३९॥
शरीरमिन्द्रियैर्युक्तं क्षेत्रमित्यभिधीयते ।
वेद तत्प्राण एवैकस् तस्मात्क्षेत्रज्ञ उच्यते ॥४०॥ ८॥
B मेघे शकस्तस्य धूमः सलिलं वास एव वा ।
B सोम उक्षा भवन्त्यस्य पावकाश्च मयोऽधिपाः ॥४१॥
B गौरीरन्तं वैश्वदेवम् उपरि स्यात्पृथक्स्तुतिः ।
B इन्द्रं मित्रमिमे सौर्यौ सौरी वान्त्या सरस्वते ॥४२॥
A सूक्तमल्पस्तवं त्वेतज् ज्ञानमेव प्रशंसति ।
A प्रवादबहुलत्वाच्च ततः सलिलमुच्यते ॥४३॥
मारुतैन्द्रस्तु संवादः कयेति परमः स्मृतः ।
मरुतामयुजस्त्वैन्द्र्यो युग्माः सर्वाः सहान्त्यया ॥४४॥
एकादशी प्रथमा च मारुतस्तृच उत्तरः ।
B तृचस्यैव तु तस्योक्तं कर्तृत्वमितरस्य तु ॥४५॥
B इतिहासः* पुरावृत्त ऋषिभिः परिकीर्त्यते ।
समागच्छन्मरुद्भिस्तु चरन्व्योम्नि शतक्रतुः ॥४६॥
दृष्ट्वा तुष्टाव तानिन्द्रस् ते चेन्द्रमृषयोऽब्रुवन् ।
तेषामगस्त्यः संवादं तपसा वेद तत्त्वतः ॥४७॥
स तानभिजगामाशु निरुप्यैन्द्रं हविस्तदा ।
मरुतश्चाभितुष्टाव सूक्तैस्त्विन्वति च त्रिभिः ॥४८॥ ९॥
महश्चिदिति चैवेन्द्रं सहस्रमिति चैतया ।

निरुप्तं तद्धविश्चेन्द्रं मरुद्भ्यो दातुमिच्छति ॥४९॥
विज्ञायावेक्ष्य तद्भावम् इन्द्रो नेति तमब्रवीत् ।
न श्वो नाद्यतनं ह्यस्ति वेद कस्तद्यदद्भुतम् ॥५०॥
कस्यचित्त्वर्थसंचारे चित्तमेव विनश्यति ।
किं न इत्यब्रवीदिन्द्रम् अगस्त्यो भ्रातरस्तव ॥५१॥
मरुद्भिः संप्रकल्पस्व वधीर्मा नः शतक्रतो ।
किं नो भ्रातरिति त्वस्याम् इन्द्रो मान्यमुपालभत् ॥५२॥
अगस्त्यस्त्वरमित्यस्यां क्षुब्धमिन्द्रं प्रशामयत् ।
प्रादात्संवननं कृत्वा तेभ्य एव च तद्धविः ॥५३॥ १०॥
सुते चकार सोमेऽथ तानिन्द्रः सोमपीथिनः ।
तस्माद्विद्यान्निपातेन ऐन्द्रेषु मरुत स्तुतान् ॥५४॥
प्रीतात्मा पुनरेवर्षिस् तांस्तुष्टाव पृथक्पृथक् ।
मरुतः प्रति सूक्ताभ्याम् इन्द्रं षड्भिः परैस्तु सः ॥५५॥
B स्तुतश्चतसृभिश्चेन्द्र स्तुतास इति तैः सह ।
B मरुद्भिः सह यत्रेन्द्रो मरुत्वांस्तत्र सोऽभवत् ॥५६॥
ऋतौ स्नातामृषिर्भार्यां लोपमुद्रां यशस्विनीम् ।
उपजल्पितुमारेभे रहःसंयोगकाम्यया ॥५७॥ ११॥
द्वाभ्यां सा त्वब्रवीदृग्भ्यां पूर्वीरिति चिकीर्षितम् ।
रिरंसुस्तामथागस्त्य उत्तराभ्यामतोषयत् ॥५८॥
विदित्वा तपसा सर्वं तयोर्भावं रिरंसतोः ।
श्रुत्वैनः कृतवानस्मि ब्रह्मचार्युत्तमे जगौ ॥५९॥
प्रशस्य तं परिष्वज्य गुरू मूर्ध्न्य*वजघ्रतुः ।
स्मित्वैनमाहतुश्चोभाव् अनागा असि पुत्रक ॥६०॥
युवो रजांसीति ततः सूक्तैः पञ्चभिरश्विनौ ।
अगस्त्य एव तुष्टाव कतरेति परेण तु ॥६१॥

द्यावापृथिव्यौ सूक्तेन आ नो विश्वान्दिवौकसः ।
पितुमन्नं समिद्धाग्न्यो अग्निमग्ने नयेति च ॥ ६२ ॥
बृहस्पतेरनर्वाणं कङ्कतोपनिषत्परम् ।
अपां तृणानां सूर्यस्य केचिदेतां स्तुतिं विदुः ॥ ६३ ॥
ददर्श तदगस्त्यो वा विषघ्नं विषशङ्कया ।
अदृष्टाख्यो नष्टरूपः सूक्तस्यान्त्योऽत्र तु तृचः ॥ ६४ ॥ १२ ॥

RV. ii. अस्तौद्गृत्समदोऽग्निं त्वं जातवेदस्यमाप्रियः ।
यज्ञेनाथ समिद्धोऽग्निर् अतोऽग्निं सप्तभिर्हुवे ॥ ६५ ॥
संयुज्य तपसात्मानम् ऐन्द्रं बिभ्रन्महद्वपुः ।
अदृश्यत मुहूर्तेन दिवि च व्योम्नि चेह च ॥ ६६ ॥
तमिन्द्रमिति मत्वा तु दैत्यौ भीमपराक्रमौ ।
धुनिश्च चुमुरिश्चोभौ सायुधावभिपेततुः ॥ ६७ ॥
विदित्वा स तयोर्भावम् ऋषिः पापं चिकीर्षतोः ।
यो जात इति सूक्तेन कर्माण्यैन्द्राण्यकीर्तयत् ॥ ६८ ॥
उक्तेषु कर्मस्वैन्द्रेषु भीस्तावाशु विवेश ह ।
इदमन्तरमित्युक्त्वा ताविन्द्रस्तु निबर्हयत् ॥ ६९ ॥ १३ ॥
निहत्य तौ गृत्समदम् ऋषिं शक्रोऽभ्यभाषत ।
यथेष्टं मां सखे पश्य प्रियत्वं ह्यागतोऽसि मे ॥ ७० ॥
वरं गृहाण मत्तस्त्वम् अक्षयं चास्तु ते तपः ।
प्रह्वस्तं प्रत्युवाचर्षिर् अस्माकं वदतां वर ॥ ७१ ॥
तनूनामस्तु चारिष्टिर् वाक् चास्तु हृदयंगमा ।
सुवीरा रयिमन्तश्च वयं त्वामिन्द्र धीमहे ॥ ७२ ॥
इन्द्र त्वां च विजानीमो वयं जन्मनि जन्मनि ।
त्वद्गतश्चैव मे भावो मापगास्त्वं रथीतर ॥ ७३ ॥

B निरुक्तं तदिदं वार्यम् इन्द्र श्रेष्ठान्यृचान्यया ।
B वव्रे वरमिदं सर्वं तदाकर्ण्य शचीपतिः ॥७४॥ १४॥
तथेत्युक्त्वा तुराषाट् तु पाणौ जग्राह दक्षिणे ।
ऋषिश्चास्य सखित्वेन पाणिना पाणिमस्पृशत् ॥७५॥
सहितौ जग्मतुश्चैवं महेन्द्रसदनं प्रति ।
तत्रैनमार्हयत्प्रीत्या स्वयमेव पुरंदरः ॥७६॥
कर्मणा विधिदृष्टेन तमृषिं चाभ्यपूजयत् ।
सखित्वाच्च पुनश्चैनम् उवाच हरिवाहनः ॥७७॥
गृणन्मादयसे यस्मात् त्वमस्मानृषिसत्तम ।
तस्माद्गृत्समदो नाम शौनहोत्रो भविष्यसि ॥७८॥
ततो द्वादशभिः सूक्तैस् तुष्टावेन्द्रं श्रुधीत्यृषिः ।
ददर्श संस्तुवन्नेव तत्र स ब्रह्मणस्पतिम् ॥७९॥ १५॥
बृहस्पतिं तु तुष्टाव दृष्टलिङ्गाभिरेव च ।
स तमप्यभितुष्टाव चतुर्भिरित उत्तरैः ॥८०॥
गणानां विश्वमित्यस्यां सहेन्द्राब्रह्मणस्पती ।
बृहस्पतिं प्रसङ्गाद्वा ब्रह्मणस्पतिमेव च ॥८१॥
A तुष्टाव कर्मणैकेन प्रभावस्यान्तरं द्वयोः ।
मित्रावरुणदक्षांशतुविजातभगार्यम्णाम् ॥८२॥
आदित्यानामिमाः सूक्तम् इदं वारुणमुच्यते ।
वारुणी यो म इत्याद्या दुःस्वप्नाद्यप्रणाशिनी ॥८३॥
धृतव्रता वैश्वदेवम् ऋतमैन्द्रं परं तु यत् ।
प्र हि क्रतुमिति त्वस्याम् इन्द्रासोमौ सह स्तुतौ ॥८४॥
सरस्वति त्वमित्यस्मिन्न् अर्धर्चे मध्यमा तु वाक् ।
बृहस्पतिस्तुतिर्यो नस् तं व* ऋङ् मरुतां स्तुतिः ॥८५॥ १६॥
अस्माकं वैश्वदेवं स्याद् आदावस्येति चास्य ऋक् ।

द्यावापृथिव्योस्त्वाष्ट्र्यौ वा अथवैन्द्र्यौ परे ततः ॥८६॥
द्वे द्वे राकासिनीवाल्योः षड् गुङ्ग्वाद्यास्तथान्यया ।
B तत्पूर्वे द्वे ऋचौ कुह्वाः कुहूमहमिति स्मृते ॥८७॥
B तदुत्तरे द्वेऽनुमतेर् अनु नोऽन्विदिति स्मृते ।
B धातुश्चतस्रस्त्वादौ धाता ददातु नो रयिम् ॥८८॥
रौद्रं मारुतं तु परम् आ ते धारावरा इति ।
वामतस्तु मृगं दृष्ट्वा बिभ्यदेत्य ऋषिः स्वयम् ॥८९॥
स्तुहि श्रुतमिति त्वस्यां तमेवास्तौत्प्रसादयन् ।
अपां नपादुपेत्यत्र स्तुतः सूक्ते ततः परे ॥९०॥ १७॥
तुभ्यमित्यार्तवे सूक्ते सावित्रादाश्विनं परम् ।
सोमः पूषादितिश्चैव सोमापौष्णेऽन्यया स्तुताः ॥९१॥
वायव्ये चैन्द्रवायवी पञ्चाथ प्राउगास्तृचाः ।
प्रेत्यृक्स्तौति हविर्धाने अग्निस्तत्र निपातभाक् ।
द्यावापृथिव्यौ द्यावेति हविर्धाने ततः परे ॥९२॥
स्तुतिं तु पुनरेवेच्छन् इन्द्रो भूत्वा कपिञ्जलः ।
ऋषेर्जिगमिषोराशां ववाशास्थाय दक्षिणाम् ॥९३॥
स तमार्षेण संप्रेक्ष्य चक्षुषा पक्षिरूपिणम् ।
पराभ्यामभितुष्टाव सूक्ताभ्यां तु कनिक्रदत् ॥९४॥ १८॥

RV. iii. प्रशास्य गां यस्तपसाभ्यगच्छद् ब्रह्मर्षितामेकशतं च पुत्रान् ।
स गाथिपुत्रस्तु जगाद सूक्तं सोमस्य मेत्याग्नेयं यत्परे च ॥९५॥
वैश्वानरीये* समित्समिदाग्न्यो द्वे आग्नेये उत्तरे त्वत्र सूक्ते ।
द्यावापृथिव्या उषसो निपाता आपोऽथ देवाः पितरश्च मित्रः ॥९६॥
आग्नेयेषु दृश्यन्ते स्तुतास्तु वैश्वानरो वरुणो जातवेदाः ।
स्तूयेतैको यत्र यत्रास्तुतिर्वा निपात्यर्थाश्चोपमार्थाश्च विद्यात् ॥९७॥

राजर्षयो गृत्समदा वसिष्ठा भरद्वाजाः कुशिका गोतमाश्च ।
विश्वेऽश्विनावङ्गिरसोऽत्रयोऽदितिर् भोजाः कण्वा भृगवो रोदसी
दिशः ॥ ९८ ॥

सावित्रसौम्याश्विनमारुतेषु ऐन्द्राग्नेये रौद्रसौर्यौषसेषु ।
आदावन्तो सूक्तमध्ये स्तुतास्तु न व्याघ्नन्ति देवताः सूक्तभाजः ॥ ९९ ॥ १९ ॥

अग्नेः सप्तदशोऽध्याय ऊर्ध्वं ऊ षु ण ऊतये ।
एते काण्व्यावृचौ यौष्याव् अञ्जन्ति त्वेति पञ्च च ॥ १०० ॥
शेषा बहुभ्यो यूपेभ्यो वैश्वदेवी तृगष्टमी ।
अस्यान्या व्रश्चनी योक्ता षष्ठमैन्द्राग्नमुच्यते ॥ १०१ ॥
अग्निमुषसं वैश्वदेवी दधिक्रामिति चैतया ।
आग्नेन्द्री त्वन्न इन्द्रश्चर्क् परो वैश्वानरस्तृचः ॥ १०२ ॥
प्र यन्तु मारुतश्चान्या शतधारं गुरुस्तवः ।
प्र वो वाजा ऋतूंस्तौति ऋत्विज स्तौति मन्यत ॥ १०३ ॥
पुरीष्यास इति त्वस्यां धिष्ण्यायात्रीन्प्रशंसति ।
ज्ञेयाश्चैव तु होतारस् ते दैव्याश्चैव तत्र तु ॥ १०४ ॥ २० ॥
त्रयोविंशतिरैन्द्राणि इच्छन्तीति पराण्यतः ।
सूक्ते प्रेति तु नद्यश्च विश्वामित्रः समूदिरे ॥ १०५ ॥
पुरोहितः सन्निज्यार्थं सुदासा सह यन्नृषिः ।
विपाट्छुतुद्र्योः संभेदं शमित्येते उवाच ह ॥ १०६ ॥
प्रवादास्तत्र दृश्यन्ते द्विवद्बहुवदेकवत् ।
अच्छेत्यर्धर्चे पच्छो वा नदीष्वप्येकवन्नि ते ॥ १०७ ॥
आद्ये तृचे द्विवत्सार्धे विश्वामित्रवचः स्तुतेः ।
एताभिर्ऋग्भिर्वा नद्य ऋषिं बहुवदूचिरे ॥ १०८ ॥
षष्ठ्याष्टम्या चतुर्थ्यां च दशम्या चेतरा ऋषेः ।
सप्तम्यामृचि षष्ठ्यां च यौ देवौ परिकीर्तितौ ॥ १०९ ॥ २१ ॥

निपातिनौ तु तौ ज्ञेयौ ऐन्द्रापार्वत्यृगुत्तमे ।
करोति पुत्रिकां नाम यथा दुहितरं तथा ॥११०॥
तस्यां सिञ्चति रेतो वा तच्छासदिति कीर्तितम् ।
रिक्थस्य दुहितुर्दानं नेत्यृचि प्रतिषिध्यते ॥१११॥
तस्याश्चाह यवीयांसं भ्रातरं ज्येष्ठवत्सुतम् ।
सुदासश्च महायज्ञे शक्तिना गाथिसूनवे ॥११२॥
निगृहीतं बलाच्चेतः सोऽवसीदद्विचेतनः ।
तस्मै ब्राह्मीं तु सौरीं वा नाम्ना वाचं ससर्परीम् ॥११३॥
सूर्यक्षयादिहाहृत्य ददुस्ते जमदग्नयः ।
कुशिकानां ततः सा वाग् अमतिं तामपाहनत् ॥११४॥ २२॥
उपेति चास्यां कुशिकान् विश्वामित्रोऽनु*बोधयत् ।
लब्ध्वा वाचं च हृष्टात्मा तानृषीन्प्रत्यपूजयत् ॥११५॥
ससर्परीरिति द्वाभ्याम् ऋग्भ्यां वाचं स्तुवन्स्वयम् ।
स्थिरावित्यनसोऽङ्गान्यनडुहश्च गृहान्व्रजन् ॥११६॥
ततश्च स्वशरीरेण गृहान्गच्छन्परीददे ।
पराश्चतस्रो यास्त्वत्र वसिष्ठद्वेषिण्यः स्मृताः ॥११७॥
विश्वामित्रेण ताः प्रोक्ता अभिशापा इति स्मृताः ।
द्विषद्वेषास्तु ताः प्रोक्ता विद्याश्चैवाभिचारिकाः ॥११८॥ २३॥
वसिष्ठास्ता न शृण्वन्ति तदाचार्यकसंमतम् ।
कीर्तनाच्छ्रवणाद्वापि महादोषश्च जायते ॥११९॥
शतधा भिद्यते मूर्धा कीर्तितेन श्रुतेन वा ।
तेषां बालाः प्रमीयन्ते तस्मात्तास्तु न कीर्तयेत् ॥१२०॥
विश्वांश्च देवांस्तुष्टाव चतुर्भिरिममित्यृषिः ।
B अस्तौद्विश्वात्मना सर्वान् मन्यमानः परं पदम् ॥१२१॥
B देवानामसुरत्वं तद् एकं महदितीरयन् ।

अश्विनौ मित्र ऋभवो धेनुर्मित्र इहेह वः ॥१२२॥

A वैश्वदेवीति विज्ञेया मैत्री मित्राय पञ्च तु ।

ऐन्द्रार्भवस्तृचस्त्वत्र आर्भवे सूक्त उत्तमः ॥१२३॥ २४॥

B पूर्वे त्वृचे निपातीन्द्र उषो वाजेन पञ्चमात् ।

औषसादुत्तरास्त्वन्ये षट् पृथग्देवतास्तृचाः ।

ऐन्द्रावरुणः प्रथमो बार्हस्पत्यस्तथापरः ॥१२४॥

पौष्णसावित्रसौम्याश्च मैत्रावरुण उत्तमः ।

तुष्टाव जमदग्निश्च तेन देवावृतावृधौ ॥१२५॥ २५॥

RV. iv. देवर्षिपितृपूजार्थं पपाचान्त्राणि यः शुनः ।

यस्य वै श्येनरूपेण आहरद्वृत्रहा मधु ॥१२६॥

सोऽग्निं तु पञ्चदशभिर् इन्द्रं षोडशभिः परैः ।

ऋषिस्त्वामिति तुष्टाव सूक्तैरेति तु गौतमः ॥१२७॥

स भ्रातरमिति त्वासु तिसृष्वग्निर्निपातभाक् ।

वरुणेनाभिसंस्तौति आहुरन्ये निपातिनम् ॥१२८॥

लिङ्गोक्तदैवते सूक्ते एके प्रत्यग्निरेव तु ।

ऋषिर्बोधदिति द्वाभ्यां स्तौति सोमकमेव तु ॥१२९॥ २६॥

तस्यैव चायुषोऽर्थाय पराभ्यामश्विनौ स्तुतौ ।

अञ्जसा न जनिष्येऽहं ब्रुवाणं गर्भमेव तु ॥१३०॥

अन्वशाददितिः पुत्रम् इन्द्रमात्महितैषिणी ।

स जातमात्रो युद्धाय ऋषिमेवाजुहाव तु ॥१३१॥

योधयन्वामदेवस्तं कृत्वात्मनि बलं तथा ।

दिनानि दश रात्रीश्च विजिग्ये चैनमोजसा ॥१३२॥

स तं क इममित्यस्यां विक्रीणन्नृषिसंसदि ।

स्वयं तेनाभितुष्टाव नकिरिन्द्रेति गौतमः ॥१३३॥

किमादुतासीति चास्यां मन्युमर्धे पराणुदत् ।
अथास्य रूपवीर्याणि धैर्यकार्याणि तान्यृषिः ॥१३४॥ २७॥
विविधानि च कर्माणि शशंसादितये तथा ।
अहमित्यात्मसंस्तावस् तृचे स्तुतिरिवास्य हि ॥१३५॥
प्र सु ष विभ्यो नवभिर् ऋग्भिः श्येनस्य संस्तवः ।
पराभिस्त्वेति पञ्चर्चे सोमेनेन्द्र स्तुतः सह ॥१३६॥
सोमप्रधानामेतां तु क्रौष्टुकिर्मन्यते स्तुतिम् ।
दिवश्चिदिति चैतेन तृचेनेन्द्रेण संस्तुताम् ॥१३७॥
उषसं मध्यमां मेने आचार्यः शाकटायनः ।
वाममृचि स्तुताश्चात्र भगः पूषेति चार्यमा ॥१३८॥
B करूळतीति पूषोक्तोऽदन्तकः स इति श्रुतेः ।
B अस्माकमुत्तमं सूर्यं स्तौतीत्याहाश्वलायनः ॥१३९॥ २८॥
इन्द्रस्य हरयो ह्यश्वा अग्नेरश्वास्तु रोहितः ।
सूर्यस्य हरितश्चैव वायोर्नियुत एव च ॥१४०॥
रासभः सहितोऽश्विभ्याम् अजाः पूष्णश्च वाजिनः ।
पृषत्योऽश्वास्तु मरुतां गावोऽरुण्यस्तथोषसाम् ॥१४१॥
सवितुर्वाजिनः श्यावा विश्वरूपा बृहस्पतेः ।
सहैते देवताभिस्तु स्तूयन्तेऽप्यल्पशोऽन्यथा ॥१४२॥
आयुधं वाहनं चापि स्तुतौ यस्येह दृश्यते ।
तमेव तु स्तुतं विद्यात् तस्यात्मा बहुधा हि सः ॥१४३॥
कनीनका सूक्तशेषो हर्यो स्तुतिरिहोच्यते ।
चत्वार्यतश्च विज्ञेयान्य् अप्रगृह्याणि विद्रधे ॥१४४॥
अप्रगृह्याणि विद्रधे ॥ २९॥

॥ इति बृहद्देवतायां चतुर्थोऽध्यायः ॥

प्रेति पञ्चार्भवं त्रीणि दाधिक्राणि पराण्यतः ।
ऋग्द्यावापृथिव्यौ स्तौति दाधिक्राणां मुखे तु या ॥१॥
परोक्षैरस्तुतो वाग्भिर् नामभिश्च स्तुतास्त्रयः ।
अग्निर्वायुश्च सूर्यश्च हंसः शुचिषदित्यृचि ॥२॥
B नियुक्ता सूर्यदेवत्या हंस इत्यैतरेयके ।
द्वे त्वैन्द्रावरुणे सूक्ते ततस्त्रीण्याश्विनानि कः ॥३॥
अयं वायो विहीत्येषु* वायव्याः सप्त कीर्तिताः ।
नव चैवैन्द्र*वायव्या इन्द्रस्तिस्रः शतेन षट् ॥४॥
इदं कथितदेवत्यं यस्तस्तम्भोत्तमो तृचः ।
स्तुतिरिन्द्राबृहस्पत्योर् अष्टावेता ऋचः स्मृताः ॥५॥
सूक्तं तु तद्बार्हस्पत्यम् इदमित्यौषसे परे ।
पुरोधातुः कर्मशंसा स इद्राजोच्यते तृचे ॥६॥ १॥
तस्याविचे द्वे तु को वैश्वदेवं मही द्यावापृथिवीयं परं तु यत् ।
क्षेत्रस्येति तिस्रस्तु क्षेत्रपत्याः शुनं वाहाः शुनदेवी त्वृगुत्तरा ॥७॥
वायुः शुनः सूर्य एवात्र सीरः शुनासीरौ वायुसूर्यौ वदन्ति ।
शुनासीरं यास्क इन्द्रं तु मेने सूर्येन्द्रौ तौ मन्यते शाकपूणिः ॥८॥
शुनासीरौ पञ्चम्यां तु स्तुतौ तौ द्वे तु सीतायै षष्ठी सप्तमी च ।
शुनं नः फालाः कृषिं स्तौति पादः शुनं कीनाशाः कृषिजीवान्मनुष्यान् ॥९॥
स्तुतः पादेऽत्र पर्जन्यस्तृतीये अन्त्यं* त्वृषिर्धनकामो जगाद ।
कृषिं वा स्तौति सर्वं हि सूक्तं समुद्रादित्यग्नेर्मध्यमस्य ॥१०॥
आदित्यं वा ब्राह्मणोक्तं प्रदिष्टम् आग्नेयं वाप्याज्यसूक्तं हि दृष्टम् ।
अपां स्तुतिं वा यदि वा घृतस्तुतिं गव्यमेके सौर्यमेतद्वदन्ति ॥११॥ २॥

RV. v. स्वर्भानुदृष्टं सूर्यस्य अपहत्य तमोऽत्रयः ।
सप्तविंशतिभिः सूक्तैर् अबोधीत्यग्निमस्तुवन् ॥१२॥
त्रैवृष्णस्त्रसदस्युश्च अश्वमेध ऋणंचयः ।
स्तूयमानाः परीक्ष्याः स्युर् अत्रिष्वेते क्वचित्क्वचित् ॥१३॥
ऐक्ष्वाकुस्त्र्यरुणो राजा त्रैवृष्णो रथमास्थितः ।
संजग्राहाश्वरश्मींश्च वृशो जानः पुरोहितः ॥१४॥
स ब्राह्मणकुमारस्य रथो गच्छञ्छिरोऽच्छिनत् ।
एनस्त्वीत्यब्रवीत्तत्रैव स राजैनं पुरोहितम् ॥१५॥
सोऽथर्वाङ्गिरसान्मन्त्रान् दृष्ट्वा संजीव्य तं शिशुम् ।
क्रोधात्संत्यज्य राजानम् अन्यदेशं समाश्रितः ॥१६॥
हरोऽप्यग्नेर्ननाशास्य तस्यापक्रमणादृषेः ।
अग्नौ प्रास्तानि हव्यानि न ह्यपच्यन्त कानिचित् ॥१७॥ ३॥
ततः प्रव्यथितो राजा सोऽभिगम्य प्रसाद्य तम् ।
आनीत्वा स वृशं जानं पुनरेव पुरोदधे ॥१८॥
स प्रसन्नो वृशोऽन्वैच्छद् धरमग्नेर्नृपक्षये ।
अविन्दत पिशाचीं तां जायां तस्य च भूपतेः ॥१९॥
निषण्णः स तया सार्धम् आसन्द्यां कशिपावपि ।
तामुपामन्त्रयां चक्रे कमेतं त्वमिति त्वृचा ॥२०॥
हरः कुमाररूपेण ब्रुवंस्तामभ्यभाषत ।
विज्योतिषेति चोक्तायां सहसाग्निरुदज्वलत् ॥२१॥
B सहमानः समायान्तं प्रकाशं च प्रकाशयन् ।
पिशाचीमदहत्तां स यत्र चोपविवेश सा ॥२२॥ ४॥
एष एव परामृष्टो भाल्लविब्राह्मणे तृचः ।
B निदानसंज्ञके ग्रन्थे छन्दोगानामिति श्रुतिः ॥२३॥
भवेदेव परामर्शः सूक्तस्यास्य व्यपेक्षया ।

भवन्ति वाह्या* मन्त्रा हि विधिदृष्टेन चोदिताः ॥२४॥
दृश्यन्ते ब्राह्मणे मन्त्रा एकदेशे प्रदर्शिताः ।
जामदग्न्यस्तथैवाप्र्य स्तोकीयाश्चैतरेयके ॥२५॥
आप्रियः सुसमिद्धाय पञ्चमं सूक्तमत्र तु ।
एदमृग्वैश्वदेवी वा अन्त्या चैन्द्राग्न्युपोत्तमे ॥२६॥
ऐन्द्राणि द्वादश त्रीति उशना त्वत्र संस्तुतः ।
उशनेति तु पादेन सं ह यद्वामनेन च ॥२७॥ ५॥
इन्द्राकुत्सेति चैतस्यां कुत्सेनेन्द्र स्तुतः सह ।
यस्त्वा सूर्येति चात्रीणां पञ्चर्चे कर्म कीर्त्यते ॥२८॥
B अनस्वन्तेति सूक्तेऽस्मिन् आत्रेयेऽत्रिर्ऋषिः स्वयम् ।
B दानतुष्टः शशंसैतान् राजर्षीनिति केचन ॥२९॥
B आशीरध्येषणाश्चैभ्यो अग्निं प्रति च दृश्यते ।
B अयुतं च गवां त्रीणि शतान्यथ च विंशतिम्* ॥३०॥
B सौवर्णं शकटं गोभ्यां त्र्यरुणोऽदान्नृपोऽत्रये ।
B अश्वमेधः शतं चोक्ष्णां त्रसदस्युर्धनं बहु ॥३१॥ ६॥
B राज्ञः प्रति च तत्सूक्तं बभाष इति केचन ।
B आत्मा हि नात्मने दद्यात् अग्रहीन्नृपतेर्ऋषिः ॥३२॥
B अत्रेः सुतमृषिं बभ्रुम् आर्त्विज्याय ऋणंचयः ।
B सहस्रदक्षिणे सोमे वव्रे तं सोऽप्ययाजयत् ॥३३॥
B ददौ च* रौशमो* राजा सहस्राणि शतानि च ।
B तस्मै चत्वारि चत्वारि महावीरं च काञ्चनम् ॥३४॥
B प्रवर्ग्येषु महावीराः सौवर्णास्तस्य चाभवन् ।
B प्रतिगृह्य ऋषिर्गच्छन् मध्यमेनाग्निना पथि ॥३५॥
B पृष्ट इन्द्रेण चाचख्यौ भद्रं चतसृभिश्च तत् ।
को नु वां वैश्वदेवानि एकादश परायतः ॥३६॥ ७॥

मारुतानि दश प्रेति इळाभीत्यृचि तु स्तुता ।
Bउदित्यृचि तृतीयायां सविता शौनकोऽब्रवीत् ॥३७॥
उपेति बार्हस्पत्यस्तु* तृचो मारुत्यृगुत्तरा ।
तमु ष्टुहीति रौद्री तु प्र सुष्टुतिरिति त्वृचि ॥३८॥
Bशौनकादिभिराचार्यैर् देवता बहुधेरिता ।
इळस्पतिं* शाकपूणिः पर्जन्याग्नी तु गालवः ॥३९॥
यास्कस्तु पूषणं मेने स्तुतमिन्द्रं तु शौनकः ।
वैश्वानरं भागुरिस्तु मारुत्येष समाश्विनी ॥४०॥
वायव्याध्वर्यवः सौमी दशेत्यैन्द्री परा तु या ।
Bअग्निं घर्मं पराञ्चन्ति अश्विनौ स्तौत्यृगछ च ॥४१॥ ८॥
Bप्रेति वायुं* पूषणं च अर्धर्चेऽग्निरिहोच्यते ।
Bप्रथमेऽथ द्वितीये च स्तुता एति दिवौकसः ॥४२॥
आ वाचं मध्यमां स्तौति ततोऽन्या तु बृहस्पतिम् ।
Bज्यायांसमिति चादित्यं प्र वो वायुरिहोच्यते ॥४३॥
Bतं प्रत्नथेति सौमी वा दैव्यैन्द्री वा प्रजापतेः ।
Bपरोक्षवैश्वदेवं तद् आह कौषीतकिः स्वयम् ॥४४॥
Bतेषु तृतीयमित्युक्तं देवान्हुव इदं परम् ।
देवानां पत्नीरिति तु देवपत्न्यो बृचे स्तुताः ॥४५॥ ९॥
अयं चतुर्णामिति चेन्द्रवायू त्रिभि स्तुतौ वायवा याहि वायुम् ।
रथं त्वृचा रोदसी स्तूयतेऽच यस्या स्तुता मरुतो रुद्रपत्न्याः ॥४६॥
आ रुद्रास इति त्वस्यां रुद्राणां संस्तुतो गणः ।
मरुतां तु गणस्यैतन् नाम रुद्रा इति स्मृताः ॥४७॥
असावग्निरयं चोभाव् अग्नी पार्थिवमध्यमौ ।
अग्ने मरुद्भिरित्यस्यां मरुद्भिः सह संस्तुतौ ॥४८॥
Bमध्यमा वाक् स्त्रियः सर्वाः पुमान् सर्वेष्व* मध्यमः ।

B गणाश्च सर्वे मरुतो गुणभेदात्पृथक् पृथक् ॥४९॥ १०॥
राजर्षिरभवद्दार्भ्यो रथवीतिरिति श्रुतः ।
स यक्ष्यमाणो राजात्रिम् अभिगम्य प्रसाद्य च ॥५०॥
आत्मानं कार्यमर्थं च ख्यापयन्प्राञ्जलि स्थितः ।
अवृणीतर्षिमात्रेयम् आर्त्विज्यायार्चनानसम् ॥५१॥
स सपुत्रोऽभ्यगच्छत्तं राजानं यज्ञसिद्धये ।
श्यावाश्वश्चात्रिपुत्रस्य पुत्रः खल्वर्चनानसः ॥५२॥
साङ्गोपाङ्गान्सर्ववेदान् यः पित्राध्यापितो मुदा ।
अर्चनानाः सपुत्रोऽथ गत्वा नृपमयाजयत् ॥५३॥
यज्ञे च विततेऽपश्यद् राजपुत्रीं यशस्विनीम् ।
स्नुषा मे राजपुत्री स्याद् इति तस्य मनोऽभवत् ॥५४॥
श्यावाश्वस्य च तस्यां वै सक्तमासीत्तदा मनः ।
संयुज्यस्व मया राजन् इति याज्यं च सोऽब्रवीत् ॥५५॥ ११॥
B श्यवाश्वाय सुतां दित्सुर् महिषीं स्वां नृपोऽब्रवीत् ।
B किं ते मतमहं कन्यां श्यावाश्वाय ददामि हि ॥५६॥
B अत्रिपुत्रोऽदुर्बलो हि जामाता त्वावयोरिति ।
B राजानमब्रवीत्सापि नृपर्षिकुलजा ह्यहम् ॥५७॥
B नानृषिर्नो तु जामाता नैष मन्त्रान् हि दृष्टवान् ।
B ऋषये दीयतां कन्या वेदस्याम्बा* भवेत्तथा ।
B ऋषिं*र्मन्त्रदृशं वेदपितरं मन्यते यतः ॥५८॥
प्रत्याचष्टे स तं राजा सह संमन्त्र्य भार्यया ।
अनृषिर्नैव जामाता कश्चिद्भवितुमर्हति ॥५९॥
प्रत्याख्यात ऋषिस्तेन वृत्ते यज्ञे न्यवर्तत ।
श्यावाश्वस्य तु कन्याया मनो नैव न्यवर्तत ॥६०॥
ततस्तौ तु निवर्तेतां*म् उभावेवाभिजग्मतुः ।

B शशीयसीं तरन्तं च पुरुमीळ्हं च पार्थिवम् ॥६१॥
तरन्तपुरुमीळ्हौ तु राजानौ वैददश्व्यृषी ।
ताभ्यां तौ चक्रतुः पूजाम् ऋषिभ्यां नृपती स्वयम् ॥६२॥
ऋषिपुत्रं महिष्याश्च दर्शयामास तं नृपः ।
तरन्तानुमता चैव प्रादाद्बहुविधं वसु ॥६३॥ १२॥
अजाविकं गवाश्वं च श्यावाश्वाय शशीयसी ।
B अत्रिं याज्यार्चितौ गत्वा पितापुत्रौ स्वमाश्रमम् ॥६४॥
B अभ्यवादयतामत्रिं महर्षिं दीप्ततेजसम् ।
B श्यावाश्वस्य मनस्यासीन् मन्त्रस्यादर्शनादहम् ॥६५॥
B न लब्धवानहं कन्यां हन्त सर्वाङ्गशोभनाम् ।
B अप्यहं मन्त्रदर्शी स्यां भवेद्धर्षो महान्मम ॥६६॥
B इत्यरण्ये चिन्तयतः प्रादुरासीन्मरुद्गणः ।
ददर्श संस्थितान्पार्श्वे तुल्यरूपानिवात्मनः ॥६७॥
समानवयसश्चैव मरुतो रुक्मवक्षसः ।
तांस्तुल्यवयसो दृष्ट्वा देवान्पुरुषविग्रहान् ॥६८॥
श्यावाश्वो विस्मितोऽपृच्छत् के ष्ठेति मरुतस्तदा ।
ततस्तु मरुतो देवान् रुद्रसूनूनबुध्यत ॥६९॥
य ईं वहन्त इत्याभिर् बुद्ध्वा तुष्टाव तांस्तथा ।
अतिक्रमं हि तं मेने ऋषिर्विपुलमात्मनः ॥७०॥
यच्च दृष्ट्वैव तुष्टाव यच्च के ष्ठेति पृष्टवान् ।
स्तुता स्तुत्या तया प्रीता गच्छन्तः पृश्निमातरः ॥७१॥ १३॥
अवमुच्य स्ववक्षोभ्यो रुक्मं तस्मै तदा ददुः ।
मरुत्सु तु प्रयातेषु श्यावाश्वः सुमहायशाः ॥७२॥
रथवीतेर्दुहितरम् अगच्छन्मनसा तदा ।
स सद्य ऋषिरात्मानं प्रवक्ष्यन् रथवीतये ॥७३॥

एतं मे स्तोममित्याभ्यां दौत्ये रात्रीं न्ययोजयत् ।
रथवीतिमपश्यन्तीं संप्रेक्ष्यार्षेण चक्षुषा ॥ ७४ ॥
रम्ये हिमवतः पृष्ठे एष क्षेतीति चाब्रवीत् ।
ऋषेर्नियोगमाज्ञाय देव्या रात्र्या प्रचोदितः ॥ ७५ ॥
आदाय कन्यां तां दार्भ्य उपेयायार्चनानसम् ।
पादौ तस्योपसंगृह्य स्थित्वा प्रह्वः कृताञ्जलिः ॥ ७६ ॥ १४ ॥
रथवीतिरहं दार्भ्य इति नाम शशंस च ।
मया संगतिमिच्छन्तं त्वां प्रत्याचक्षिँ यत्पुरा ॥ ७७ ॥
तत्क्षमस्व नमस्तेऽस्तु मा च मे भगवन्क्रुधः ।
ऋषेः पुत्रः स्वयमृषिः पितासि भगवन्नृषेः ॥ ७८ ॥
हन्त प्रतिगृहाणेमां स्नुषामित्येवमब्रवीत् ।
पाद्यार्घ्यमधुपर्कैश्च पूजयित्वा स्वयं नृपः ॥ ७९ ॥
शुक्लमश्वशतं दत्त्वा अनुजज्ञे गृहान्प्रति ।
शशीयसीं तरन्तं च पुरुमीळ्हं च पार्थिवम् ॥ ८० ॥
षड्भिः सनदिति स्तुत्वा जगामर्षिरपि क्षयम् ।
ऋतेन मैत्रावरुणान्य् एकादश पराणि तु ॥ ८१ ॥ १५ ॥
षळाश्विनानि गर्भार्थे पञ्चर्चोपनिषत्स्तुतिः ।
सप्त कृत्वापराधान्वै विफले दारसंग्रहे ॥ ८२ ॥
ऋषिः कृतोऽश्वमेधेन भारतेनेति वै श्रुतिः ।
तमष्टमेऽपराधे तु वृक्षद्रोण्यां स पार्थिवः ॥ ८३ ॥
ऋ*बीसे ह विनिक्षिप्य स्कन्नं रात्रौ न्यधारयत् ।
सोऽश्विनाविति सूक्तेन तुष्टावर्षिः शुभस्पती ॥ ८४ ॥
तौ तं तस्मात्समुद्धृत्य चक्रतुः सफलं पुनः ।
तृचः स्वस्यैव गर्भार्थे स्वपतस्तस्य गर्भवत् ॥ ८५ ॥
यथा वात इति ज्ञेये त्वश्विभ्यामितरे ऋचौ ।

B स्रवतामपि गर्भाणां दृष्टं तदनुमन्त्रणम् ॥८६॥ १६॥
B भाववृत्तं तु तद्वत्स्यात् तथारूपं हि दृश्यते ।
B जरायुगर्भशब्दाभ्याम् एतद्रूपं हि दृश्यते ॥८७॥
महे उषस्ये साविचे युञ्जतेऽछेति वै स्तुतः ।
पर्जन्यो बळिति त्वस्मिन् पृथिवी मध्यमा स्तुता ॥८८॥
B अद्या नो देव सवितर् इयं दुःस्वप्ननाशनी ।
वारुणं तु प्र सम्राजे इन्द्राग्न्यैन्द्राग्नमुत्तरम् ॥८९॥
विष्णोंन्यङ्गं परं प्रेति मारुतं सूक्तमुत्तमम् ।
B एवयामरुदाख्यातं द्यौर्नैन्द्रे* प्रतिपूर्वकम् ॥९०॥
श्रीसूक्तमाशीर्वादस्तु श्रीपुत्राणां पराणि षट् ।
तस्याद्यालक्ष्म्यपनुदम् अग्निस्तत्र निपातभाक् ॥९१॥ १७॥
प्रजावज्जीवपुत्रौ वा गर्भकर्मणि संस्तुतौ ।
नानारूपा पयस्विन्यः संस्रवन्तीति संस्तुताः ॥९२॥
आशीर्वादेषु संज्ञासु कर्मसंस्थासु देवता ।
निपातभाग् लिङ्गवाक्यात् परीक्षेतेह मन्त्रवित् ॥९३॥
मन्त्रप्रयोगमन्त्रयोः प्रयोगो बलवत्तरः ।
विधेस्तयोः परीक्षा स्यान् मन्त्राः स्युरभिधायकाः ॥९४॥
तस्मात्तेन विसंवादो मन्त्राणां तन्नतानि तु ।
गुणाभिधायकानि स्युः संविज्ञानपदानि तु ॥९५॥
मन्त्रेषु गुणभूतेषु प्रधानेषु च कर्मसु ।
प्रधानगुणभूताः स्युर् देवता इति गम्यते ॥९६॥ १८॥
त्रिसांवत्सरिकं सत्त्रं प्रजाकामः प्रजापतिः ।
आहरत्सहितः साध्यैर् विश्वैर्देवैः सहेति च ॥९७॥
तत्र वाग्दीक्षणीयायाम् आजगाम शरीरिणी ।
तां दृष्ट्वा युगपत्तत्र कस्याथ वरुणस्य च ॥९८॥

शुक्रं चस्कन्द तद्वायुर् अग्नौ प्रास्यद्यदृच्छया ।
ततोऽर्चिभ्यो भृगुर्जज्ञे अङ्गारेष्वङ्गिरा ऋषिः ॥९९॥
प्रजापतिं* सुतौ दृष्ट्वा दृष्टा वागभ्यभाषत ।
आभ्यामृषिस्तृतीयोऽपि भवेदत्रैव मे सुतः ॥१००॥
प्रजापतिस्तथेत्युक्तः प्रत्यभाषत भारतीम् ।
ऋषिरत्रिस्ततो जज्ञे सूर्यानलसमद्युतिः ॥१०१॥ १९॥
योऽङ्गारेभ्य ऋषिर्जज्ञे तस्य पुत्रो बृहस्पतिः ।
बृहस्पतेर्भरद्वाजो विदथीति य उच्यते ॥१०२॥
मरुत्स्वासीद्गुरुर्यश्च स एवाङ्गिरसो नपात् ।

RV. vi. सपुत्रस्य तु तस्यैतन् मण्डलं षष्ठमुच्यते ॥१०३॥
त्वं ह्यग्न इति तत्रादाव् आग्नेयानि त्रयोदश ।
सूक्तानि त्रीणि मूर्धानम् अग्नेर्वैश्वानरस्य तु ॥१०४॥
एकान्नत्रिंशदेवात्र पिबेत्यैन्द्राण्यतः परम् ।
अग्ने स क्षेषदित्यस्यां देवौ यौ तु निपातितौ ॥१०५॥
प्रोतये नू म इत्येते वैश्वदेव्यावृचौ स्मृते ।
ऋग्द्वितीया पदं चान्यम् ऐन्द्रमेति गवां स्तुतिः ॥१०६॥ २०॥
आसस्राणास इत्यस्यां वायुरिन्द्रश्च संस्तुतौ ।
B इन्द्रः प्राधान्यतो वात्र स्तुतो वायुर्निपातभाक् ॥१०७॥
B अयं देवस्तृचं सौम्यम् ऐन्द्रमेके प्रचक्षते ।
य आनयदिति त्वस्य तृचोऽधीति बृबुस्तुतिः ॥१०८॥
पितरं स्तौति शंयुश्च तृचस्यान्त्ये पदे स्वकम् ।
स्वादुष्किलायमिति तु सौम्यः पञ्चर्च उत्तरः ॥१०९॥
B इन्द्रः प्रधानतो वात्र स्तुतः सोमो निपातभाक् ।
B इन्द्रस्यैन्द्र्योऽनुपानीयाः श्रूयन्ते ह्यैतरेयके ॥११०॥

अगव्यूति स्तौति देवान् पादो भूमिमथोत्तरः ।
बृहस्पतिं तृतीयस्तु इन्द्रमेवोत्तमं पदम् ॥१११॥ २१॥
वनस्पते वीड्वङ्गः परं यत् तदाचार्या भाववृत्तं वदन्ति ।
ऋचस्तु तिस्रस्तु रथाभिमर्शना उपेति तिस्रो दुन्दुभेः संस्तवोऽत्र ॥११२॥
समश्वपर्णा इति चार्धमैन्द्रं दशादितोऽग्नेस्तृणपाणिकस्य ।
तृचः परो मारुतः पृश्निसूक्ते त्र्यृचः परो वैश्वदेवः पुनश्च ॥११३॥
आदित्यो वा मारुत एव वा स्याद् आ मा पूषन्निति पौष्णी*श्चतस्रः ।
त्र्यृचं परं मारुतं तत्र विद्याद् अन्त्या द्युभ्वोः कीर्तना पृश्नये वा ॥११४॥ २२॥
स्तुषे सूक्तानि चत्वारि वैश्वदेवान्यतः परम् ।
द्वितीयाग्निं चतुर्थी च वायुं पञ्चम्यथाश्विनौ ॥११५॥
स्तौत्यृक् तु सप्तमी वाचम् अत्र पूषणमष्टमी ।
त्वष्टारं नवमी रुद्रं भुवनस्येत्यथोत्तरे ॥११६॥
मारुत्यौ यो रजांसीति विष्णुमेव जगावृषिः ।
अभ्यैन्*द्र्येति च सावित्री रौदस्याग्नेय्यु*ताश्विनी ॥११७॥
अग्नीपर्जन्यावनयोः सौर्यौ* चोदु त्यदित्यृचौ ।
वयं चत्वारि पौष्णानि त्वैन्द्रापौष्णस्य चोत्तरम् ॥११८॥
B रथीतमं कपर्दिनं रौद्रमेके प्रचक्षते ।
ऐन्द्राग्ने प्र नु वोचेति इयं सारस्वतं स्तुषे ॥११९॥ २३॥
आश्विने चौषसे चैव मारुतं तु वपुर्न्विति ।
B उपेति च त्र्यृचेऽश्विभ्याम् आ*राधनं च शंसति ॥१२०॥
मैत्रावरुणमेवैकं विश्वेषां वः सतामिति ।
श्रुष्टीति चैन्द्रावरुणं समैन्द्रावैष्णवं परम् ॥१२१॥
द्यावापृथिव्यौ सविता इन्द्रासोमौ बृहस्पतिः ।
पृथक्पृथक् परैः सूक्तैः सोमारुद्रेति तौ स्तुतौ ॥१२२॥
B चक्रं रथो मणिर्भार्या भूमिरश्वो गजस्तथा ।

B एतानि सप्त रत्नानि सर्वेषां चक्रवर्तिनाम् ॥१२३॥ २४॥
अभ्यावर्ती चायमानः प्रस्तोकश्चैव सार्ञ्जयः ।
आजग्मतुर्भरद्वाजं जितौ वारशिखैर्युधि ॥१२४॥
अभिगम्योचतुस्तौ तं प्रसाद्याख्याय नामनी ।
युधि वारशिखैर्ब्रह्मन् आवां विद्धि विनिर्जितौ ॥१२५॥
भवत्पुरोहितावावां क्षत्रबन्धूञ्जयेवहि ।
क्षत्रं तदपि विज्ञेयं ब्रह्म यत्पाति शाश्वतम् ॥१२६॥
ऋषिस्तौ तु तथेत्युक्त्वा पायुं पुत्रमभाषत ।
अधर्षणीयौ शत्रूणां कुरुष्वैतौ नृपाविति ॥१२७॥
पितरं स तथेत्युक्त्वा युद्धोपकरणं तयोः ।
जीमूतस्येति सूक्तेन पृथक्त्वेनान्वमन्त्रयत् ॥१२८॥ २५॥
प्रथमा त्वस्य सूक्तस्य योद्धारं स्तौति वर्मिणम् ।
धनुषश्च द्वितीया तु तृतीया ज्याभिमन्त्रिणी ॥१२९॥
स्तौत्यृगार्त्नी चतुर्थी तु इषुधिं स्तौति पञ्चमी ।
अर्धेन सारथिः* षष्ठ्या रश्मयोऽर्धेन संस्तुताः ॥१३०॥
अश्वांस्तु सप्तमी स्तौति आयुधागारमष्टमी ।
नवमी रथगोपांस्तु दशमी रणदेवताः ॥१३१॥
इषुं चैकादशी स्तौति द्वादशी कवचस्तुतिः ।
त्रयोदशी कशां स्तौति हस्तत्राणं चतुर्दशी ॥१३२॥
प्रथमे पञ्चदश्यास्तु पादे दिग्ध इषु स्तुतः ।
अयोमुखी द्वितीये तु अर्धेऽस्त्रं वारुणं परे ॥१३३॥ २६॥
षोळश्यां त्वस्य सूक्तस्य धनुर्मुक्त इषु स्तुतः ।
सप्तदश्यां तु युद्धादेः कवचस्य तु बध्यतः ॥१३४॥
स्तुतिरष्टादशी ज्ञेया युयुत्सो स्तुतिरुत्तमा ।
आशास्ते चोत्तमे पादे ऋषिरात्मन आशिषः ॥१३५॥

सूक्तेनानेन तु स्तुत्वा संग्रामाज्ञान्यृषिस्तयोः ।
ततः प्रस्थापयामास पुनर्वारशिखान्प्रति ॥१३६॥
Bएतत्त्यत्ते चतसृभी राज्ञो साहाय्यकाम्यया ।
Bभरद्वाजोऽभितुष्टाव प्रीतस्तेन पुरंदरः ॥१३७॥
Bअभ्यावर्तिनमभ्येत्य हर्युपीयानदीतटे ।
Bसहितश्चायमानेन जघानैनाञ्छचीपतिः ॥१३८॥ २७॥
तौ तु वारशिखाञ्जित्वा ततोऽभ्यावर्तिसार्ञ्जयौ ।
भरद्वाजाय गुरवे ददतुर्विविधं वसु ॥१३९॥
भरद्वाजश्च गर्गश्च दृष्टाविन्द्रेण वै पथि ।
द्वयान् प्रस्तोक इत्याभिर् दानं तद्वै शशंसतुः ॥१४०॥
Bऋषिरप्यभितुष्टाव दानं तच्च च तस्य तु ।
Bऋचैकया द्वयाँ अग्ने दत्तं संकीर्तयन् स्वयम् ॥१४१॥
प्रसङ्गात्त्विह याः सूक्ते देवताः परिकीर्तिताः ।
ता एव सूक्तभाजस्तु मेने राथीतर स्तुतौ ॥१४२॥ २८॥

RV. vii. प्राजापत्यो मरीचिर्हि मारीचः कश्यपो मुनिः ।
तस्य देव्योऽभवञ्जाया दाक्षायण्यस्त्रयोदश ॥१४३॥
Bअदितिर्दितिर्दनुः काला दनायुः सिंहिका मुनिः ।
Bक्रोधा विश्वा* वरिष्ठा च सुरभिर्विनता तथा ॥१४४॥
Bकद्रूश्चैवेति दुहितॄः कश्यपाय ददौ स च ।
तासु देवासुराश्चैव गन्धर्वोरगराक्षसाः ॥१४५॥
वयांसि च पिशाचाश्च जज्ञिरेऽन्याश्च जातयः ।
तत्रैका त्वदितिर्देवी द्वादशाजनयत्सुतान् ॥१४६॥
Bभगश्चैवार्यमांशश्च मित्रो वरुण एव च ।
Bधाता चैव विधाता च विवस्वांश्च महाद्युतिः ॥१४७॥ २९॥

B त्वष्टा पूषा तथैवेन्द्रो द्वादशो विष्णुरुच्यते ।
द्वन्द्वं तस्यास्तु तज्जज्ञे मित्रश्च वरुणश्च ह ॥१४८॥
तयोरादित्ययोः सत्त्रे दृष्ट्वाप्सरसमुर्वशीम् ।
रेतश्चस्कन्द तत्कुम्भे न्यपतद्वासतीवरे ॥१४९॥
तेनैव तु मुहूर्तेन वीर्यवन्तौ तपस्विनौ ।
अगस्त्यश्च वसिष्ठश्च तत्रर्षी संबभूवतुः ॥१५०॥
B बहुधा पतिते शुक्रे कलशेऽथ जले स्थले ।
B स्थले वसिष्ठस्तु मुनिः संभूत ऋषिसत्तमः ॥१५१॥
B कुम्भे त्वगस्त्यः संभूतो जले मत्स्यो महाद्युतिः ।
उदियाय ततोऽगस्त्यः शम्यामात्रो महायशाः ॥१५२॥ ३०॥
मानेन संमितो यस्मात् तस्मान्मान्य इहोच्यते ।
यद्वा कुम्भादृषिर्जातः कुम्भेनापि हि मीयते ॥१५३॥
कुम्भ इत्यभिधानं तु परिमाणस्य लक्ष्यते ।
ततोऽप्सु गृह्यमाणासु वसिष्ठः पुष्करे स्थितः ॥१५४॥
सर्वत्र पुष्करं तत्र विश्वे देवा अधारयन् ।
उत्थाय सलिलात्तस्माद् अथ तेपे महत्तपः ॥१५५॥
नामास्य गुणतो जज्ञे वसतेः श्रैष्ठ्यकर्मणः ।
अदृश्यमृषिभिर्हीन्द्रं सोऽपश्यत्तपसा पुरा ॥१५६॥
सोमभागानथो तस्मै प्रोवाच हरिवाहनः ।
B ऋषयो वा इन्द्रमिति ब्राह्मणात्तद्धि दृश्यते ॥१५७॥ ३१॥
वसिष्ठश्च वसिष्ठाश्च ब्राह्मणा ब्रह्मकर्मणि ।
सर्वकर्मसु यज्ञेषु दक्षिणीयतमास्तथा ॥१५८॥
तस्माद्येऽद्यापि वासिष्ठाः सदस्याः स्युस्तु कर्हिचित् ।
अर्हयेद्दक्षिणाभिस्तान् भाल्लवेयी श्रुतिस्त्वियम् ॥१५९॥
ऋषिस्तु मैत्रावरुणिः सूक्तैः षोळशभिः परैः ।

तुष्टावाग्निमिति त्वग्निम् आग्नेयस्तत्र जुषस्व नः ॥१६०॥
प्राग्नयेऽथ प्र सम्राजो द्वितीयं प्राग्नये तृचम् ।
वैश्वानरीयाख्येतानि त्वे हैन्द्राणि पराण्यतः ॥१६१॥
दश पञ्च च सूक्तानि निपातो मरुतां स्तुतिः ।
नकिः सुदास इत्यस्यां दानं पैजवनस्य तु ॥१६२॥ ३२॥
वसिष्ठेन चतुर्भिस्तु द्वे नभुरिति कीर्तितम् ।
संवादं सूक्तमैन्द्रं वा श्वित्यञ्चस्तु प्रचक्षते ॥१६३॥
वसिष्ठागस्त्ययोरत्र कीर्त्यते तनयैः सह ।
इन्द्रेण चैव संवादो महिमा जन्म कर्म च ॥१६४॥
पराणि प्रेति चत्वारि वैश्वदेवानि तत्र तु ।
स्तौत्यृगब्जामहिं तत्र मा नोऽहिं बुध्न्यमेव च ॥१६५॥
B अहिराहन्ति मेघान्स एति वा तेषु मध्यमः ।
B योऽहिः स बुध्न्यो बुध्ने हि सोऽन्तरिक्षेऽभिजायते ॥१६६॥
उदु ष्य सवितुः सूक्तं शं नो वाजिनदैवतः ।
तृचोऽर्धर्चश्च भागोऽत्र भगमुग्र इति श्रुतिः ॥१६७॥ ३३॥
पादश्चैव तृतीयोऽत्र पञ्चम्यामहिदैवतः ।
B यथार्धर्चो भगमुग्रस् तथा नूनं भगोऽपि च ॥१६८॥
B स हि रत्नानि सविता सुवातीति भगः स वा ।
वैश्वदेवानि पञ्चोर्ध्वः पञ्चर्चो भगदैवतः ॥१६९॥
प्रातर्जितमुषस्यान्या द्रष्टॄ*ण्योऽत्राशिरेव वा ।
एके तु प्रातरित्यस्यां भगमेव प्रचक्षते ॥१७०॥
आदावन्ते तु ऋषयः कीर्तयन्ति प्रसङ्गतः ।
सूक्तेऽस्मिन्देवतास्त्वन्या अन्यास्तत्र भवन्ति च ॥१७१॥
सालोक्यात्साहचर्याद्वा संस्तवादथवा पुनः ।
गणस्थानात्प्रभक्तितो वा कीर्त्यन्तेऽन्यास्तु देवताः ॥१७२॥ ३४॥

दाधिक्रमथ सावित्रं रौद्रमित्यनुपूर्वशः ।
दाधिक्रे प्रथमायास्तु देवताः परिकीर्तिताः ॥१७३॥
ता ज्ञेया आप आप्यं स्याद् आर्भवः प्रथमस्तृचः ।
उत्तमा वैश्वदेवी वा आर्भवी वा निगद्यते ॥१७४॥
वैश्वदेवे तथा शस्त्रे आर्भवं शस्यते हि तत् ।
दशमेऽह्नि समस्तं समुद्रज्येष्ठा अपां स्तुतिः ॥१७५॥
समुद्रज्येष्ठा अपां स्तुतिः ॥ ३५॥

॥ इति बृहद्देवतायां पञ्चमोऽध्यायः ॥

आ मामिति तु सूक्तेन प्रत्यृचं देवता स्तुताः ।
B मित्रावरुणावग्निश्च देवा नद्यस्तथैव च ॥ १ ॥
तृचावादित्यदेवत्यौ रोदस्योः प्रेति यस्तृचः ।
वास्तोष्पत्यास्ततस्तस्तु सप्त प्रस्वापिन्यः स्मृताः ॥ २ ॥
परं चत्वारि सूक्तानि मारुतानि क ईमिति ।
तेषां तु पितरं देवं त्र्यम्बकं स्तौत्यृगुत्तमा ॥ ३ ॥
स्तुतौ तु मित्रावरुणौ सूक्तैर्यदिति सप्तभिः ।
अश्विनौ तु परैर्देवाव् अष्टभिः प्रति वामिति ॥ ४ ॥
यदद्यैकोत्सूर्यस्तिस्र उद्वेतीत्यर्धपञ्चमाः ।
सौर्यस्तच्चक्षुरिति तु गीयते चक्षुर्देवता ॥ ५ ॥ १ ॥
B आदित्यानां तद्वो अद्य द्वे ऋचौ शौनकोऽब्रवीत् ।
B अन्याः सर्वा ऋचः सौर्या यदद्याद्याः प्रकीर्तिताः ॥ ६ ॥
B इमे चेतार इत्याद्याः † † † ।
B अर्यम्णो वरुणस्यापि मित्रस्यैता नव स्मृताः ॥ ७ ॥
B यदद्य सूर इत्याद्या दशादित्या ऋचः स्मृताः ।
B सविता वादितिर्मित्रो वरुणश्चार्यमा भगः ॥ ८ ॥
B स्तुता उदु त्यदित्येतास् तिस्रः सौर्यस्ततः पराः ।
B आशीस्तच्चक्षुरित्येताम् आचार्यः शौनकोऽब्रवीत् ॥ ९ ॥
उषास्तु सप्तभिर्व्युषाः सूक्तान्येभ्यः पराणि तु ।
चत्वारीन्द्रावरुणेति इन्द्रावरुणयो स्तुतिः ॥ १० ॥ २ ॥
B उदु ज्योतिरिति तस्मिन्न् अर्धर्चे मध्यम स्तुतः ।
वरुणस्य गृहानात्रो वसिष्ठः स्वप्न आचरत् ॥ ११ ॥

प्राविवेशाथ तं तत्र श्वा नदन्नभ्यधावत ।
B क्रन्दन्तं सारमेयं स धावन्तं दष्टुमुद्यतम् ॥१२॥
B यदर्जुनेति च द्वाभ्यां सान्त्वयित्वा व्यसुष्वपत् ।
स तं प्रस्वापयामास जनमन्यं च वारुणम् ॥१३॥
ततस्तु वरुणो राजा स्वैः पाशैः प्रत्यबध्यत ।
स बद्धः पितरं सूक्तैश् चतुर्भिरित उत्तरैः ॥१४॥
अभितुष्टाव धीरेति मुमोचैनं ततः पिता ।
A ध्रुवासु त्वेति चोक्तायां पाशा अस्मात्प्रमोचिरे ॥१५॥ ३॥
पराणि त्रीणि सूक्तानि वायव्यानि प्र वीरया ।
अथ तास्वैन्द्रवायव्या स्तुतौ यासु द्विवत्स्तुतिः ॥१६॥
B प्र वीरयोक्ता वायव्या प्राउगीत्यैतरेयके ।
B पदस्य व्यत्ययं कृत्वा वायोः प्राधान्यमुच्यते ॥१७॥
B ते सत्येन तृचो यावत् तरश्चतुर्ऋचः पुनः ।
B उशन्तीका प्र सीता चर्ग् द्वयोरेता नव स्मृताः ॥१८॥
ऐन्द्राग्ने शुचिमित्येते प्रेति सारस्वते परे ।
*ऋचा सरस्वान् स इति जनीयन्तश्च तिसृभिः ॥१९॥ ४॥
राजा वर्षसहस्राय दीक्षिष्यन्नाहुषः पुरा ।
चचारैकरथेनेमां ब्रुवन् सर्वाः समुद्रगाः ॥२०॥
यक्ष्ये वहत भागान्मे द्वन्द्वशो वाथवैकशः ।
प्रत्यूचुस्तं नृपं नद्यः स्वल्पवीर्याः कथं वयम् ॥२१॥
वहेम भागान्सर्वांस्ते सत्त्रे वार्षसहस्रिके ।
सरस्वतीं प्रपद्यस्व सा ते वक्ष्यति नाहुष ॥२२॥
तथेत्युक्त्वा जगामाशु आपगां स सरस्वतीम् ।
सा चैनं प्रतिजग्राह दुदुहे च पयो घृतम् ॥२३॥
एतदत्यद्भुतं कर्म सरस्वत्या नृपं प्रति ।

वारुणिः कीर्तयामास प्रथमस्य द्वितीयया ॥२४॥ ५*॥
यज्ञे बार्हस्पत्यमैन्द्रं वैष्णवे तु परे ततः ।
उरुमैन्द्र्यश्च तिस्रः स्युः पार्जन्ये तिस्र उत्तरे ॥२५॥
A स्तौतीन्द्रं प्रथमा त्वत्र द्वितीयाद्या बृहस्पतिम् ।
B यज्ञ आद्येन्द्रमेवास्तौद् अन्या त्विन्द्राबृहस्पती ॥२६॥
तृतीया नवमी चैव स्तौतीन्द्राब्रह्मणस्पती ।
संवत्सरं तु मण्डूकान् ऐन्द्रासोमं परं तु यत् ॥२७॥
ऋषिर्ददर्श राक्षोघ्नं पुत्रशोकपरिप्लुतः ।
हते पुत्रशते तस्मिन् सौदासैर्दुःखितस्तदा ॥२८॥ ६॥
ये पाकशंसमृक्सौम्या आग्नेयी तत उत्तरा ।
एकादशी वैश्वदेवी सौम्यस्तस्याः परो तृचः ॥२९॥
यदि वाहमृगाग्नेयी ऐन्द्री यो मेति तु स्मृता ।
ग्राव्णी प्र या जिगातीति वि तिष्ठध्वं तु मारुती ॥३०॥
प्र वर्तयेति पञ्चैन्द्र्य ऐन्द्रासोमी तृगुत्तमा ।
ऋषिस्त्वाशिषमाधास्ते मा नो रक्ष इति तृचि ॥३१॥
दिवि चैव पृथिव्यां च तथा पालनमात्मनः ।
उलूकयातुं जह्येतान् नानारूपान्निशाचरान् ॥३२॥
पञ्चदश्यां तु सूक्तस्य अष्टम्यां चैव वारुणिः ।
दुःखशोकपरीतात्मा शपते विलपन्निव ॥३३॥
हते पुत्रशते तस्मिन् वसिष्ठो दुःखितस्तदा ।
रक्षोभूतेन शापात्तु सुदासेनेति वै श्रुतिः ॥३४॥ ७॥

RV. viii. कण्वश्चैव प्रगाथश्च घोरपुत्रौ बभूवतुः ।
गुरुणा तावनुज्ञाताव् ऊषतुः सहितौ वने ॥३५॥
वसतोस्तु तयोस्तत्र कण्वपत्न्याः शिरः स्वपत् ।

कृत्वा कनीयान्काण्वस्य उत्सङ्गे नान्वबुध्यत ॥३६॥
शप्तुकामस्तु तं काण्वः क्रुद्धः पापाभिशङ्कया ।
बोधयामास पादेन दिधक्षन्निव तेजसा ॥३७॥
विदित्वा तस्य तं भावं प्रगाथः प्राञ्जलि स्थितः ।
मातृत्वे च पितृत्वे च वरयामास तावुभौ ॥३८॥
स घौरो वाथ काण्वो वा वंशजैर्बहुभिः सह ।
ददर्शान्यैश्च सहित ऋषिर्मण्डलमष्टमम् ॥३९॥ ८॥
माचिदैन्द्राणि चत्वारि अन्त्यस्य स्थूरमित्यृचि ।
तुष्टावाङ्गिरसी नारी वसन्ती शश्वती पतिम् ॥४०॥
स्त्रियं सन्तं पुमांसं तम् आसङ्गं* कृतवानृषिः ।
स्वस्य दानं स्तुहीत्यृग्भिश् चतुर्भिः परिकीर्तितम् ॥४१॥
शिक्षेत्यृग्भ्यां तु काश्यस्य विभिन्दोः परिकीर्तितम् ।
पाकस्थाम्नस्तु भोजस्य चतुर्भिर्यमिति स्तुतम् ॥४२॥
पौष्णौ प्रेति प्रगाथौ द्वौ मन्यते शाकटायनः ।
ऐन्द्रमेवाथ पूर्वं तु गालवः पौष्णमुत्तरम् ॥४३॥
ऐन्द्राणामिह सूक्तानाम् उत्तमस्योत्तमे तृचे ।
दानं राज्ञः कुरुङ्गस्य स्थूरं राध इति स्तुतम् ॥४४॥ ९॥
दूरादित्याश्विने सूक्ते सप्तविंशत्तमी यथा ।
इत्यर्धर्चो तृचश्चान्त्यः कशोर्दानस्तुतिः स्मृता ॥४५॥
महानिन्द्रं प्रत्नवत्याम् अग्निं वैश्वानरं स्तुतम् ।
मन्यते शाकपूणिस्तु भार्म्यश्वश्चैव मुद्गलः ॥४६॥
तृचे तु शतमित्यस्मिन् दानं तैरिन्दिरं स्मृतम् ।
परं तु मारुतं प्रेति आ नस्त्रीण्याश्विनानि च ॥४७॥
त्वमाग्नेयं य इन्द्रेति षडैन्द्राण्युत्तमस्य तु ।
उपोत्तमायामर्धर्चे देवो वास्तोष्पति स्तुतः ॥४८॥

इदमादित्यदेवत्यं तिसृभिस्त्वदिति स्तुता ।
षष्ठ्या चतुर्थ्या सप्तम्या उतेत्याश्विन्यृगष्टमी ॥४९॥ १०॥
स्तुताः शमिति पञ्चस्तु अग्निसूर्यानिलास्त्रयः ।
वरुणार्यममित्राणां प्रगाथो यमिति स्तुतिः ॥५०॥
आग्नेये स्तुती राजर्षेस् त्रसदस्योरदादिति ।
B पञ्चाशतं वधूनां च गवां तिस्रश्च सप्ततीः ॥५१॥
B अश्वोष्ट्राणां तथैवासौ वासांसि विविधानि च ।
B रत्नानि वृषभं श्यावं तासामग्रेसरं पतिम् ॥५२॥
B कृत्वा दारानृषिर्गच्छन् इन्द्रायैतच्छशंस च ।
B वयं सूक्तेन शक्रं च प्रीतस्तेन शचीपतिः ॥५३॥
B ऋषे वरं वृणीष्वेति प्रहृष्टस्तमृषिरब्रवीत् ।
B काकुत्स्थकन्याः पञ्चाशद् युगपद्रमये प्रभो ॥५४॥ ११॥
B कामतो बहुरूपत्वं यौवनं चाक्षयां रतिम् ।
B शङ्खनिधिं पद्मनिधिं मद्गृहेष्वनपायिनम् ॥५५॥
B प्रासादान् विश्वकर्मासौ सौवर्णांस्त्वत्प्रसादतः ।
B कुर्वीत पुष्पवाटीं च पृथक्तासां सुरद्रुमैः ॥५६॥
B मा भूत्सपत्नीस्पर्धासां सर्वमस्त्विति चाब्रवीत् ।
आ गन्त मारुतं सूक्तं वयमित्यैन्द्रमुत्तरम् ॥५७॥
काण्वस्य सोभरेश्चैव यजतो वंशजैः सह ।
कुरुक्षेत्रे यवाञ्जक्षुर् हवींषि विविधानि च ॥५८॥
आस्रवः सोऽभितुष्टाव इन्द्रं चित्रं सरस्वतीम् ।
B इन्द्रो वेत्यनयर्चा स दानशक्तिं प्रकाशयन् ॥५९॥ १२॥
B आसुराजोऽभिमानाच्च प्रहर्षितमनाः स्वयम् ।
संस्तुतो देववच्चित्र ऋषये तु गवां ददौ ॥६०॥
अयुतानां सहस्रं वै निजयाह स्तुवन्नृषिः ।

ऋषिं चोवाच हृष्टात्मा नाहमर्हाम्यृषे स्तुतिम् ॥६१॥
तिर्यग्योनौ समुत्पन्नो देवता स्तोतुमर्हसि ।
तमन्त्यया पुनश्चास्तौद् ओ त्यं सूक्तेन चाश्विनौ ॥६२॥
ईळिष्वेत्येतदाग्नेयं सखायश्चैन्द्रमुत्तरम् ।
यथा वरो सुषाम्ण इत्य् उत्तमस्त्वौषसस्तृचः ॥६३॥
अष्टौ तु सहितास्त्वेता देवता बिभिदुर्वलम् ।
उषाश्चेन्द्रश्च सोमश्च अग्निः सूर्यो बृहस्पतिः ॥६४॥
अङ्गिराः सरमा चैव ता वामित्युत्तरस्य तु ।
आदौ मैत्रावरुण्यस्तु नव द्वादश तूत्तराः ॥६५॥ १३॥
वैश्वदेव्यो वरू राजा यस्मादादृषये वसु ।
कीर्तितं तत्तृचे त्वस्मिन्न् ऋज्रमुक्षण्यायने ॥६६॥
B अश्विनौ ददतुः प्रीतौ तदिहोक्तं सुषामणि ।
आश्विनं तु युवोर्मुक्ष्व वायव्या उत्तरास्तु याः ॥६७॥
यं सवर्णा मनुर्नाम लेभे पुत्रं विवस्वतः ।
वैश्वदेवानि पञ्चैतान्य् अग्निरुक्थे जगाद सः ॥६८॥
बभ्रुरेक इति त्वेता लिङ्गतो द्विपदा दश ।
स्तूयन्ते देवता ह्यासु कर्मभिः स्वैः पृथक्पृथक् ॥६९॥
स्तुताः कर्मगुणैः स्वैः स्वैर् देवता यत्र तत्र तु ।
पृथक्कर्मस्तुतिर्नाम वैश्वदेवं तदेव तु ॥७०॥ १४॥
तासां बभ्रुरिति त्वाद्या सौम्याग्नेयी त्वृगुत्तरा ।
त्वाष्ट्री चैन्द्री च रौद्री च पौष्णी वैष्णव्यृगाश्विनी ॥७१॥
नवमी मैत्रावरुणी ऋग्दशम्यर्थि*संस्तवः ।
यजमानप्रसङ्गाच्च य इ*ज्याच प्रकीर्तिता ॥७२॥
B यो यजाति द्वृचे शक्रो यजतां पतिरीळितः ।
B तस्य द्युमान् द्वृचे यज्वा चतसृष्वपि मह्विति ॥७३॥

B यज्वनोरेव दंपत्योः पञ्च या दंपती ऋचः ।
B आ शर्मोर्शीरितु *पौष्ण्यौ परे मित्रोऽर्यमा यथा ॥७४॥
B वरुणश्च स्तुतास्त्वत्र आदित्या अग्निमग्नये ।
सूक्तानि प्र कृतानीति चौरयैन्द्राणि पराण्यतः ॥७५॥ १५॥
अध इत्यत्र कन्या तं स्त्रीलिङ्गेनेन्द्रमब्रवीत् ।
स हि तां कामयामास दानवीं पाकशासनः ॥७६॥
ज्येष्ठां स्वसारं व्यंसस्य तस्यैव युवकाम्यया ।
अग्निनेत्याश्विनं सूक्तम् ऐन्द्रसूक्ते परे ततः ॥७७॥
ऐन्द्राग्नं परमाग्नेयम् ऐन्द्राग्नं वारुणे परे ।
उत्तरे वारुणे त्वन्त्य आ वामित्याश्विनस्तृचः ॥७८॥
सूक्ते इमे समाग्नेये ताभ्यामिन्द्रे ततः परे ।
वशाया*श्व्याय यस्मादात् कानीतस्तु पृथुश्रवाः ॥७९॥
तदत्र संस्तुतं दानम् आ स इत्येवमादिभिः ।
आ नः प्रगाथौ वायव्यौ सूक्तस्योपोत्तमा च या ॥८०॥ १६॥
B मित्रार्यमाणौ मरुतः सुनीथो घ वृचे स्तुताः ।
B त्रिचत्वारिंशकात्प्रीतस् त्रिशोकाय पुरंदरः ॥८१॥
B गिरिं निकृत्य वज्रेण गा ददावसुरैर्हृताः ।
B यः कृन्तदिति चैतस्याम् ऋषिस्तु स्वयमब्रवीत् ॥८२॥
स्तुता नवम्या त्वदितिर् महीत्यादित्यदैवते ।
अन्त्याः पञ्चोषसेऽपि स्युः सौम्यं स्वादोरिति स्मृतम् ॥८३॥
पराण्यष्टौ तु सूक्तानि ऋषीणां तिग्मतेजसाम् ।
ऐन्द्राण्यत्र तु षड्विंशः प्रगाथो बहुदेवतः ॥८४॥
ऋगन्त्याग्नेरचेत्यग्निः सूर्यमन्त्यं पदं जगौ ।
प्रस्कण्वश्च पृषध्र*स्य प्रादाद्यद्वसु किंचन ॥८५॥ १७॥
तन्नूरीदिति सूक्ताभ्याम् अखिलं त्विह संस्तुतम् ।

A ऐन्द्राण्युभयमित्यत्र षळाग्नेयात्पराणि तु ।
निपातमाह देवानां दाता म इति भागुरिः ॥८६॥
ऋचं यास्कस्तृचं त्वेतं मन्यते वैश्वदेवतम् ।
आदित्यदैवतं सूक्तं त्यान्न्वित्यत्र परं तु यत् ॥८७॥
B धीवराः सहसा मीनान् दृष्ट्वा सारस्वते जले ।
B जालं प्रक्षिप्य तान्बद्ध्वोद् अक्षिपन्सलिलात्स्थलम् ॥८८॥
B शरीरपातभीतास्ते तुष्टुवुश्चादितेः सुतान् ।
B मुमुचुस्तांस्ततस्ते च प्रसन्नास्तान् समूदिरे ॥८९॥
B धीवराः क्षुद्भयं मा वो भूत् स्वर्गं प्राप्स्यथेति च ।
उतेति माता तत्रैषां तृचेनाभिष्टुतादितिः ॥९०॥ १८॥
मातृत्वादभिसंबन्धात् स्तूयेतैषां स्तुतौ स्तुतौ ।
ऐन्द्राण्या त्वा रथं त्रीणि स्तौत्यृतूनुप मेति षट् ॥९१॥
ऋक्षाश्वमेधयोरत्र पञ्च दानस्तुतिः पराः ।
अपादिन्द्रस्य चाग्नेश्च विश्वेषां चैव संस्तवः ॥९२॥
तृचस्य प्रथमोऽर्धर्चः शेषो वरुणदैवतः ।
त्वमाग्नेयेऽथवा सूक्तम् उत्तरं हविषां स्तुतिः ॥९३॥
पयःपश्वोषधीनां च तथारूपं हि दृश्यते ।
उदित्याश्विनमाग्नेये परे सूक्ते विशोविशः ॥९४॥
ऋग्भ्यामहमिति द्वाभ्यां स्तौत्यात्मानमृषिः स्वयम् ।
B आत्मानमात्मना स्तुत्वा स्तौति दानं श्रुतर्वणः ॥९५॥ १९॥
B आत्मादानाभिसंबन्धात् परुष्णीं च महानदीम् ।
परया परुष्णीमिन्द्रं त्रिभिः सूक्तैरिमं न्विति ॥९६॥
अयं कृत्नुरिदं सौम्यं त्रीण्यैन्द्राणि पराण्यतः ।
नहीति तेषां प्रथमे वैश्वदेव्यृगवीवृधत् ॥९७॥
देवानामिति देवानां प्रेष्ठमाग्नेयमुत्तरम् ।

त्रीण्याश्विनान्या म इति ऐन्द्राणि नमितीति च ॥९८॥ २०॥
अपालात्रिसुता त्वासीत् कन्या त्वग्दोषिणी पुरा ।
तामिन्द्रश्चकमे दृष्ट्वा विजने पितुराश्रमे ॥९९॥
तपसा बुबुधे सा तु सर्वमिन्द्रचिकीर्षितम् ।
उदकुम्भं समादाय अपामर्थे जगाम सा ॥१००॥
Bदृष्ट्वा सोममपामन्ते तुष्टावर्चा वने तु तम् ।
Bकन्या वारिति चैतस्याम् एषोऽर्थः कथितस्ततः ॥१०१॥
सा सुषाव मुखे सोमं [Bसुत्वेन्द्रं चाजुहाव तम् ।
असौ य एषीत्यनया] पपाविन्द्रश्च तन्मुखात् ॥१०२॥
अपूपांश्चैव सक्तूंश्च भक्षयित्वा स तद्गृहात् ।
ऋग्भिस्तुष्टाव सा चैनं जगादैनं तृचेन तु ॥१०३॥ २१॥
सुलोमामनवद्याङ्गीं कुरु मां शक्र सुत्वचम् ।
Bतस्यास्तद्वचनं श्रुत्वा प्रीतस्तेन पुरंदरः ॥१०४॥
रथच्छिद्रेण तामिन्द्रः शकटस्य युगस्य च ।
प्रक्षिप्य निश्चकर्ष त्रिः सुत्वक् सा तु ततोऽभवत् ॥१०५॥
तस्यास्त्वगपहता या पूर्वा सा शल्यकोऽभवत् ।
उत्तरा त्वभवद्गोधा कृकलासस्त्वगुत्तमा ॥१०६॥
इतिहासमिदं सूक्तम् आहतुर्यास्कभागुरी ।
कन्येति शौनकस्त्वैन्द्रं पान्तमित्युत्तरे च ये ॥१०७॥
Bउत्तमा त्वार्भवी प्रोक्ता उत्तरस्यैतरेयके ।
Bछान्दोमिके तृतीये तद् आर्भवं शस्यते यतः ॥१०८॥ २२॥
मारुतं गौः परं सूक्तम् आ त्विन्द्राणि पराणि षट् ।
Bसूक्ते द्वितीय एतेषाम् इतिहासं प्रचक्षते ।
अपक्रम्य तु देवेभ्यः सोमो वृत्रभयार्दितः ॥१०९॥
नदीमंशुमतीं नाम्ना अभ्यतिष्ठत्कुरून्प्रति ।

तं बृहस्पतिनैकेन अभ्ययाद्वृत्रहा सह ॥११०॥
योत्स्यमानः सुसंहृष्टैर् मरुद्भिर्विविधायुधैः ।
दृष्ट्वा तानायतः सोमः स्वबलेन व्यवस्थितः ॥१११॥
मन्वानो वृत्रमायान्तं जिघांसुमरिसेनया ।
व्यवस्थितं धनुष्मन्तं तमुवाच बृहस्पतिः ॥११२॥
मरुत्पतिरयं सोम एहि देवान्पुनर्विभो ।
B श्रुत्वा देवगुरोर्वाक्यम् अनर्थं वृत्रशङ्कया ॥११३॥ २३॥
सोऽब्रवीन्नेति तं शक्रः स्वर्ग एव बलाद्बली ।
इयाय देवानादाय तं पपुर्विधिवत्सुराः ॥११४॥
जघ्नुः पीत्वा च दैत्यानां समरे नवतीर्नव ।
तदेतदप्सवेत्यस्मिंस् तृचे सर्वं निगद्यते ॥११५॥
B इन्द्रं च मरुतश्चैव तथैव च बृहस्पतिम् ।
तृचस्य देवता होता इन्द्रमेवाह शौनकः ॥११६॥
B ऐन्द्राबार्हस्पत्य उक्तो ब्राह्मणे त्वैतरेयके ।
तृचेनेन्द्रमपश्यंस्तं* नेमोऽयमिति भार्गवः ॥११७॥
तुष्टावेन्द्रो बृचेनायम् अहं पश्य च मामृषे ।
B स हि स्तुवन्नेमं* एको नेन्द्रो अस्तीति चाब्रवीत् ॥११८॥ २४॥
B तदाकर्ण्येन्द्र आत्मानम् ऋग्भ्यां तुष्टाव दर्शयन् ।
ऋषिस्तं दृष्ट्वा सुप्रीतो विश्वेत्ता त इति बृचे ॥११९॥
विविधानि च कर्माणि दानमैन्द्रं च शंसति ।
मनोजवास्तु सौपर्णी समुद्रे वज्रसंस्तवः ॥१२०॥
वाचं सर्वगतां देवीं स्तौति यद्वागिति बृचे ।
त्रींल्लोकानभितप्येमान् वृत्रस्तस्थौ स्वया त्विषा ॥१२१॥
तं नाशकद्धन्तुमिन्द्रो विष्णुमभ्येत्य सोऽब्रवीत् ।
वृत्रं हनिष्ये तिष्ठस्व विक्रम्याद्य ममान्तिके ॥१२२॥

उद्यतस्यैव वज्रस्य द्यौर्ददातु ममान्तरम् ।
तथेति विष्णुस्तच्चक्रे द्यौश्चास्य विवरं ददौ ॥१२३॥ २५॥
तदेतदखिलं प्रोक्तं सखे विष्णविति त्वृचि ।
मैत्रावरुण्यः सूक्ताद्याश् चतस्रस्त्वृधगित्यृचः ॥१२४॥
प्रेति मित्राय पादाश्च अर्यम्णो वरुणस्य च ।
त्रयश्चतुर्थः सर्वेषाम् आदित्यानामिति स्तुतिः ॥१२५॥
परा त्वादित्यदेवत्या आ म इत्याश्विनो तृचः ।
वायव्ये सौर्ये उषस्या प्रभां वा चन्द्रसूर्ययोः ॥१२६॥
पावमानी प्रजा हेति मातेत्यृग्भ्यां तु गौ स्तुता ।
त्वमग्ने बृहदाग्नेये परेऽग्निस्त्वृचि संस्तुतः ॥१२७॥
मरुद्भिः सह रुद्रैश्च आग्ने याहीति मध्यमः ।
B प्रजा हेत्यपि वार्धर्चे प्रथमेऽग्निरिहोच्यते ॥१२८॥
B पादे तृतीय आदित्यस् तुरीये मध्यम स्तुतः ।
B रहस्ये ब्राह्मणेऽप्येवं व्याख्यातं ह्यैतरेयके ॥१२९॥ २६॥

RV. ix. पवमान स्तुतः सोमो नवमे त्विह मण्डले ।
पवमानवदाप्र्यस्तु समिद्ध इति संस्तुताः ॥१३०॥
अग्न आयूंषीति चासु तिसृष्वग्निर्निपातभाक् ।
अविता न इति त्वस्मिंस् तृचे पूष्णा सह स्तुतः ॥१३१॥
आग्नेय्यौ द्वे ऋचावत्र यत्त इत्युत्तरे ततः ।
उभाभ्यामिति सावित्री आग्निसावित्र्यृगुत्तरा ॥१३२॥
पुनन्तु मां वैश्वदेवी आग्नेयी त्वृगुप प्रियम् ।
उत्तरे च य इत्येते स्वाध्यायाध्येतृसंस्तवः ॥१३३॥
सूक्ते निरुक्ते स्त्रक्तेऽग्नी रक्षोहा घर्मसंस्तवः ।
सूर्यवच्चात्मवच्चापि पवित्रमिति चोच्यते ॥१३४॥ २७॥

B आर्भवस्तु भवेत्पाद् ऋभुर्धीर इति स्मृतः ।
B निपातैस्तु त्रिभिः पादैस् त्रयो देवा इहोदिताः ॥१३५॥
ब्रह्मा देवानां तिस्रोक्तास् त्रिभिस्त्वेतैर्ऋचैर्ऋचैः ।
सूर्यवच्चात्मवच्चापि स्तूयते सोम एव वा ॥१३६॥
अनावृष्ट्यां तु वर्तन्त्यां पप्रच्छर्षीञ्छचीपतिः ।
काले दुर्गे महत्यस्मिन् कर्मणा केन जीवथ ॥१३७॥
B शकटं शाकिनी गावः कृषिरस्यन्दनं वनम् ।
B समुद्रः पर्वतो राजा एवं जीवामहे वयम् ॥१३८॥
स्तुवन्नेव शशंसास्य ऋषिराङ्गिरसः शिशुः ।
नानानीयेन सूक्तेन ऋषीणामेव संनिधौ ॥१३९॥ २८॥
तानिन्द्रस्त्वाह सर्वांस्तु तपध्वं सुमहत्तपः ।
न ह्यृते तपसः शक्यम् इदं कृच्छ्रं व्यपोहितुम् ॥१४०॥
अथ ते वै तपस्तेपुः सर्वे स्वर्गजिगीषवः ।
ततस्ते तपसोग्रेण पावमानीर्ऋचोऽब्रुवन् ॥१४१॥
अनसूयुरधीयानः शुश्रूषुस्तपसान्वितः ।
दश पूर्वापरान् वंश्यान् पुनात्यात्मानमेव च ॥१४२॥
पापं यच्चाकरोत्किंचिन् मनोवाग्देहभोजनैः ।
पूतः स तस्मात्सर्वस्मात् स्वाध्यायफलमश्नुते ॥१४३॥
A पावमान्यः परं ब्रह्म शुक्रं ज्योतिः सनातनम् ।
A गायत्र्योऽन्तेऽत्र यश्चासां प्राणानायम्य तन्मनाः ॥१४४॥
पावमानं पितॄन्देवान् ध्यायेद्यश्च सरस्वतीम् ।
पितॄंस्तस्योपवर्तेत क्षीरं सर्पिर्मधूदकम् ॥१४५॥
B एतत्सूक्त*शतं सौम्यं मण्डलं सचतुर्दशम् ।
B पावमानमिति ख्यातम् अनुवाकास्तु सप्त वै ॥१४६॥ २९॥

RV. x. सप्ताग्नेयानि सूक्तानि ददर्शाग्य इति त्रितः ।
प्र केतुनेति त्वाष्ट्रस्तु त्रिशिराः सूक्तमुत्तरम् ॥१४७॥
ऋचस्त्वस्य षळाग्नेय्यस् तृचस्त्वस्येति यः परः ।
तेनेन्द्रमभितुष्टाव स्वप्नान्त इति नः श्रुतिः ॥१४८॥
अभवत्स हि देवानां पुरोधाः प्रियकाम्यया ।
असुराणां स्वसुः पुत्रस् त्रिशिरा विश्वरूपधृक् ॥१४९॥
तमृषिं प्रहितं त्विन्द्रो देवेषु बुबुधेऽसुरैः ।
सोऽस्य वज्रेण तान्याशु शिरांसि त्रीण्यथाछिदत् ॥१५०॥
तस्य यत्सोमपानं तु मुखं सोऽभूत्कपिञ्जलः ।
कलविङ्कः सुरापाणम् अन्नादं तित्तिरिस्त्वभूत् ॥१५१॥ ३०॥
तं वागभ्यवदद्ब्राह्मी ब्रह्महासि शतक्रतो ।
प्रपन्नं हतवान्यस्माद् विश्वरूपं पराङ्मुखम् ॥१५२॥
तमभ्यसिञ्चत्सूक्तेन ऋषिराप इति स्वयम् ।
सिन्धुद्वीपोऽपनुत्त्यर्थं तस्याश्लीलस्य पाप्मनः ॥१५३॥
मैथुनार्थमभीप्सन्तीं प्रत्याचष्टे यमीं यमः ।
तदो चिदिति संवादो विवस्वत्सुतयोस्तयोः ॥१५४॥
वृषाग्नेये हविर्धाने युजे वामत्र संस्तुते ।
परेयिवांसमित्यत्र स्तूयते मध्यमो यमः ॥१५५॥
अथर्वाणोऽथ भृगवोऽङ्गिरसः पितरः सह ।
षष्ठ्यां देवगणास्तत्र संस्तूयन्ते द्युभक्तयः ॥१५६॥ ३१॥
B पितृभिश्चाङ्गिरोभिश्च संस्तुतो दृश्यते यमः ।
B मन्त्रेषु बहुशः पादे विवस्वन्तं पिता हि सः ॥१५७॥
B संस्कार्यप्रेतसंयुक्तैः पितृभि स्तूयते यमः ।
B प्रेहि प्रेहीति तिसृषु प्रेताशिष उदाहृताः ॥१५८॥
B पितॄणां हि पतिर्देवो यमस्तस्मात्स सूक्तभाक् ।

अति द्रव तृचे श्वानौ परं पित्र्यमुदीरताम् ॥१५९॥

A उत्तरेण तु सूक्तेन श्मशाने कर्म शंसति ।

पितृदेवासुराणां च अभवन्नग्नयस्त्रयः ।

हव्यकव्यवहौ चोभौ सहरक्षाश्च नाम यः ॥१६०॥

तत्र मैनमिति त्वेतत् कव्यवाहनसंस्तुतिः ।

इतराणि तु दैवस्य स्तुतिर्नास्यासुरस्य च ॥१६१॥ ३२॥

अभवन्मिथुनं त्वष्टुः सरण्यूस्त्रिशिराः सह ।

स वै सरण्यूं प्रायच्छत् स्वयमेव विवस्वते ॥१६२॥

ततः सरण्य्वां जज्ञाते यमयम्यौ विवस्वतः ।

तौ चाप्युभौ यमावेव ज्यायांस्ताभ्यां तु वै यमः ॥१६३॥ ३३॥

ज्यायांस्ताभ्यां तु वै यमः ॥

॥ इति बृहद्देवतायां षष्ठोऽध्यायः ॥

सृष्ट्वा भर्तुः परोक्षं तु सरण्यूः सदृशीं स्त्रियम् ।
निक्षिप्य मिथुनं तस्याम् अश्वा भूत्वापचक्रमे ॥१॥
अविज्ञानाद्विवस्वांस्तु तस्यामजनयन्मनुम् ।
राजर्षिरभवत्सोऽपि विवस्वानिव तेजसा ॥२॥
स विज्ञाय त्वपक्रान्तां सरण्यूमश्वरूपिणीम् ।
त्वाष्ट्रीं प्रति जगामाशु वाजी भूत्वा सलक्षणः ॥३॥
सरण्यूश्च विवस्वन्तं विदित्वा हयरूपिणम् ।
मैथुनायोपचक्राम तां च तत्रारुरोह सः ॥४॥
ततस्तयोस्तु वेगेन शुक्रं तदपतद्भुवि ।
उपाजिघ्रच्च सा त्वश्वा तच्छुक्रं गर्भकाम्यया ॥५॥ १॥
आघ्रातमात्राच्छुक्रात्तु कुमारौ संबभूवतुः ।
नासत्यश्चैव दस्रश्च यौ स्तुतावश्विनाविति ॥६॥
इतिहासमिमं यास्कः सरण्यूदेवते त्वृचे ।
विवस्वतश्च त्वष्टुश्च त्वष्टेति सह मन्यते ॥७॥
पूषेति पादौ पौष्णौ द्वाव् आग्नेयावुत्तरौ तु यौ ।
स्यात्तृतीयोऽपि वा पौष्णस् तिस्रश्चान्याः परास्तु याः ॥८॥
अपां स्तुतिस्त्वृगर्धैका तृचात्सारस्वतात्परा ।
स्तुतः परोक्षः सोमस्तु द्रप्स इत्युत्तरे तृचे ॥९॥
अब्देवताशीर्वादो वा पयस्वत्युत्तरा तु या ।
चतस्रस्ता स्तुतिर्मृत्योर् अन्त्ये क्रुप्ताश्च कर्मणि ॥१०॥ २॥
B मृतशिष्टेभ्य आशास्ते इमे ज्योग्जीवनं पुनः ।
B इमं जीवेभ्य आशास्ते तेभ्यः परिधिकर्मणि ॥११॥

यथा धाय्युत्तरा त्वाष्ट्री ततो याम्या इमास्त्विति ।
स्त्रीणामाशिषमाशास्ते तयैवाञ्जनकर्मणि ॥१२॥
उदीर्ष्व नारीत्यनया मृतं पत्न्यनुरोहति ।
भ्राता कनीयान्प्रेतस्य निगद्य प्रतिषेधति ॥१३॥
B कुर्यादेतत्कर्म होता देवरो न भवेद्यदि ।
B प्रेतानुगमनं न स्याद् इति ब्राह्मणशासनात् ॥१४॥
B वर्णानामितरेषां च स्त्रीधर्मोऽयं भवेन्न वा ।
शान्त्यर्थं धनुरादाने प्रेतस्यर्चं धनुर्जपेत् ।
यस्मादेताः प्रयुज्यन्ते श्मशाने चान्यकर्मणि ॥१५॥ ३॥
तस्माद्वदेत्तृचस्यास्य देवतां मृत्युमेव तु ।
मन्त्रेषु ह्यनिरुक्तेषु देवतां कर्मतो वदेत् ॥१६॥
मन्त्रतः कर्मतश्चैव प्रजापतिरसंभवे ।
पराश्चतस्रो यास्त्वत्र उप सर्पेति पार्थिवी ॥१७॥
तासां प्रयोगः प्रेतस्य अस्थिसंचयकर्मणि ।
प्रतीचीने यथाहानि अपहृत्येतराणि तु ॥१८॥
अहःसु पितरो दधुर् इत्याशास्तेऽन्ययाशिषः ।
B अहःस्वागामिषु च मां प्रय*न्तं समजीवयन् ॥१९॥
नि वर्तध्वमितीदं तु गवां केचिदपां विदुः ।
अर्धर्चः प्रथमायास्तु अग्नीषोमीय उत्तरः ॥२०॥ ४॥
ऐन्द्री षष्ठी द्वितीयायाम् उभौ देवौ निपातितौ ।
दशाक्षरं तु शान्त्यर्थं मानसं सूक्तमुच्यते ॥२१॥
त्रीण्यैन्द्राणि कुहेत्यत्र आग्नेयाभ्यां पराणि तु ।
तृचोऽत्रास्त्याश्विनस्त्वेक ऐन्द्राणामुत्तमे युवम् ॥२२॥
भद्रं सौम्यं प्र हि पौष्णं त्रीण्यैन्द्राणि पराण्यसत् ।
तेषामाद्येन मत्तः सन् स्वानि कर्माणि शंसति ॥२३॥

यथा चरति भूतेषु यथा वर्षति पाति च ।
सूक्ते तदस्मिन्नष्टाभिर् ऋग्भिरुक्तमभूर्विति ॥ २४ ॥
सप्तेति मरुत स्तौति स्तौति वज्रमृगुत्तरा ।
अग्निमिन्द्रं च सोमं च पीवानं मेषमर्चेति ॥ २५ ॥ ५ ॥
पूर्वोऽर्धर्चोऽपरस्तस्याः पर्जन्यं वायुना सह ।
वि क्रोशनास इत्यग्निम् उत्तरा सूर्यमेव तु ॥ २६ ॥
एतौ मेऽयं य इत्येते स्तुतिश्चैवेन्द्रवज्रयोः ।
वृक्षेवृक्षे धनुश्चैन्द्रं देवानामिति तु त्रयः ॥ २७ ॥
शीतोष्णवर्षदातारः पर्जन्यानिलभास्कराः ।
अन्त्ये सूर्यानिलौ चोभौ स्तूयेते च पदे सह ॥ २८ ॥
सा ते जीवातुरित्यस्याम् इन्द्रो वा सूर्य एव वा ।
विश्वो ह्यन्यस्तु संवाद ऋषेः शक्रस्य चैव हि ॥ २९ ॥
युग्माः शक्रस्य विज्ञेया वसुक्रस्येतरा ऋचः ।
B स्नुषेन्द्रस्यागतान्देवान् दृष्ट्वा शक्रमनागतम् ॥ ३० ॥ ६ ॥
B यज्ञं परोक्षवत्प्राह श्वशुरो नागतो मम ।
B यद्यागच्छेद् भक्षयेत्स धानाः सोमं पिबेदपि ॥ ३१ ॥
B इति तस्या वचः श्रुत्वा तत्क्षणादेत्य वज्रधृक् ।
B तिष्ठन्वेद्यामुत्तरस्याम् उच्चैराह स रोरुवत् ॥ ३२ ॥
तृतीयया चतुर्थ्या च प्र देवत्रेत्यपां स्तुतौ ।
अपांनपादित्यनेन नाम्नाग्निर्मध्यम स्तुतः ॥ ३३ ॥
एति यद्वैश्वदेवं तु तस्य प्रेत्यैन्द्रमुत्तरम् ।
वैश्वदेवी प्र मेत्येका सं मेत्यैन्द्रो तृचः परः ॥ ३४ ॥
कुरुश्रवणमर्चतः परे द्वे त्रासदस्यवम् ।
मृते मित्रातिथौ राज्ञि तन्नपातमृषिः परैः ॥ ३५ ॥ ७ ॥
उपमश्रवसं यस्य चतुर्भिः स व्यशोकयत् ।

प्रावेपा इति सूक्तं यत् तदक्षस्तुतिरुच्यते ॥३६॥
अत्राक्षान्द्वादशी स्तौति नवम्याद्या च सप्तमी ।
A त्रयोदशी कृषिं स्तौति कितवं चानुशासति ।
अक्षांस्तु शेषा निन्दन्ति अबुध्नं वैश्वदेवते ॥३७॥
B सावित्रमेके मन्यन्ते महो अग्ने स्तवं परम् ।
B आचार्याः शौनको यास्को गालवश्चोत्तमामृचम् ॥३८॥
नमः सौर्यमैन्द्रमस्मिन् सौर्ये षष्ठ्या तु या स्तुताः ।
निपातिन्यँस्ताः सूक्तान्ते वैश्वदेवोऽत्र तु त्वृचः ॥३९॥
आश्विनानि तु यस्त्रीणि ऐन्द्राण्यस्त्वेव सु प्र च ।
ऐन्द्राणामुत्तमायास्तु स्तुतोऽर्धर्चे बृहस्पतिः ॥४०॥ ८॥
परे दिवस्पर्याग्नेये प्रथमस्योत्तमेन तु ।
द्यावापृथिव्यौ विश्वे च पच्छोऽर्धर्चेन संस्तुताः ॥४१॥
B आसीत्काक्षीवती घोषा पापरोगेण दुर्भगा ।
B उवास षष्टिं वर्षाणि पितुरेव गृहे पुरा ॥४२॥
B आतस्थे महतीं चिन्तां न पुत्रो न पतिर्मम ।
B जरां प्राप्ता मुधा तस्मात् प्रपद्येऽहं शुभस्पती ॥४३॥
B यथैतौ मामकस्तात आराध्यावाप यौवनम् ।
B आयुरारोग्यमैश्वर्यं सर्वभूतहने विषम् ॥४४॥
B रूपवत्तां च सौभाग्यम् अहं तस्य सुता यदि ।
B ममापि मन्त्राः प्रादुःस्युर् यै स्तोष्येते मयाश्विनौ ॥४५॥ ९॥
B चिन्तयन्तीति सूक्ते द्वे यो वां परि ददर्श सा ।
B स्तुतौ तावश्विनौ देवौ प्रीतौ तस्या भगान्तरम् ॥४६॥
B प्रविश्य विजरारोगां सुभगां चक्रतुश्च तौ ।
B भर्तारं ददतुस्तस्यै सुहस्त्यं च सुतं मुनिम् ॥४७॥
B ददतुस्तत्सुपर्णाभ्यां यन्नासत्येति कीर्त्यते ।

B काक्षीवत्यै च घोषायै न तस्यामाजुँ*रोऽनया ॥४८॥
प्राजापत्यासुरी त्वासीद् विकुण्ठा नाम नामतः ।
सेच्छन्तीन्द्रसमं पुत्रं तेपेऽथ सुमहत्तपः ॥४९॥ १०॥
सा प्रजापतितः कामांल् लेभेऽथ विविधान् वरान् ।
तस्यां चेन्द्रः स्वयं जज्ञे जिघांसुर्दैत्यदानवान् ॥५०॥
एकदा दानवैः सार्धं समरे समसज्यत ।
जघान तेषां नवतीर् नव सप्त च सप्तकान् ॥५१॥
भित्त्वा स्वबाहुवीर्येण हैमरौप्यायसीः पुरीः ।
हत्वा सर्वान् यथास्थानं पृथिव्यादिव्यवस्थितान् ॥५२॥
पृथिव्यां कालकेयांश्च पौलोमांश्चैव धन्विनः ।
तांश्च व्युत्सादयामास प्रह्लादतनयान्दिवि ॥५३॥ ११॥
राज्यं प्राप्य स दैत्येषु स्वेन वीर्येण दर्पितः ।
देवान्बाधितुमारेभे मोहितोऽसुरमायया ॥५४॥
बाध्यमानास्तु तेनापि असुरेणामितौजसा ।
उपाधावन्नृषिश्रेष्ठं तत्प्रबोधाय सप्तगुम् ॥५५॥
ऋषिस्तु सप्तगुर्नाम तस्यासीत्सुप्रियः सखा ।
स चैनमभितुष्टाव जगृभ्मेति करे स्पृशन् ॥५६॥
ततः स बुद्ध्वा चात्मानं सप्तगुस्तुतिहर्षितः ।
आत्मानमेव तुष्टाव अहं भुवमिति त्रिभिः ॥५७॥
कीर्तयन्स्वानि कर्माणि यानि स्म कृतवान्पुरा ।
यथाकरोच्च वैदेहं व्यंसं सोमपतिं नृपम् ॥५८॥ १२॥
वसिष्ठशापादभवद् वैदेहो नृपतिः पुरा ।
इन्द्रप्रसादादीजे च सत्त्रैः सारस्वतादिभिः ॥५९॥
B प्रभूतां शक्तिमस्त्रां च शत्रूणामप्यपाक्रियाम् ।
नृषु सर्वेषु चैश्वर्यं प्रभुत्वं भुवनेषु च ।

प्र वो मह इति त्वस्याम् आत्मनो वीर्यमक्षयम् ॥ ६० ॥
वैश्वानरे गृहपतौ यविष्ठेऽग्नौ च पावके ।
वषट्कारेण वृक्णेषु भ्रातृ*ष्वग्नौ सहःसुते ॥ ६१ ॥
अपचक्राम देवेभ्यः सौचीकोऽग्निरिति श्रुतिः ।
स प्राविशदपक्रम्य ऋतूनपो वनस्पतीन् ॥ ६२ ॥
ततोऽसुराः प्रादुरासन् नष्टेऽग्नौ हव्यवाहने ।
तेऽग्निमेवान्वैक्षन्त देवा हत्वासुरान्युधि ॥ ६३ ॥ १३ ॥
तं तु दूराद्यमश्चैव वरुणश्चान्वपश्यताम् ।
उभावेनं समादाय देवानेवाभिजग्मतुः ॥ ६४ ॥
दृष्ट्वा देवास्त्वेनमूचुर् अग्ने हव्यानि नो वह ।
वरान् गृहाण चास्मत्तश् चित्रभानो भजस्व नः ।
B देवयानान् सुगान् पथः कुरुष्व सुमनाः स्वयम् ॥ ६५ ॥
प्रत्युवाचाथ तानग्निर् विश्वे देवा यदूच माम् ।
तत्करिष्ये जुषन्तां तु होत्रं पञ्च जना मम ॥ ६६ ॥
शालामुख्यः प्रणीतश्च पुत्रो गृहपतेश्च यः ।
उत्तरो दक्षिणश्चाग्निर् एते पञ्च जनाः स्मृताः ॥ ६७ ॥ १४ ॥
मनुष्याः पितरो देवा गन्धर्वोरगराक्षसाः ।
B गन्धर्वाः पितरो देवा असुरा यक्षराक्षसाः ॥ ६८ ॥
यास्कौपमन्यवावेतान् आहतुः पञ्च वै जनान् ।
निषादपञ्चमान् वर्णान् मन्यते शाकटायनः ॥ ६९ ॥
ऋत्विजो यजमानं च शाकपूणिस्तु मन्यते ।
B होताध्वर्युस्तथोद्गाता ब्रह्मा चेति वदन्ति तान् ॥ ७० ॥
B चक्षुः श्रोत्रं मनो वाक् च प्राणश्चेत्यात्मवादिनः ।
B गन्धर्वाप्सरसो देवा मनुष्याः पितरस्तथा ॥ ७१ ॥
B सर्पाश्च ब्राह्मणे चैव श्रूयन्ते ह्यैतरेयके ।

B ये चान्ये पृथिवीजाता देवाश्चान्येऽथ यज्ञियाः ॥७२॥ १५॥
आयुरस्तु च मे दीर्घं हवींषि विविधानि च ।
अरिष्टिः पूर्वजानां च भ्रातॄणामध्वरेऽध्वरे ॥७३॥
प्रयाजाश्चानुयाजाश्च घृतं सोमे च यः पशुः ।
मद्देवत्यानि वै सन्तु यज्ञो मद्देवतोऽस्तु च ॥७४॥
तवाग्ने यज्ञ इत्येतत् प्रत्यार्धि स्विष्टकृच्च सः ।
यस्य त्रीणि सहस्राणि नव त्रीणि शतानि च ॥७५॥
त्रिंशच्चैव तु देवानां सर्वानेव वरान्ददुः ।
ततोऽग्निः सुमनाः प्रीतो विश्वैर्देवैः पुरस्कृतः ॥७६॥
विधूयाङ्गानि यज्ञेषु चक्रे होत्रमतन्द्रितः ।
भ्रातृभिः सहितः प्रीतो दिव्यात्मा हव्यवाहनः ॥७७॥ १६॥
तस्यास्थि देवदार्वासीन् मेदो मांसं च गुग्गुलुः ।
सुगन्धितेजनं स्नायु शुक्रं रजतकाञ्चने ॥७८॥
रोमाणि काशाः केशास्तु कुशाः कूर्मा नखानि च ।
अन्त्राणि चैवाप्यवका मज्जा सिकतशर्कराः ॥७९॥
असृक् पित्तं च विविधा धातवो गैरिकादयः ।
एवमग्निश्च देवाश्च सूक्तैर्महदिति त्रिभिः ॥८०॥
समूदिरे परे त्वस्माद् ऐन्द्रे सूक्ते तु तां सु ते ।
B विधुं दद्राणमित्यस्यां सूर्याचन्द्रमसौ स्तुतौ ॥८१॥
B प्राणवच्चात्मवच्चापि स्तुतिरप्यत्र दृश्यते ।
इदं द्वे वैश्वदेवे च द्वितीये *मनसस्तृचः ॥८२॥ १७*॥
प्रथमैन्द्री द्वितीयाग्नेय्य् अन्त्या तत्सोमदेवता ।
B अपि स्तौति पितॄनेतद् आर्त्विजं यत्तदुत्तरम् ॥८३॥
B सूक्तमाख्यानसंयुक्तं वक्तुकामस्य मे शृणु ।
B संमोहान्नष्टसंज्ञस्य शत्रुणाभिहतस्य तु ॥८४॥

जीवावृत्तिः सुबन्धोर्वा यदि वा मनस स्तवः ।
राजासमातिरैक्ष्वाकू रथप्रोष्ठः पुरोहितान् ॥ ८५ ॥
व्युदस्य बन्धुप्रभृतीन् द्वैपदा येऽभिमण्डले ।
द्वौ किराताकुली नाम ततो मायाविनौ द्विजौ ॥ ८६ ॥
असमातिः पुरोऽधत्त वरिष्ठौ तौ हि मन्यते ।
तौ कपोतौ द्विजौ भूत्वा गत्वा गौपायनानभि ॥ ८७ ॥ १८* ॥
मायाबलाच्च योगाच्च सुबन्धुमभिपेततुः ।
स दुःखादभिघाताच्च मुमोह च पपात च ॥ ८८ ॥
तौ ततोऽस्यासुमालुच्य राजानमभिजग्मतुः ।
ततः सुबन्धौ पतिते गतासौ भ्रातरस्त्रयः ॥ ८९ ॥
जेपुः स्वस्त्ययनं सर्वे मेति गौपायनाः सह ।
मनआवर्तनं तस्य सूक्तं यदिति तेऽभ्ययुः ॥ ९० ॥
A जेपुश्च भेषजार्थं यं प्र तारीति परं ततः ।
सूक्तस्याद्यस्तृचस्तत्र निर्ऋतेरपनोदनः ॥ ९१ ॥
त्रयः पादा मो ष्विति तु सौम्या नैर्ऋत उत्तमः ।
ऋक् सौम्या नैर्ऋती चैषा असुनीते स्तुतिः परे ॥ ९२ ॥
तृचे त्वानुमतं पादम् अन्त्यं यास्कस्तु मन्यते । १९ ॥
भूर्द्यौः सोमश्च पूषा च खं पथ्या स्वस्तिरेव च ॥ ९३ ॥
सुबन्धोरेव शान्त्यर्थं पुनर्न ऋचि तु स्मृताः ।
तृचः शमिति रोदस्योर् ऐन्द्रोऽर्धर्चः समित्यृचि ॥ ९४ ॥
रपसो नाशनार्थं वै तुष्टुवुस्तत्र रोदसी ।
रप इत्यभिधानं तु गदितं पापकृच्छ्रयोः ॥ ९५ ॥
ऋग्भिरेति चतसृभिस् तत ऐक्ष्वाकुमस्तुवन् ।
इन्द्र क्षत्रेत्यृचा चास्य स्तुत्वाशंसिषुराशिषः ॥ ९६ ॥
अगस्त्यस्येति माता च तेषां तुष्टाव तं नृपम् ।

स्तुतः स राजा सव्रीळस् तस्थौ गौपायनानभि ॥९७॥
सूक्तेनाप्यस्तुवन्नग्निं द्वैपदेन यथार्चिषु ।
अग्निरप्यब्रवीदेतान् अयमन्तःपरि*ध्यसुः ॥९८॥ २०॥
सुबन्धोरस्य चैक्ष्वाकोर् मया गुप्तो हितार्थिना ।
सुबन्धवे प्रदायासुं जीवेत्युक्त्वा च पावकः ॥९९॥
स्तुतो गौपायनैः प्रीतो जगाम त्रिदिवं प्रति ।
अयं मातेति हृष्टास्ते सुबन्धोरसुमाह्वयन् ॥१००॥
शरीरमभिनिर्दिश्य सुबन्धोः पतितं भुवि ।
सूक्तशेषं जगुश्चास्य चेतसो धारणाय ते ॥१०१॥
लब्धासुं चायमित्यस्यां पृथक् पाणिभिरस्पृशन् ।
षळिदं वैश्वदेवानि द्वितीयेऽङ्गिरसां स्तुतिः ॥१०२॥
जन्म कर्म च सख्यं च इन्द्रेण सह कीर्तयन् ।
स्तौति प्र नूनमित्याद्याः सावर्ण्यस्य मनो स्तुतिः ॥१०३॥ २१॥
तस्यैव चायुषोऽर्थाय देवान्स्तौत्यभ्ययादृषिः ।
सुत्रामाणं महीमू षु दक्षस्येत्यदिते स्तुतिः ॥१०४॥
पथ्यास्वस्तेः स्वस्तिरिद्धि स्वस्ति नो मरुतां स्तुतिः ।
मारुतीमृचमन्वाहेत्य् उक्तमाध्वर्यवेषु हि ॥१०५॥
या गौरिति तथैवास्यां स्तूयते मध्यमा तु वाक् ।
मित्राय मैत्रावरुणी भुज्युमंहस आश्विनी ॥१०६॥
A स्तौत्यं*पि च मनुं स्वस्ति द्व्यृचे वाचं च मध्यमाम् ।
अथेमां द्वे बार्हस्पत्ये भद्रा आग्नेयमाप्रियः ॥१०७॥
B प्रथमे बार्हस्पत्ये तु अर्धर्चे ब्रह्मणस्पतिः* ।
B वैश्वदेवेऽपि सूक्तेऽच स्तुतोऽर्धर्चे बृहस्पतिः ।
B ब्रह्मणस्पतिरित्यस्मिन् लिङ्गवाक्यविकारतः* ॥१०८॥ २२॥
यज्ज्योतिरमृतं ब्रह्म यद्योगात्समुपाश्नुते ।

तज्ज्ञानमभितुष्टाव सूक्तेनाथ बृहस्पतिः ॥ १०९ ॥
जीवनार्थं प्रयोगस्तु मन्त्राणां प्रतिषिध्यते ।
वेदतत्त्वार्थविज्ञानं प्रायेणात्र हि दृश्यते ॥ ११० ॥
आचार्याः केचिदित्याहुर् अत्र वाग्विदुषां स्तवः ।
यथाभिर्निन्द्यतेऽत्रर्ग्भिः सूक्तेऽन्याभिरनर्थवित् ॥ १११ ॥
यथैतामन्वविन्दन्त विद्वांसर्षिगतां सतीम् ।
यथा च व्यभजन् यज्ञे तदत्रोक्तं तृतीयया ॥ ११२ ॥
प्रशस्यते दशम्या तु विद्वानुत्तमया त्वृचा ।
यज्ञे महर्त्विजामाह विनियोगं च कर्मणाम् ॥ ११३ ॥ २३ ॥
परे तु स्तूयते *दक्षो अष्टौ चैवादितेः सुताः ।
धातेन्द्रो वरुणो मित्रो अंशः सूर्योऽर्यमा भगः ॥ ११४ ॥
ऐन्द्रे जनिष्ठाः सूक्ते द्वे प्र स्वित्यत्र परं तु यत् ।
तत्र प्राच्यः प्रतीच्यश्च स्रवन्त्यो दक्षिणाश्च याः ॥ ११५ ॥
ताः सप्त सप्तकैर्वर्गैः संस्तूयन्ते प्रधानतः ।
ग्राव्णामा वो मारुते द्वे अभ्रप्रुष इति स्मृते ॥ ११६ ॥
अपश्यमिति चाग्नेये य इमा वैश्वकर्मणे ।
मान्यवे यस्त इत्येते परं यत्तु मम व्रते ॥ ११७ ॥
तदाशीर्वादबहुलं स्तौति विश्वान्दिवौकसः ।
पराकदास आग्नेयं यदुदित्यष्टकं परम् ॥ ११८ ॥ २४ ॥
मैत्रावरुण्यृक् तत्रास्ति चतुर्थ्यैन्द्रा*ग्न्युपोत्तमा ।
सावित्री चैव सूर्या च सैव पत्नी विवस्वतः ॥ ११९ ॥
स्तुता वृषाकपायीति उषा इति च योच्यते ।
उषा एषा त्रिधात्मानं विभज्य प्रैति गोपतिम् ॥ १२० ॥
उषाः पुरोदयाद् भूत्वा सूर्या मध्यंदिने स्थिते ।
भूत्वा वृषाकपायी च दिनान्तेष्ववगच्छति ॥ १२१ ॥

सत्यसूर्यर्तसोमानां सौर्याद्याच ह्यृगुच्यते ।
पराभिस्त्रिसृभिस्त्वृग्भिर् उच्यते सोम ओषधिः ॥१२२॥
विस्पष्टमुत्तरा त्वासाम् ऋक् चन्द्रमसमर्चति ।
सूर्यायै भाववृत्तं तु रैभीत्यष्टाभिरुच्यते ॥१२३॥ २५॥
यदश्विनौ तृच स्तौति सूर्यमेवोत्तरार्चति ।
सप्तदशी वैश्वदेवी सौर्याचान्द्रमसी परा ॥१२४॥
परस्याः प्रथमौ पादौ सौर्यौ चान्द्रमसौ परौ ।
और्णवाभो तृचे त्वस्मिन्न् अश्विनौ मन्यते स्तुतौ ॥१२५॥
सूर्याचन्द्रमसौ तौ हि प्राणापानौ च तौ स्मृतौ ।
अहोरात्रौ च तावेव स्यातां तावेव रोदसी ॥१२६॥
अप्नुवाते हि तौ लोकाञ् ज्योतिषा च रसेन च ।
पृथक्पृथक् च चरतो दक्षिणेनोत्तरेण च ॥१२७॥
B सूर्यः सरति भूतेषु सु वीरयति तानि वा ।
B सु ईर्यत्वाय यात्येषु सर्वकार्याणि संदधत् ॥१२८॥ २६॥
B चारु द्रमति वा चायंश् चायनीयो* द्रमत्युत ।
B चमेः पूर्वे समेतानि निर्मिमीतेऽथ चन्द्रमाः ॥१२९॥
सुकिंशुकमिति त्वस्यां सूर्यामारोहतीं पतिम् ।
स्तौति विश्वावसुं चैव तृचे गन्धर्वमुत्तरे ॥१३०॥
अनृक्षरा इत्यनया यातौ स्तौतीह दंपती ।
गृहान्प्रपद्यमानां तु पराभिः पञ्चभिर्वधूम् ॥१३१॥
वाससश्च वधूनां च वरदानं प्रचक्षते ।
तत स्त्रि*या विरागस्य विभवे सति वाससः ॥१३२॥ २७॥
अन्यच मैथुनाद्भर्तुर् हरणं प्रतिषिध्यते ।
ये यक्ष्मनाशिनी स्तौति तृचे मा परिपन्थिनः ॥१३३॥
तृष्टमेतदिति त्वाह यादृग्वाधूयमर्हति ।

आशास्ते चैव विविधं ज्ञातिभ्यश्चानुशासनम् ॥१३४॥
बद्धा स्त्री भाववृत्तिश्च परया त्वत्र कथ्यते ।
B गृभ्णामि त ऋचा हस्तं गृह्णन्नथ धनाशिषः ॥१३५॥
B आशास्ते परया तस्याः संयोगार्थास्तथाशिषः ।
पराभिराशीश्चाशास्ते पृथक् ताभ्यां सहैव च ॥१३६॥
B अघोरेति तृचे तस्याः समिहेति द्वयोर्द्वयोः ।
B आ नः प्रजापतेर् ई*माम् ऐन्द्री चा*न्त्या बृहस्पतेः ॥१३७॥ २८॥
मन्त्रा वैवाहिका ह्येते निगद्यन्ते नृणामपि ।
आर्त्विजा* याजमानाश्च यथारूपं विशेषतः ॥१३८॥
प्रत्यृचं प्रतिकीर्त्यन्ते देवताश्चेह यासु याः ।
वदेत्तां देवतां तासु नाराशंसीर्वदेत वा ॥१३९॥
औषसीः सर्वथा चैता भाववृत्तं प्रचक्षते ।
सूर्यया सह सूक्तेऽस्मिन् पादश्चैवात्र लक्ष्यते ॥१४०॥
वि हि वार्षाकपं सूक्तम् असौ हि कपिलो वृषा ।
इन्द्रः प्रजापतिश्चैव विश्वस्मादिन्द्र उत्तरः ॥१४१॥
रक्षोहणादि चाग्नेयं त्रीन् स्तौत्यग्नीन् परं हविः ।
इमं च मध्यमं चैव असौ वैश्वानरं च यः ॥१४२॥ २९॥
ऐन्द्रात्पुरुषसूक्तं च अन्त्यया पौरुषस्य तु ।
यथैनमभजन्साध्या यज्ञार्थे सोऽर्थ उच्यते ॥१४३॥
आपान्तमन्युरित्यैन्द्यां स्तुतः सोमोऽत्र दृश्यते ।
सालोक्यात्साहचर्याद्वा स्तूयते सोम एव वा ॥१४४॥
निपातभाजं सोमं च अस्यां रथीतरोऽब्रवीत् ।
ऐन्द्रेषु हि निपातोऽत्र स्तुतोऽग्निररुणेन सम् ॥१४५॥
यज्ञस्य वो वैश्वदेवे प्रेत इत्युत्तरं तु यत् ।
तत्रार्बुदस्तु ग्रावाणं मूर्तिमन्तमिवार्चति ॥१४६॥

B प्र तद्दुःसीम इत्यृग्भ्यां राज्ञां दानं च शंसति ।
पुरूरवसि राजर्षाव् अप्सरास्तूर्वशी पुरा ।
न्यवसत्संविदं कृत्वा तस्मिन्धर्मं चचार च ॥१४७॥ ३०॥
तया तस्य च संवासम् असूयन् पाकशासनः ।
पैतामहं चानुरागम् इन्द्रवज्रापि तस्य तु ॥१४८॥
स तयोस्तु वियोगार्थं पार्श्वस्थं वज्रमब्रवीत् ।
प्रीतिं भिन्द्धि तयोर्वज्र मम चेदिच्छसि प्रियम् ॥१४९॥
तथेत्युक्त्वा तयोः प्रीतिं वज्रोऽभिनत्*स्वमायया ।
ततस्तया विहीनस्तु चचारोन्मत्तवन्नृपः ॥१५०॥
चरन्सरसि सोऽपश्यद् अभिरूपामिवोर्वशीम् ।
सखीभिरभिरूपाभिः पञ्चभिः पार्श्वतो वृताम् ॥१५१॥
तामाह पुनरेहीति दुःखात्सा त्वब्रवीन्नृपम् ।
अप्राप्याहं त्वयाद्येह स्वर्गे प्राप्स्यसि मां पुनः ॥१५२॥ ३१॥
आह्वानं प्रति चाख्यानम् इतरेतरयोरिदम् ।
संवादं मन्यते यास्क इतिहासं तु शौनकः ॥१५३॥
हय इति परमैन्द्रं प्र ते या ओषधीस्तवः ।
B प्रयोगे भिषजस्त्वेतद् यक्ष्मनाशाय कल्पते ॥१५४॥
आर्ष्टिषेणस्तु देवापिः कौरव्यश्चैव शंतनुः ।
भ्रातरौ कुरुषु त्वेतौ राजपुत्रौ बभूवतुः ॥१५५॥
ज्येष्ठस्तयोस्तु देवापिः कनीयांश्चैव शंतनुः ।
त्वग्दोषी राजपुत्रस्तु ऋष्टिषेणसुतोऽभवत् ॥१५६॥
राज्येन छन्दयामासुः प्रजाः स्वर्गं गते गुरौ ।
स मुहूर्तमिव ध्यात्वा प्रजास्ताः प्रत्यभाषत ॥१५७॥
प्रजास्ताः प्रत्यभाषत ॥ ३२॥

॥ इति बृहद्देवतायां सप्तमोऽध्यायः ॥

न राज्यमहमर्हामि नृपतिर्वोऽस्तु शंतनुः ।
तथेत्युक्त्वाभ्यसिञ्चंस्ताः प्रजा राज्याय शंतनुम् ॥१॥
ततोऽभिषिक्ते कौरव्ये वनं देवापिराविशत् ।
न ववर्षाथ पर्जन्यो राज्ये द्वादश वै समाः ॥२॥
ततोऽभ्यगच्छद्देवापिं प्रजाभिः सह शंतनुः ।
प्रसादयामास चैनं तस्मिन्धर्मव्यतिक्रमे ॥३॥
शिशिक्ष चैनं राज्येन प्रजाभिः सहितस्तदा ।
तमुवाचाथ देवापिः प्रह्वं तु प्राञ्जलिस्थितम् ॥४॥
न राज्यमहमर्हामि त्वग्दोषोपहतेन्द्रियः ।
याजयिष्यामि ते राजन् वृष्टिकामेज्यया स्वयम् ॥५॥ १॥
ततस्तं तु पुरोऽधत्त आर्त्विज्याय स शंतनुः ।
स चास्य चक्रे कर्माणि वार्षिकाणि यथाविधि ॥६॥
बृहस्पते प्रतीत्यृग्भिर् ईजे चैव बृहस्पतिम् ।
B द्वितीययास्य सूक्तस्य बोधिते जातवेदसा ॥७॥
B आस्ये ते द्युमतीं वाचं दधामि स्तुहि देवताः ।
ततः सोऽस्मै ददौ प्रीतो वाचं देवीं तया च सः ॥८॥
ऋग्भिश्चतसृभिर्देवाञ् जगौ वृष्ट्यर्थमेव तु ।
अग्निं च सूक्तशेषेण कमैन्द्रं सूक्तमुत्तरम् ॥९॥
इन्द्र दृह्येति विश्वेषाम् उदित्यृत्विक्स्तुतिः परम् ।
शक्तिप्रकाशनेनैषां विनियोगोऽत्र कीर्त्यते ॥१०॥ २॥
प्रेतीतिहाससूक्तं तु मन्यते शाकटायनः ।
यास्को द्रौघणमैन्द्रं वा वैश्वदेवं तु शौनकः ॥११॥

आजावनेन भार्म्यश्व* इन्द्रासोमौ तु मुद्गलः ।
अजयद्वृषभं युक्त्वा ऐन्द्रं च द्रुघणं रथे ॥१२॥
B युध्यन् संख्ये जयं प्रेप्सुर् ऐन्द्रोऽप्रतिरथो* जगौ ।
आशुरैन्द्रमप्वा* देवी अमीषामित्यृचि स्तुता ॥१३॥
B चतुर्थी बार्हस्पत्या स्यान् नाकुले च महानिति* ।
तृचस्तु मारुतः प्रेतेत्य्* ऐन्द्री वा ब्रह्म यत्परम् ॥१४॥
तत्रानिरुक्तसूक्तादाव् ऋगेका सूर्यमर्चति ।
घर्मपराश्चतस्रस्तु सवितारमभीति या ॥१५॥ ३॥
सूक्तशेषस्य षळृचः सूर्याचन्द्रमसौ सह ।
तुष्टावेन्द्रमसावीति अष्टकोऽस्मात्परेण तु ॥१६॥
कौत्सः कदा वसो सूक्तं दुर्मित्रो नाम नामतः ।
सुमित्रश्चैव नाम स्याद् गुणार्थमितरत्पदम् ॥१७॥
भूतांशस्तु प्रजाकामः कर्माणि कृतवान्पुरा ।
न हि लेभे प्रजाः काश्चित् काश्यपो मुनिसत्तमः ॥१८॥
उवाच भार्या भूतांशं सुतानिच्छसि यावतः ।
तावतो जनयिष्यामि देवता द्वन्द्वश स्तुहि ॥१९॥
तमभ्ययुस्तु सर्वाणि द्वन्द्वानि स्तुतिकाम्यया ।
तान्यवेक्ष्याथ तश्चक्रे नासत्यौ सूक्तभागिनौ ॥२०॥ ४॥
तदेतदन्ततो भावाद् आश्विनं सूक्तमुच्यते ।
न ह्यस्मिन्देवतालिङ्गं प्रागन्त्याद्दृश्यते पदात् ॥२१॥
सूक्तेन तु परेणाथ स्वयमाविरभूदिति ।
आत्मानमेव तुष्टाव प्राजापत्याथ दक्षिणा ॥२२॥
दातॄनथ स्तुतानेके दक्षिणानां वदन्ति तु ।
दातृत्वाद्दक्षिणानां च भोजाश्चतसृभि स्तुताः ॥२३॥
असुराः पणयो नाम रसापारनिवासिनः ।

गास्तेऽपजह्रुरिन्द्रस्य न्यगूहंश्च प्रयत्नतः ॥२४॥
बृहस्पतिस्तथापश्यद् दृष्ट्वेन्द्राय शशंस च ।
प्राहिणोत्तम दूत्येऽथ सरमां पाकशासनः ॥२५॥ ५॥
किमित्यचायुजाभिस्तां पप्रच्छुः पणयोऽसुराः ।
कुतः कस्यासि कल्याणि किं वा कार्यमिहास्ति ते ॥२६॥
अथाब्रवीत्तान्सरमा दूत्यैन्द्री विचराम्यहम् ।
युष्मान्व्रजं चान्विष्यन्ती गाश्चैवेन्द्रस्य पृच्छतः ॥२७॥
विदित्वेन्द्रस्य दूतीं ताम् असुराः पापचेतसः ।
ऊचुर्मा सरमे गास्त्वम् इहास्माकं स्वसा भव ॥२८॥
B विभजामो गवां भागं माहिता ह ततः पुनः ।
सूक्तस्यास्यान्यया चर्चा युग्माभिस्त्वेव सर्वशः ॥२९॥
साब्रवीन्नाहमिच्छामि स्वसृत्वं वा धनानि वा ।
पिबेयं तु पयस्तासां गवां यास्ता निगूहथ ॥३०॥ ६॥
असुरास्तां तथेत्युक्त्वा तदाजह्रुः पयस्ततः ।
सा स्वभावाच्च लौल्याच्च पीत्वा तत्पय आसुरम् ॥३१॥
परं संवननं हृद्यं बलपुष्टिकरं ततः ।
शतयोजनविस्ताराम् अतरत्तां रसां पुनः ॥३२॥
यस्याः पारे परे तेषां पुरमासीत्सुदुर्जयम् ।
पप्रच्छेन्द्रश्च सरमां कच्चिद्गा दृष्टवत्यसि ॥३३॥
सा नेति प्रत्युवाचेन्द्रं प्रभावादासुरस्य तु ।
तां जघान पदा क्रुद्धः उद्गिरन्ती पयस्ततः ॥३४॥
जगाम सा भयोद्विग्ना पुनरेव पणीन्प्रति ।
पदानुसारिपद्धत्या रथेन हरिवाहनः ॥३५॥ ७॥
गत्वा जघान च पणीन् गाश्च ताः पुनराहरत् ।
तेऽबदन्वैश्वदेवं तु ब्रह्मजाया जुहूर्जगौ ॥३६॥

B जामद*ग्न्यं समिद्धोऽद्य आप्रीसूक्तमतः परम् ।
युगपद्वै व्रजन्तं तं वैरूपा ऋषयस्त्रिभिः ॥३७॥
इन्द्रं प्रतिजगुः सूक्तैः पणीन्प्रति मनीषिणः ।
वैश्वदेवं परं सूक्तं घर्मेत्येकेऽत्र तु स्तुतान् ॥३८॥
देवानिन्द्रं च मन्यन्ते छन्दांस्यग्निं च मध्यमम् ।
आग्नेयं चित्र इत्येतज् जगादर्षिरुपस्तुतः ॥३९॥
पिबेन्द्रं स्तौति नेत्यन्नं राक्षोघ्नाग्नेयमुत्तरम् ।
इति वै लाब*मैन्द्रं तद् आस्याः षष्ठ्यां निपातिताः ॥४०॥ ८॥
प्राजापत्यमथाग्नेयं वैन्यमित्यनुपूर्वशः ।
वरुणेन्द्राग्निसोमानाम् इमं न इति संस्तवः ॥४१॥
चतस्रस्त्वत्र सूक्तादाव् अग्निरात्मस्तवं जगौ ।
स्तुतः सोमस्तु षष्ठ्या च नवम्या च पदैस्त्रिभिः ॥४२॥
वारुण्यस्त्वितरास्तिस्र ऐन्द्रमेवोत्तमं पदम् ।
अहं वाक्सूक्तमर्यम्णो मित्रस्य वरुणस्य च ॥४३॥
न तं राज्याः परं सूक्तं वैश्वदेवं ममेति यत् ।
नमस्ते वैद्युतं सूक्तम् आशीर्वादः परं तु यत् ॥४४॥
यां कल्पयन्ति नोऽरयः कृत्यानाशनमात्मनः ।
हिरण्यस्तुतिरायुष्यं नासद्यत्परमेष्ठिनः ॥४५॥ ९॥
वदन्ति भाववृत्तं तद् यो यज्ञ इति चोत्तरम् ।
अपैन्द्रमत्र त्वाश्विन्यौ चतुर्थी पञ्चमी स्मृते ॥४६॥
मैत्रावरुणमीजानं प्रथमायामृचि स्तुताः ।
अर्धर्चे द्यौश्च भूमिश्च अश्विनौ चोत्तरे ततः ॥४७॥
प्रो ष्वैन्द्रे वैश्वदेव्यृक् तु नकिर्देवा मिनीमसि ।
यस्मिन्वृक्ष इति त्वस्मिन् द्युस्थान स्तूयते यमः ॥४८॥
केश्यग्निं कै*शिनं सूक्तम् उत देवाः परं तु यत् ।

देवानामत्र चाद्या स्याद् वातदेवस्तृचः परः ॥४९॥
चायन्तां वैश्वदेव्यृक् तु शेषस्त्वब्दैवतः परः ।
स्यादेतद्विश्वभैषज्यं रपसो वा विनाशनम् ॥५०॥ १०॥
भूमिर्लाक्षं परं सूक्तं तवैन्द्रं सूक्तमुत्तरम् ।
सूर्यरश्मिरिति त्वस्मिन् सावित्रः प्रथमस्तृचः ॥५१॥
आत्मा स्तुतः परोक्षस्तु गन्धर्वेणोत्तरे तृचे ।
इन्द्रो वैष निपातेन अथवा सूर्य उच्यते ॥५२॥
B सूक्तेऽस्मिन्देवतास्तिस्र एता एव प्रकीर्तिताः ।
B आग्नेयं त्वग्ने तवेति* अग्ने अच्छेति यत्परम् ॥५३॥
आग्नेयं वैश्वदेवं च अयमित्यत्र तु द्वृचाः ।
शार्ङ्गाश्चत्वार ऋषयो अग्निमार्चन्पृथक्पृथक् ॥५४॥ ११॥
आश्विनं त्यं चिदित्येतद् अयमैन्द्रं ततः परम् ।
इमां खनामीति सूक्तम् इन्द्राणी यत्स्वयं जगौ ॥५५॥
तदौपनिषदं षट्कं भाववृत्तं प्रचक्षते ।
B उत्तानपर्णी पाठां तु स्तौति सूक्ते महौषधिम् ॥५६॥
B पतिसंवननी त्वन्त्यान्याः सपत्न्यपनोदिकाः* ।
अरण्यानीत्यरण्यान्या स्तुतिरैन्द्रे श्रदुत्तरे ॥५७॥
सावित्रं सविता यन्त्रैः समिद्धश्चित्समिध्यसे ।
आग्नेयं श्रद्धया श्राद्धं मेधासूक्तमतः परम् ॥५८॥
आग्नेयमा सूरि*त्वेतच्च छास ऐन्द्रे ततः परे ।
सोम एकेभ्य इत्येतद् भाववृत्तं प्रचक्षते ॥५९॥ १२॥
यदरायीत्यलक्ष्मीघ्नं तत्र चत्तो इति द्वृचे ।
प्राधान्याद्वा निपाताद्वा स्तूयते ब्रह्मणस्पतिः ॥६०॥
इन्द्रश्चैव यदित्यस्यां विश्वे देवाः परीत्यृचि ।
आग्नेयं चाग्निमित्येतद् वैश्वदेवमिमा नु कम् ॥६१॥

इन्द्रः प्राधान्यतस्तत्र विश्वैर्देवैः सह स्तुतः ।
आदित्यैश्च मरुद्भिश्च तथारूपं हि दृश्यते ॥६२॥
सूर्यो न इति सौर्यं तु यस्त्वेतदुदसाविति ।
पौलोमी स्वान्गुणांस्तत्र सपत्नीनां च शंसति ॥६३॥ १३॥
ऐन्द्रं तीव्रस्य मुञ्चामि भेषज्यं यक्ष्मनाशनम् ।
राजयक्ष्महणं सूक्तं प्राजापत्यं तदुच्यते ॥६४॥
ऐन्द्राग्नं मन्यते यास्क एके लिङ्गोक्तदैवतम् ।
राक्षोघ्नाग्नेयमित्युक्तं यस्त्वेतद्ब्रह्मणेति तु ॥६५॥
स्रवतामपि गर्भाणां दृष्टं तदनुमन्त्रणम् ।
वैन्यं तु वेनस्तत्पश्यद् अक्षीभ्यां यक्ष्मनाशनम् ॥६६॥
दुःस्वप्नघ्नमपेहीति निपातीन्द्रोऽग्निरेव च ।
आसीदृषिर्दीर्घतपाः कपोतो नाम नैर्ऋतः ॥६७॥
अकरोत्कपोतस्तस्याश्वाम् अभिधाने पदं किल ।
स तमात्महितैर्वाक्यैः कपोतं स्तुतवानृषिः ॥६८॥ १४॥
देवा इति तु सूक्तेन प्रायश्चित्तार्थमुच्यते ।
ऋषभं मा सपत्नघ्नं येनेदमिति मानसम् ॥६९॥
तुभ्येत्यृषी ददृशतुर् ऐन्द्रं गाथिनभार्गवौ ।
वरुणो विधातानुमतिर् धाता सोमो बृहस्पतिः ॥७०॥
षळेता देवतास्तत्र तृतीयायामृचि स्तुताः ।
वातस्येति परेणास्तौद् अनिलः पितरं स्वकम् ॥७१॥
मयोभूरिति यत्सूक्तम् अपश्यच्छबर ऋषिः ।
नानारूपाः पयस्विन्यो गावस्तत्र तु संस्तुताः ॥७२॥
विभ्राट् सौर्यं त्वं त्यमैन्द्रम् आ याहीत्युषस स्तुतिः ।
आ त्वा राज्ञेऽभिषिक्ताय द्वे सूक्ते चानुमन्त्रणे ॥७३॥ १५॥
प्र व इत्युत्तरं ग्राव्णां ददर्श स्तुतिमार्बुदिः ।

यस्त्वतः परमाग्नेयं तत्रार्भव्यृक् प्र सूनवः ॥७४॥
ऋषिर्जगौ पतंगस्तु पतंगमिति यत्परम् ।
तत्सौर्यमेके मन्यन्ते मायाभेदं तथापरे ॥७५॥
B मायाभेदे द्वितीयायां वाक् स्तुतेत्याह शौनकः ।
B देवी बिभर्ति मनसा या वाचं विदितां सतीम् ॥७६॥
त्यमू षु तार्क्ष्यदैवत्यं सूक्तं स्वस्त्ययनं विदुः ।
उदैन्द्रे वैश्वदेवं तु प्रथश्चेति च यत्परम् ॥७७॥
आत्मप्रभावमाचख्युस् तत्राद्या ऋषयस्त्रयः ।
रथंतरं यथा स्तोत्रं स्तोत्रं चैव यथा बृहत् ॥७८॥ १६॥
यथा च संभूतो घर्मः सवितुश्चोपलक्ष्यते ।
बृहस्पतिरिति त्वस्मिन् स्तुतः सूक्ते बृहस्पतिः ॥७९॥
आशिषो यजमानस्य केचिदेतां स्तुतिं विदुः ।
प्राजापत्यस्य यत्सूक्तम् अपश्यं त्वा प्रजावतः ॥८०॥
प्रत्यृचं देवता स्तौति लिङ्गैरेवात्र लक्षिताः ।
आशिषः पुत्रकामस्य प्रथमा हि वदत्यथ ॥८१॥
द्वितीया पुत्रकामायास् तृतीयात्मस्तवं त्वृषेः ।
यद्विष्णुरिति सूक्तं तु वैश्वदेवं प्रचक्षते ॥८२॥
तस्मिन्स्वदारगर्भार्थम् ऋषिराशास्त आशिषः ।
परं तु नेजमेषेति गर्भार्थं वा तदुच्यते ॥८३॥ *१७॥
अस्यै मे पुत्रकामायै *गर्भमा धेहि यः पुमान्* ।
आशिषो योगमेतं हि सर्व*र्गर्धेन मन्यते ॥८४॥
एकारमनुकम्पार्थे नाम्नि स्मरति माठरः ।
आख्याते भूतकरणं बाष्कला आव्ययोरिति ॥८५॥
माहिषं यन्महि त्रीणाम् आदित्यानां स्तुतिं विदुः ।
*वरुणार्यममित्राणाम् आदित्येष्वितरेषु तु ॥८६॥

एत एव त्रयो देवा स्तुताः स्वल्पेष्वतोऽन्यथा ।
शान्त्यर्थं सूक्तमेतद्धि पावनं चैव वै श्रुतम् ।
B यातां*मपि स्वस्त्ययने दृष्टं तदनुमन्त्रणम् ॥८७॥
उलोऽस्तौत्पितरं वातं वात आग्नेयमुत्तरम् ।
विस्पष्टं जातवेदस्यं प्रेति दाशतयीषु तु ॥८८॥ *१८॥
यत्किंचिदन्यच्चाग्नेयं जातवेदस्यमुच्यते ।
आयं गौरिति यत्सूक्तं सार्पराज्ञी स्वयं जगौ ॥८९॥
तस्मात्सा देवता तत्र सूर्यमेके प्रचक्षते ।
मुद्गलः शाकपूणिश्च आचार्यः शाकटायनः ॥९०॥
त्रिस्थानाधिष्ठितां वाचं मन्यन्ते प्रत्यृचं स्तुताम् ।
भाववृत्तं परं सूक्तं ददर्शाथाघमर्षणः ॥९१॥
परं न विद्यते यस्माच् छान्त्यै वा पावनाय वा ।
यथाश्वमेधः क्रतुराट् सर्वरिप्रप्रणोदनः ॥९२॥
तथाघमर्षणं ब्रह्म सर्वरिप्रप्रणोदनम् ।
तदादीनीति यच्चातः संज्ञानं ज्ञानसंस्तवः ॥९३॥ *१९॥
चतुर्थं यत्तु नैर्हस्त्यं तत्सपत्ननिबर्हणम् ।
संसमित् प्राध्वराणां चेत्य् आग्नेय्यावेव* ते स्मृते ॥९४॥
उशना वरुणश्चेन्द्रश् चाग्निश्च सविता स्तुताः ।
संज्ञाने प्रथमस्यां तु द्वितीयस्यामथाश्विनौ ॥९५॥
तृतीया चोत्तमे च द्वे आशिषोऽभिवदन्ति ताः ।
इन्द्रः पूषा सपत्नघ्ने द्वितीयस्यामृचि स्तुतौ ॥९६॥
देवानामितराः प्रोक्ता आशीर्वादपराश्च याः ।
संसं संज्ञानमित्येते परं संवननं विदुः ॥९७॥
महानाम्न्य ऋचो गुह्यास् ता एन्द्र्यश्चैव यो वदेत् ।
सहस्रयुगपर्यन्तम् अ*हर्ब्राह्मं स राध्यते ॥९८॥ २०॥

B तृचाधमं याज्ञिकाः सूक्तमाहुस् तस्मिन्स्तुतो दृश्यन्ते याः सूक्तभाजः।
B प्रधानमुक्तं किल देवता याः सूक्तभाजः सर्वदा शौनकेन ॥९९॥
B ऐन्द्रीर्ऋचो महानाम्नीस्तु विद्यात् तथा हि दृष्टं ब्राह्मणे सूक्तशब्दः।
B न दृश्यते सूक्तवादो निवित्सु यथा प्रैषेष्वाह सूक्ताभिधानम् ॥१००॥
B सूक्तैकदेशा इति तान्प्रतीयाद् अन्याश्च कुन्त्याः पदशो निशास्ताः।
B यथैतशो देवनीथादिसंज्ञा कुन्तापे तत्सर्वमेकं हि सूक्तम् ॥१०१॥

पुरीषपदमासां तु प्रथमं स्यात्प्रजापतेः।
आग्नेयमैन्द्रं वैष्णवं पौष्णं चैव तु पञ्चमम् ॥१०२॥
अग्नेः प्रयाजानुयाजाः प्रैषा ये च हवींषि च।
यद्दैवतं हविस्तु स्यात् प्रैषास्तद्दैवताश्च ते ॥१०३॥ २१॥
निविदां निगदानां च स्वैः स्वैर्लिङ्गैश्च देवताः।
निगदेन निगद्यन्ते याश्च कल्पानुगा ऋचः ॥१०४॥
अग्नेरेव तु गायत्र्य उष्णिहः सवितुः स्मृताः।
अनुष्टुभस्तु सोमस्य बृहत्यस्तु बृहस्पतेः ॥१०५॥
पङ्क्तयस्त्रिष्टुभश्चैव विद्यादैन्द्र्यश्च सर्वशः।
विश्वेषां चैव देवानां जगत्यो यास्तु काश्चन ॥१०६॥
विराजश्चैव मित्रस्य स्वराजो वरुणस्य च।
इन्द्रस्य निचृतः प्रोक्ता वायोश्च भुरिजः स्मृताः ॥१०७॥
A विषये यस्य वा स्यातां स्यातां वा वायुदेवते।
यास्त्वतिछन्दसः काश्चित् ताः प्रजापतिदेवताः ॥१०८॥ २२॥
A विछन्दसस्तु वायव्या मन्त्राः पादैश्च ये मिताः।
पौरुष्यो द्विपदाः सर्वा ब्राह्म्य एकपदाः स्मृताः ॥१०९॥
समस्ता ऋच आग्नेय्यो वायव्यानि यजूंषि च।
सौर्याणि चैव सामानि सर्वाणि ब्राह्मणानि च ॥११०॥
वैश्वदेवो वषट्कारो हिंकारो ये यजामहे।

रूपं वज्रस्य वाक्पूर्वं स्वाहाकारोऽग्निदेवतः ॥१११॥
देवानां च पितॄणां च नमस्कारः स्वधैव च ।
क्रुष्टो मूर्धनि विज्ञेयस् तालव्यः प्रथमः स्वरः ॥११२॥
द्वितीयस्तु भ्रुवोर्मध्ये तृतीयः कर्णसंश्रितः ।
चतुर्थो नासिकाग्रे स्याद् औरसो मन्द्र उच्यते ।
मन्द्रकर्षणसंयुक्तम् अतिस्वारं प्रशंसति ॥११३॥ २३॥
वदन्ति देवताः क्रुष्टं मनुष्याः प्रथमं स्वरम् ।
द्वितीयं पशवः सर्वे गन्धर्वाप्सरसः स्वरम् ॥११४॥
अण्डजाः पक्षिणः सर्पाश् चतुर्थमुपभुञ्जते ।
मन्द्रं पिशाचा रक्षांसि असुराश्चोपभुञ्जते ॥११५॥
अतिस्वारस्तु सर्वस्य जङ्गमस्थावरस्य च ।
वैश्वदेवः स्वरः क्रुष्टो नित्यं यो मूर्ध्नि तिष्ठति ॥११६॥
तालव्यः प्रथमः साम्नां स्वर आदित्यदैवतः ।
स्वरो द्वितीयः साध्यानां भ्रुवोर्देशं समाश्रितः ॥११७॥
आश्विनस्तु तृतीयोऽत्र स्वरः कर्णौ समाश्रितः ।'
चतुर्थस्त्वत्र वायव्यो नासिक्यः स्वर उच्यते ॥११८॥ २४॥
पञ्चमस्तु स्वरः प्रोक्तश् चाक्षुषः सूर्यदैवतः ।
यस्तु सामस्वरः षष्ठः स सौम्यो मन्द्र उच्यते ॥११९॥
विकर्षेण तु मन्द्रस्य युक्तोऽतिस्वार्य उच्यते ।
स मैत्रावरुणो ज्ञेयो मन्द्रस्थानसमाहितः ॥१२०॥
सामस्वराणां सप्तानाम् एते देवा इहोदिताः ।
त्रयाणामितरेषां तु लोकाधिपतयस्त्रयः ॥१२१॥
वाग्देवत्योऽथवाग्नेयः प्रस्तावश्चैव सामसु ।
उद्गीथोपद्रवावैन्द्रौ स्यातां वा वायुदेवतौ* ॥१२२॥
सौर्यः स्यात्प्रतिहारोऽत्र निधनं वैश्वदेवतम् ।

हिंकारप्रणवाभ्यां तु पुरस्तादेव कीर्तनात् ॥१२३॥ २५॥

इति व्यस्तसमस्तानां मन्त्राणामिह दैवतम् ।
देवताविदवेक्षेत प्रयोगे सर्वकर्मणाम् ॥१२४॥

सप्तर्षयो वसवश्चापि देवा अथर्वाणो भृगवः सोमसूर्याः ।
पथ्या स्वस्ती रोदसी चोक्तमन्त्रे कुहूर्गुङ्गूरदितिर्धेनुरघ्न्या ॥१२५॥

असुनीतिरिळा चाशा विधातानुमतिर्ह्रे* या ।
अङ्गिरोभिः सहैताः स्युर् उक्तमन्त्राश्च देवताः ॥१२६॥

वैश्वानरो हि सुपर्णो विवस्वान् प्रजापतिर्द्यौः* सुधन्वा नगोह्यः* ।
अपांनपादर्यमा वातजूतिर् इळस्पतिश्चापि रथस्पतिश्च ॥१२७॥

ऋभवः पर्जन्यः पर्वता ग्नाश्च * दक्षो भगो देवपत्नीर्दिशश्च ।
आदित्या रुद्राः पितरोऽथ साध्या निपातिनो वैश्वदेवेषु सर्वे ॥१२८॥ २६॥

अनुक्रान्ता देवताः सूक्तभाजो हविर्भाजश्चोभयथा निपातैः ।
अप्येवं स्यादुभयथान्यथा वा न प्रत्यक्षमनृषेरस्ति मन्त्रम् ॥१२९॥

योगेन दाक्ष्येण दमेन बुद्ध्या बाहुश्रुत्येन तपसा नियोगैः ।
उपास्यास्ताः कृत्स्नशो देवता या ऋचो ह यो वेद स वेद देवान् ।
A यजूंषि यो वेद स वेद यज्ञान् सामानि यो वेद स वेद तत्त्वम् ॥१३०॥

मन्त्राणां देवताविद्यः प्रयुङ्क्ते कर्म कर्हिचित् ।
जुषन्ते देवतास्तस्य हविर्नादेवताविदः ॥१३१॥

अविज्ञानप्रदिष्टं हि हविर्नेहेत दैवतम् ।
तस्मान्मनसि संन्यस्य देवतां जुहुयाद्धविः ॥१३२॥ *२७॥

स्वाध्यायमपि योऽधीते मन्त्रदैवतविच्छुचिः ।
स सत्त्वसदिव स्वर्गे सत्त्वसद्भिरपीड्यते ॥१३३॥

A नियमोऽयं जपे होमे ऋषिश्छन्दोऽथ दैवतम् ।
A अन्यथा चेत्प्रयुञ्जानस् तत्फलाच्चाच हीयते ॥१३४॥

A ऋषिछन्दोदैवतादि ज्ञानं यज्ञादिषु श्रुतम् ।

A तदाश्रित्य प्राणदृष्टिर् विहितावेति गम्यताम् ॥१३५॥
A अविदित्वा ऋषिं छन्दो दैवतं योगमेव च ।
A योऽध्यापयेज्जपेद्वापि पापीयाञ्जायते तु सः ॥१३६॥
A अर्थेप्सवः खल्वृषयश् छन्दोभिर्देवताः पुरा ।
A अभ्यधावन्निति छन्दो मध्ये त्वाहुर्महर्षयः ॥१३७॥
A ऋषिं तु प्रथमं ब्रूयाच् छन्दस्तु तदनन्तरम् ।
A देवतामथ मन्त्राणां कर्मस्वेवमिति श्रुतिः ॥१३८॥
आधारं वाप्यनाधारं विविच्यात्मानमात्मनि ।
ईक्षमाणो ह्युभौ संधिम् ऋचो दैवतवित्पठेत् ॥१३९॥
स ब्रह्मामृतमत्यन्तं योनिं सदसतोर्ध्रुवम् ।
महच्चाणु च विश्वेशं विशति ज्योतिरुत्तमम् ॥१४०॥
विशति ज्योतिरुत्तमम् ॥ २८॥

॥ इति बृहद्देवतायामष्टमोऽध्यायः ॥

॥ इति शौनकीया बृहद्देवता समाप्ता ॥

I. INDEX OF VEDIC PRATĪKAS CITED IN THE BṚHADDEVATĀ.

[The citations in black-faced type refer to the Ṛg-veda, except where a specific indication to the contrary is made; and the other citations refer to chapter and verse of the Bṛhaddevatā.]

II. INDEX OF AUTHORITIES CITED IN THE BṚHADDEVATĀ.

III. INDEX OF THE DEITIES OF THE ṚG-VEDA ACCORDING TO THE BṚHADDEVATĀ.

[The deviations of the Sarvānukramaṇī are stated in the footnotes.]

Maṇḍala i.

1 Agni.

2 [1–3] Vāyu, [4–6] Indra-Vāyu, [7–9] Mitra-Varuṇa.

3 [1–3] Aśvinau, [4–6] Indra, [7–9] Viśve devāḥ, [10–12] Sarasvatī.

4 Indra.

5–11 Indra.

6 [4–9] Marutaḥ, [5.7 a] Indra and Marutaḥ [a].

12 Agni, [6 a] Nirmathya and Āhavanīya.

13 Āpriyaḥ :

[1] Idhma [b], [2] Tanūnapāt, [3] Narāśaṃsa, [4] Iḷa, [5] Barhis, [6] Dvāro devyaḥ, [7] Naktoṣāsā [c], [8] Daivyau hotārau [d], [9] Tisro devyaḥ [e], [10] Tvaṣṭṛ, [11] Vanaspati, [12] Svāhākṛtayaḥ.

14 Visve devāḥ.

15 Ṛtavaḥ :

[1] Indra, [2] Marutaḥ, [3] Tvaṣṭṛ, [4] Agni, [5] Śakra (Indra), [6] Mitra-Varuṇa, [7–10] Agni Draviṇodas, [11] Nāsatyau, [12] Agni.

16 Indra.

17 Indra-Varuṇa.

18 [1–5] Brahmaṇaspati, [4] also Soma-Indra, [5] also Soma, Indra, Dakṣiṇā, [6–8] Sadasaspati, [9] Narāśaṃsa [f].

19 Agni pārthiva [g] and Marutaḥ.

20 Ṛbhavaḥ.

21 Indra-Agni.

22 [1–4] Aśvinau, [5–8] Savitṛ, [9.10] Agni, [11] Devyaḥ [h], [12] Devapatnyaḥ: Indrāṇī, Varuṇānī, Agnāyī [i], [13.14] Dyāvāpṛthivyau, [15] Pṛthivī, [16] Viṣṇu or Devāḥ, [17–21] Viṣṇu.

23 [1] Vāyu, [2.3] Indra-Vāyu, [4–6] Mitra-Varuṇa, [7–9] Indra Marutvat, [10–12] Viśve devāḥ, [13–15] Pūṣan Āghṛṇi [j], [16–23 ab] Āpaḥ, [23 cd. 24] Agni.

24 [1] Ka, [2] Agni, [3–5] Savitṛ, [5] or Bhaga, [6–15] Varuṇa.

25 Varuṇa.

26–27 Agni.

---

[a] [5.7] Sarvānukramaṇī. [b] *Idhmaḥ samiddho vāgniḥ*, Sarv. [c] *Uṣāsānaktā*, Sarv. [d] *Pracetasau* added in Sarv. [e] Their names, *Sarasvatīḷābhāratyaḥ*, added in Sarv.

[f] Narāśaṃsa or Sadasaspati, Sarv. [g] *Agnimārutam*, Sarv. [h] See note on iii. 92. [i] *Devapatnyaḥ* omitted in Sarv. [j] Simply Pūṣan, Sarv.

27 ^{10} Agni madhyama[a], ^{13} Viśve devāḥ[b].

28 $^{1-4}$ Indra (Bhāguri), Indra-Ulūkhala (Yāska and Kātthakya)[c], $^{5.6}$ Ulūkhala, $^{7.8}$ Ulūkhala and[d] Musala, ^{9} Carma͜adhiṣavaṇīya or Soma[e].

29–30 Indra.

30 $^{17-19}$ Aśvinau, $^{20-22}$ Uṣas.

31 Agni.

32–33 Indra.

34 Aśvinau.

35 Savitṛ:

^{1a} Agni, ^{1b} Mitra-Varuṇa, ^{1c} Rātri.

36 Agni:

$^{13.14}$ Yaupyau.

37–39 Marutaḥ.

40 Brahmaṇaspati.

41 $^{1-3.7-9}$ Varuṇa, Aryaman, Mitra, $^{4-6}$ Ādityāḥ.

42 Pūṣan.

43 $^{1-6}$ Rudra, ^{3} also Mitra, Varuṇa, Viśve devāḥ[f], $^{7-9}$ Soma (B).

44–45 Agni (B):

44 $^{1.2}$ also Aśvinau and Uṣas (B)[g].

45 ^{10cd} Devāḥ (B).

46–47 Aśvinau:

46 ^{5} also Āditya (Yāska: B)[h].

48–49 Uṣas.

50 Sūrya:

^{6} Varuṇa[h] (dyubhakti), $^{11-13}$ rogaghna (tṛca), ^{13cd} dviṣaddveṣaḥ.

51–57[i] [not stated].

58 Jātavedas[j].

59 Vaiśvānara.

60 Agni.

61–63 Indra.

64 Marutaḥ.

65–73 Agni.

Khilas (eleven):

1–4, 6–11 (*śaśvad dhi vām*) Aśvinau, 5 (*imāni* = viii. 59)[k], Indra-Varuṇa.

74–79 Agni.

79 $^{1-3}$ Agni madhyama.

80–84 Indra.

80 ^{16} Dadhyañc, Manu, Atharvan[l] (nipātitāḥ).

85–88 Marutaḥ.

89–90 Viśve devāḥ.

89 $^{1.2.8.9}$ Devāḥ[m], ^{10} Aditi.

91 Soma.

92 Uṣas:

$^{16-18}$ Aśvinau.

93 Agni with Soma.

94 Jātavedas[n]:

^{8abc} Devāḥ, ^{16cd} Agni or the six deities mentioned (Mitra-Varuṇa, Aditi, Sindhu, Pṛthivī, Dyu).

95 Agni Auṣasa[o].

96 Agni Draviṇodas[p].

97 Agni Śuci.

98 Agni Vaiśvānara.

99 Jātavedas.

---

[a] Not specified in Sarv. [b] *Vaiśvadevī*, Sarv. *daivī*. [c] Simply Indra, Sarv. [d] See note[b] on iii. 101. [e] No reference to Soma in Sarv., Prajāpati Hariścandra appearing instead: see note on iii. 101. [f] No mention of Viśve devāḥ in Sarv. [g] The text (iii. 111) does not expressly state which two stanzas; Sarv.: *ādyo dvṛcaḥ*. [h] No reference to this stanza in Sarv. [i] See note[d] on iii. 114. [j] Agni, Sarv. [k] Omitted in its usual place: see note[a] on vi. 86. [l] No reference to this stanza in Sarv. [m] There is no reference to these stanzas in Sarv. [n] Agni, Sarv. [o] Or Agni, Sarv. [p] This and the following three deities are identical with those stated in the Sarv.; but Ṣaḍguruśiṣya (on i. 95) would supply 'or Agni' in these four cases (96–99) from i. 95.

100–104 Indra[a].
105–107 Viśve devāḥ.
108–109 Indra-Agni.
110–111 Ṛbhavaḥ.
112 Aśvinau:
[1a] Dyāvāpṛthivyau, [1b] Agni.
113 Rātryuṣasau[b].
114 Rudra.
115 Sūrya.
116–120 Aśvinau.
120 [12] duḥsvapnanāśinī.
121 Indra; Viśve devāḥ in the Svara-sāmans[c].
122 Viśve devāḥ.
123–124 Uṣas.
125 Praise of Svanaya Bhāvayavya's gifts.
126 [1–5] Bhāvayavya, [6.7] jāyāpatyoḥ sampravādaḥ[d].
127–128 Agni.
129–133 Indra.
129 [6] Indu.
132 [6] Indra-Parvata[e].
134 Vāyu.
135 [1–3.9] Vāyu, [4–8] Indra-Vāyu.
136 [1–5] Mitra-Varuṇa, [6.7] Dyu and the other deities mentioned.
137 Mitra-Varuṇa.
138 Pūṣan.
139 Viśve devāḥ:
[1] Viśve devāḥ, [2] Mitra-Varuṇa, [3–5] Aśvinau, [6] Indra, [7] Agni, [8] Marutaḥ, [9] Indra-Agni; or the seer praises the Rishis or himself, Indra-Agni being incidental[f]; [10] Bṛhaspati, [11] Devāḥ[g].
140–141, 143–144 Jātavedas[h].
142 Āpriyaḥ:
[13] Indra.
145–150 Agni.
151–153 Mitra-Varuṇa.
151 [1] Mitra.
152 [6] Aditi or Agni; Aditi = Agni (Śaunaka)[i].
154–156 Viṣṇu.
155 [1–3] Indra-Viṣṇu.
157–158 Aśvinau.
159–160 Dyāvāpṛthivyau.
161 Ṛbhavaḥ.
162–163 Medhyasya aśvasya saṃstavaḥ.
163 [10] also many and various steeds[i].
164 [1–41] Viśve devāḥ (B), [46.47] Sūrya (B), [52] Sarasvat or Sūrya (B)[j].
165 Mārutaindraḥ saṃvādaḥ[k]: Marutaḥ deity in [1.2.4.6.8.10–15], Indra in [3.5.7.9].
166–168 Marutaḥ.
167 [1] Indra.
169 Indra.
170 [2.4] Indra, [1.3] Agastya[l].

[a] Sarv. on i. 101 adds *ādyā garbhasrāviṇy upaniṣat.* [b] According to the Sarv. the whole hymn is to Uṣas only, except 1[cd] in which Rātri is associated with her: *uṣasyaṃ; dvitīyo 'rdharco rātreś ca.* [c] See note on iii. 141. Sarv.: Indra or Viśve devāḥ. [d] *Bhāvayavyaromaśayor daṃpatyoḥ saṃvādaḥ*, Sarv. [e] Sarv.: [6ab] Indra-Parvata. [f] There is no reference in the Sarv. to the Rishis or the self-praise of the seer. [g] Viśve devāḥ, Sarv. [h] Agni, Sarv. [i] There is no reference to this stanza in Sarv. [j] Various other deities are mentioned as addressed in this hymn, but they are not assigned to specific stanzas, as is done by Sarv. for the last eleven. [k] *Saṃvādo 'gastyendramarutām*, Indra Marutvat being the deity, and the last triplet being spoken by Agastya, Sarv. [l] No statement about [5]; *indrāgastyayoḥ saṃvāda aindraḥ,*

171–172 Marutaḥ.
171 [3–6] Indra Marutvat (B).
173–178 Indra.
179 Dialogue: [1.2] Lopāmudrā speaks. [3.4] Agastya, [5.6] a Brahmacārin.
180–184 Aśvinau.
185 Dyāvāpṛthivyau.
186 Viśve divaukasaḥ (=devāḥ).
187 Anna.
188 Āpryaḥ.
189 Agni.
190 Bṛhaspati.
191 Upaniṣat:
apāṃ tṛṇānāṃ sūryasya stutiḥ kecit; tad vā viṣaghnam [a].

Maṇḍala ii.

1 Agni.
2 Jātavedas [b].
3 Āpriyaḥ.
4–10 Agni.
11–22 Indra.
23–26 Brahmaṇaspati; Bṛhaspati where that form of the name appears.
24 [12] Indra-Brahmaṇaspati.
27 Ādityāḥ: Mitra-Varuṇa, Dakṣa, Aṃśa, Tuvijāta, Bhaga, Aryaman [c].
28 Varuna:
[10] Duḥsvapnādyapraṇāśinī.
29 Viśve devāḥ.
30 Indra:
[6] Indra-Soma, [8ab] Vāc madhyamā [d], [9] Bṛhaspati, [11] Marutaḥ.
31 Viśve devāḥ.
32 [1] Dyāvāpṛthivyau, [2.3] Indra or Tvaṣṭṛ, [4.5] Rākā, [6.7] Sinīvālī, [8] Six goddesses, Guṅgū, &c. [e]
33 Rudra:
[11] ṛṣir mṛgam astaut [f].
34 Marutaḥ.
35 Apāṃ napāt.
36–37 Ṛtavaḥ.
38 Savitṛ.
39 Aśvinau.
40 Soma-Pūṣan:
[6] also Aditi [g].
41 [1.2] Vāyu, [3] Indra-Vāyu, [4–18] (five triplets to) the Praüga deities [h], [19] Havirdhāne; Agni incidental [i], [20] Dyāvāpṛthivyau, [21] Havirdhāne [j].
42–43 Indra in the form of a kapiñjala.

Sarv., where [4] is stated to be optionally spoken by Indra. According to the Ārṣānukramaṇī, Indra is Rishi of [1.3], Indra *and* Agastya, or Indra *or* Agastya, of [4]. [a] There is no reference in the Sarv. to its being *viṣaghna*. [b] Agni, Sarv. [c] The individual names are not stated in the Sarv. [d] Sarasvatī, Sarv. [e] *Liṅgoktadevatāḥ*, Sarv. [f] No reference to this in the Sarv. [g] Only in the second hemistich, Sarv. [h] See Maṇḍala i. 2–3. [i] The third pāda optionally to Agni, Sarv. [j] [19–21] Dyāvāpṛthivyau or Havirdhāne, Sarv. (cp. Ṣaḍguruśiṣya).

Maṇḍala iii.

1 Agni.
2–3 Vaiśvānara.
4 Āpryaḥ.
5–6 Agni:
Dyāvāpṛthivyau, Uṣasaḥ, Āpaḥ, Devāḥ, Pitaraḥ, Mitraḥ (nipātitāḥ)[a].
7–29 Agni:
8 $^{1-5}$ Yūpa, in the rest Yūpāḥ, ^{8} Viśve devāḥ[b], ^{11} vraścanī.
12 Indra-Agni.
20 $^{1.5}$ Viśve devāḥ.
22 ^{4} Dhiṣṇyā Agnayaḥ[c].
25 ^{4} Agni-Indra.
26 $^{1-3}$ Vaiśvānara, $^{4-6}$ Marutaḥ[d], ^{9} Gurustavaḥ[e].
27 ^{1} Ṛtavaḥ[f].
29 ^{5} Ṛtvijaḥ[g].
30–53 Indra.
33 Dialogue of Viśvāmitra and the rivers:
$^{1-3.5.7.9.11-13}$ Nadyaḥ, $^{4.6.8.10}$ Viśvāmitra, $^{6.7}$ the two deities praised [i. e. Indra and Savitṛ] are incidental[h].
53 ^{1} Indra-Parvata[i], $^{15.16}$ Vāc[j], $^{17-20}$ anaso 'ṅgāni, $^{21-24}$ Vasiṣṭhadveṣiṇyaḥ.
54–57 Viśve devāḥ.
58 Aśvinau.
59 Mitra:
^{8} Viśve devāḥ (B)[k].
60 Ṛbhavaḥ:
$^{5-7}$ Indra and Ṛbhavaḥ, $^{3.4}$ Indra incidental (B)[k].
61 Uṣas.
62 $^{1-3}$ Indra-Varuṇa, $^{4-6}$ Bṛhaspati, $^{7-9}$ Pūṣan, $^{10-12}$ Savitṛ, $^{13-15}$ Soma, $^{16-18}$ Mitra-Varuṇa.

Maṇḍala iv.

1–15 Agni:
1 $^{2-4}$ Agni, or Agni and Varuṇa[l].
13–14 liṅgoktadaivata (eke).
15 $^{7.8}$ Somaka, $^{9.10}$ Aśvinau.
16–32 Indra:
26 $^{1-3}$ Self-praise of the seer as if Indra[m], $^{4-7}$ Śyenastuti.
27 $^{1-5}$ Śyenastuti[n].
28 Indra and Soma[o].

---

[a] *Anyāsām api nipāto dṛśyate*, Sarv. [b] Yūpāḥ or Viśve devāḥ, Sarv. [c] *Purīṣyebhyo 'gnibhyaḥ*, Sarv. [d] Sarv.: *mārutas (tṛcaḥ)*, which Ṣaḍguruśiṣya explains by *dvitīyasya (tṛcasya) māruto 'gniḥ*. The deity of $^{7.8}$ would be Agni only according to the BD., but according to the Sarv. it is alternatively in praise of the Ātman: *ātmastutir vā pūrvātmagītā (agniḥ paraṃ brahma vā*, Ṣaḍg.). [e] *Upādhyāyastutiḥ*, Sarv. [f] *Ṛtavyā vā*, Sarv. [g] *Ṛtvigbhyo vā*, Sarv. [h] $^{4.6.8.10}$ spoken by the rivers, $^{6.7}$ in praise of Indra, Sarv. [i] The stanza is not specified, but the first is doubtless meant. [j] Vāc sasarparī, Sarv. [k] No statement in the Sarv. [l] Sarv.: $^{2-5}$; cp. note [a] on iv. 128. [m] Sarv.: *indram ivātmānam ṛṣis tuṣṭāvendro vātmānam.* [n] Sarv.: ^{5} Indra or Śyena (Ṣaḍg.). [o] Indra or Indra-Soma, Sarv.

30 [9–11] Uṣā madhyamā (Śākaṭāyana), [24] Bhaga, Pūṣan, Aryaman[a].
31 [15] Sūrya (Āśvalāyana: B)[a].
32 [23.24] Indra's two steeds (haryo stutiḥ).
33–37 Ṛbhavaḥ.
38–40 Dadhikrā.
38 [1] Dyāvāpṛthivyau.
40 [5] Agni, Vāyu, Sūrya; Sūrya[b] (Aitareya Brāhmaṇa: B).
41–42 Indra-Varuṇa[c].
43–45 Aśvinau.
46 [1] Vāyu, [2–7] Indra-Vāyu.
47 [1] Vāyu, [2–4] Indrā-Vāyu.
48 Vāyu.
49 Indra-Bṛhaspati.
50 Bṛhaspati:
[7–9] purodhātuḥ karmaśaṃsā[d], [10.11] Indra-Bṛhaspati.
51–52 Uṣas.
53–54 Savitṛ.
55 Viśve devāḥ.
56 Dyāvāpṛthivyau.
57 [1–3] Kṣetrapati, [4] Śuna, [5] Śunāsīrau, [6.7] Sītā, [8a] Kṛṣi, [8b] Kṛṣijīvā manuṣyāḥ, [8c] Parjanya, [8d] Dhana[e]. Or the whole hymn praises agriculture (Kṛṣi)[f].

Maṇḍala v.

1–4 Agni[g].
5 Āpriyaḥ.
6–28 Agni.
26 [9] Viśve devāḥ.
27 [6] Indra-Agni.
29–40 Indra.
29 [9a] Uśanā.
31 [8d] Uśanā[h], [9] Indra and Kutsa.
40 [5–9] Atrīṇāṃ karma kīrtyate[i].
41–51 Viśve devāḥ.
41 [19] Iḷā[j].
42 [3] Savitṛ (Śaunaka), [7–9] Bṛhaspati, [10] Marutaḥ, [11] Rudra, [14] Iḷaspati (Śākapūṇi), Parjanya-Agni (Gālava), Pūṣan (Yāska), Indra (Śaunaka), Vaiśvānara (Bhāguri), [15] Marutaḥ, [18] Aśvinau[k].
43 [3] Vāyu, [4] Soma, [5] Indra, [6] Agni, [7] Gharma, [8] Aśvinau, [9] Vāyu and Pūṣan: [10ab] Agni, [10cd] Divaukasaḥ, [11] Vāc madhyamā, [12] Bṛhaspati[l].

---

[a] No reference to this stanza in Sarv. [b] Sūrya only, Sarv. [c] 42 [1–6] Self-praise of Trasadasyu, Sarv. [d] No reference to this triplet in Sarv. [e] Sarv.: [8] Śunāsīrau. [f] No reference to this in Sarv. [g] Aufrecht in his index, RV.[2], p. 477, states 'Marutaḥ, Rudra und Vishṇu' to be the deities of v. 3[8]. Though these three names occur in that stanza, there is no mention of them in the BD. or the Sarv. [h] Sarv.: [8c] Indra or Kutsa, [8d] Indra or Uśanā. [i] Sarv.: [5] Sūrya, [6–9] Atri (because his deed is praised): cp. Ṣaḍg. [j] No mention of this stanza in Sarv. [k] Of all these individual deities the only one specified in the Sarv. is Rudra. [l] None of these individual deities are mentioned in Sarv.

44 [1] Soma, or Devāḥ, or Indra, or Prajāpati, [4] Vāyu, [8] Āditya [a].
46 [7.8] Devapatnyaḥ.
51 [4.6.7] Indra-Vāyu, [5] Vāyu [a].
52–61 Marutaḥ.
56 [8] Rodasī (sing.) [b].
57 [1] Rudrāḥ [c].
60 [8] Terrestrial and Middle Agni with the Marutaḥ.
62–72 Mitra-Varuṇa.
73–78 Aśvinau.
78 [5–9] garbhārtham upaniṣatstutiḥ [d].
79–80 Uṣas.
81–82 Savitṛ.
82 [4] duḥsvapnanāśinī (B) [b].
83 Parjanya.
84 Pṛthivī madhyamā [e].
85 Varuṇa.
86 Indra-Agni.
87 Marutaḥ, with incidental mention of Viṣṇu [f].
Khila 1: Śrīsūktam; Agni incidental.
Khila 2: Prajāvat.
Khila 3: Jīvaputra.
Khila 4 (*saṃsravanti*): payasvinyaḥ.

Maṇḍala vi.

1–6 Agni.
7–9 Agni Vaiśvānara.
10–16 Agni.
17–27 Indra:
21 [9.11] Viśve devāḥ.
27 [8] Dānastuti of Abhyāvartin and Sārñjaya [g].
28 Gavāṃ stutiḥ, [2.8d] Indra [h].
29–46 Indra:
37 [3] Vāyu and Indra [i].
44 [22–24] Soma; according to some, Indra (B) [j].
Khila (*cakṣuḥ*: B): śarīra.
45 [31–33] Bṛbustutiḥ.
47 [1–5] Soma; or Indra with incidental Soma (B) [k], [20a] Devāḥ, [20b] Bhūmi, [20c] Bṛhaspati, [20d] Indra, [22–25] Dānastuti of Abhyāvartin and Sārñjaya [l], [26a] Bhāvavṛttam [m], [26–28] rathābhimarśanāḥ, [29–31ab] dundubheḥ saṃstavaḥ, [31cd] Indra [n].
48 Tṛṇapāṇikaṃ Pṛśnisūktam: [1–10] Agni, [11–13] Marutaḥ, [14.15] Marutaḥ or Adityāḥ or Viśve devāḥ [o], [16–19] Pūṣan, [20.21] Marutaḥ, [22] Dyu-Bhū or Pṛśni [p].

---

[a] No individual deities are mentioned in Sarv. [b] No reference to this stanza in Sarv. [c] There is no reference to this stanza in the Sarv., but the whole hymn is stated to be addressed to the Maruts or the Maruts and Agni. [d] *Antyāḥ pañca garbhasrāviṇy upaniṣat*, Sarv. [e] Simply Pṛthivī, Sarv. [f] No reference to Viṣṇu in Sarv. [g] *Cāyamānasyābhyāvartino dānastutiḥ*, Sarv. [h] Sarv.: [2.8d] Gāvaḥ or Indra. [i] No reference to this stanza in Sarv. [j] No reference to this triplet in Sarv. [k] Soma only, Sarv. [l] The number of the dānastuti stanzas (22–25) is not stated in the BD. (v. 140), while the Sarv. makes no mention of Abhyāvartin. [m] No reference to this in Sarv. [n] There is no statement as to the deity (Indra) of [6–19.21] (see note on BD. v. 109). In Sarv. the deity results from the paribhāṣā *anādeśe tv indro devatā*. [o] Sarv.: [11.12] Marutaḥ, [13–15] Marutaḥ or liṅgoktadevatāḥ. [p] Or Maruts, Sarv.; but this is probably an interpolation: see note on RV. vi. 48 in Sarv.

49–52 Viśve devāḥ:
49 [2] Agni, [4] Vāyu, [5] Aśvinau, [7] Vāc, [8] Pūṣan, [9] Tvaṣṭṛ, [10] Rudra, [11.12] Marutaḥ, [13] Viṣṇu [a].
50 [5] Ródasī, [6] Indra, [8] Savitṛ, [9] Agni, [10] Aśvinau [a].
51 [1.2] Sūrya [b].
52 [16] Agni-Parjanya [b].
53–56 Pūṣan:
55 [2] Rudra according to some (B) [b].
57 Indra-Pūṣan.
58 Pūṣan.
59–60 Indra-Agni.
61 Sarasvatī.
62–63 Aśvinau.
64–65 Uṣas.
66 Marutaḥ.
67 Mitra-Varuṇa.
68 Indra-Varuṇa.
69 Indra-Viṣṇu.
70 Dyāvāpṛthivyau.
71 Savitṛ.
72 Indra-Soma.
73 Bṛhaspati.
74 Soma-Rudra.
75 Yuddhopakaraṇam, saṃgrāmāṅgāni:
[1] yoddhā varmī [c], [2] dhanuḥ, [3] jyā, [4] ārtnī, [5] iṣudhiḥ, [6ab] sārathiḥ, [6cd] raśmayaḥ, [7] aśvāḥ, [8] āyudhāgāram [d], [9] rathagopāḥ, [10] raṇadevatāḥ [e], [11] iṣuḥ [f], [12] kavacaḥ [f], [13] kaśā [g], [14] hastatrāṇam [h], [15a] digdha iṣuḥ, [15b] ayomukhī, [15cd] Vāruṇam astram, [16] dhanurmukta iṣuḥ [i], [17] yuddhādiḥ, [18] kavacasya badhyataḥ stutiḥ, [19] yuyutsuḥ, [19d] ātmana (ṛṣer) āśiṣaḥ [j].

Maṇḍala vii.

1 Agni.
2 Āpryaḥ.
3–17 Agni:
5, 6, 13 Vaiśvānara.
18–32 Indra: Marutaḥ incidental [k].
18 [22–25] Dānastuti of Paijavana.
32 [10] the same [l].
33 Indra hymn or dialogue of Vasiṣṭha and Agastya [m] with their sons and with Indra.
34–37 Viśve devāḥ:
34 [16] Ahi, [17] Ahi budhnya [n].
38 Savitṛ:
[1cd] (B) [o], [5c] Ahi [o], [6cd] Bhaga [p], [7-8] vājinaḥ.
39–43 Viśve devāḥ:
41 [2–6] Bhaga, [7] Uṣas, or a prayer for the seers [q].

---

[a] None of these individual deities are mentioned in Sarv. [b] No reference to this in Sarv. [c] Varma, Sarv. [d] Ratha, Sarv. [e] Liṅgoktadevatāḥ, Sarv. [f] Iṣavaḥ, Sarv. [g] Pratoda, Sarv. [h] Hastaghna, Sarv. [i] Sarv.: [15.16] iṣavaḥ. [j] [17-19] liṅgoktadevatāḥ, saṃgrāmāśiṣaḥ, Sarv. [k] No reference to the Maruts in Sarv. [l] No reference to this stanza in Sarv. [m] There is no reference to Agastya in the Sarv. (*saṃstavo Vasiṣṭhasya saputrasyendreṇa vā saṃvādaḥ*). [n] Sarv.: [17ab] only. [o] No reference to this pāda in Sarv. [p] Sarv.: [6cd] Savitṛ or Bhaga. [q] Sarv.: [1] liṅgoktadevatāḥ, [7] Uṣas.

44 Dadhikrā:
 ^{1} devatāḥ parikīrtitāḥ[a].
45 Savitṛ.
46 Rudra.
47 Āpaḥ.
48 $^{1-3}$ Ṛbhavaḥ, ^{4} Viśve devāḥ or Ṛbhavaḥ.
49 Āpaḥ.
50 ^{1} Mitra-Varuṇa, ^{2} Agni, ^{3} Viśve devāḥ, ^{4} Nadyaḥ.
51–52 Ādityāḥ.
53 Rodasī (=Heaven and Earth).
54 Vāstoṣpati.
55 ^{1} Vāstoṣpati, $^{2-8}$ prasvāpinyaḥ.
56–59 Marutaḥ.
 59 ^{12} Tryambaka[b].
60–66 Mitra-Varuṇa:
 60 ^{1} Sūrya, ^{5} Aryaman, Mitra-Varuṇa (B)[c].
 62 $^{1-3}$ Sūrya.
 63 $^{1-5ab}$ Sūrya.
 66 $^{4-13}$ Ādityāḥ or Savitṛ, Aditi, Mitra, Varuṇa, Aryaman, Bhaga (B)[d], $^{14-16}$ Sūrya (B), ^{16} cakṣuḥ (sūryasya): a prayer (B)[e].
67–74 Aśvinau.
75–81 Uṣas:
 76 ^{1ab} Madhyama (Agni: B)[f].
82–85 Indra-Varuṇa.
86–89 Varuṇa.
90–92 Vāyu.
 90 $^{5-7}$, 91 $^{2.4-7}$, 92 ^{2} Indra-Vāyu (B).
93–94 Indra-Agni.
95–96 Sarasvatī.
 95 ^{3}, 96 $^{4-6}$ Sarasvat.
97 Bṛhaspati:
 ^{1} Indra, $^{3.9}$ Indra and Brahmaṇaspati, ^{10} Indra and Bṛhaspati.
98 Indra[g].
99–100 Viṣṇu.
 99 $^{4-6}$ also Indra.
101–102 Parjanya.
103 Frogs.
104 Indra-Soma[h] (rākṣoghnam):
 ^{9} Soma, ^{10} Agni, ^{11} Viśve devāḥ, $^{12.13}$ Soma, ^{14} Agni, ^{16} Indra, ^{17} Grāvāṇaḥ, ^{18} Marutaḥ, $^{19-22}$ Indra, ^{23} ātmana (ṛṣer) āśīḥ[i], ^{24} Indra[j].

Maṇḍala viii.

1–4 Indra:
 1 $^{30-33}$ Dānastuti of Āsaṅga, ^{34} Āsaṅga.
 2 $^{41.42}$ Dānastuti of Vibhindu.
 3 $^{21-24}$ Dānastuti of Pākasthāman.
 4 $^{15-18}$ Pūṣan (Śākaṭāyana), $^{15.16}$ Indra, $^{17.18}$ Pūṣan (Gālava)[k], $^{19-21}$ Dānastuti of Kuruṅga.
5 Aśvinau:
 $^{37cd-39}$ Dānastuti of Kaśu.

[a] Liṅgoktadevatāḥ, Sarv. [b] *Raudrī mṛtyuvimocanī*, Sarv. [c] No reference to this stanza in Sarv. See note on vi. 7. [d] No reference to individual deities in Sarv. [e] No reference to this statement about stanza 16 in Sarv. [f] No reference to this stanza in Sarv. [g] Sarv. adds: *uktadevatāntyā*, i.e. Indra and Bṛhaspati are its deities (98 ^{7} being = 97 ^{10}). [h] The eighth stanza is by implication meant to be addressed to Indra-Soma; Sarv.: Indra only. [i] Sarv.: ^{23ab} only, ^{23cd} Pṛthivī and Antarikṣa. [j] In ^{8} and ^{15} the seer utters a curse. [k] Sarv.: $^{15-18}$ Indra or Pūṣan.

6 Indra:

^{30} Agni Vaiśvānara (Śākapūṇi and Mudgala)[a], $^{46-48}$ Dānastuti of Tirindira.

7 Marutaḥ.

8–10 Aśvinau.

11 Agni.

12–17 Indra:

17 ^{14ab} Vāstoṣpati[b].

18 Ādityāḥ:

$^{4.6.7}$ Aditi[c], ^{8} Aśvinau, ^{9a} Agni, ^{9b} Sūrya, ^{9c} Anila[d].

19 $^{34.35}$ Varuṇa, Aryaman, Mitra[e], $^{36.37}$ Trasadasyu.

20 Marutaḥ.

21 Indra:

$^{17.18}$ Dānastuti of Citra.

22 Aśvinau.

23 Agni.

24 Indra:

$^{28-30}$ Uṣas[f].

25 $^{1-9}$ Mitra-Varuṇa, $^{10-21}$ Viśve devāḥ[g], $^{22-24}$ Dānastuti of Varu[h].

26 Aśvinau:

$^{20-25}$ Vāyu.

27–31 Viśve devāḥ.

29 Pṛthakkarmastuti:

^{1} Soma, ^{2} Agni, ^{3} Tvaṣṭṛ, ^{4} Indra, ^{5} Rudra, ^{6} Pūṣan, ^{7} Viṣṇu, ^{8} Aśvinau, ^{9} Mitra-Varuṇa, ^{10} Atrayaḥ[i].

31 ijyā:

$^{1.2}$ Śakra, yajatāṃ pati (B), $^{3.4}$ yajvan (B)[j], $^{5-9}$ dampatī (B), ^{10} āśīḥ (B)[k], $^{11.12}$ Pūṣan (B), ^{13} Mitra, Aryaman, Varuṇa: Ādityāḥ (B), ^{14} Agni, $^{15-18}$ yajvan (B).

32–34 Indra:

33 ^{19} Indra addressed by a Dānavī[l].

35 Aśvinau.

36–37 Indra.

38 Indra-Agni.

39 Agni.

40 Indra-Agni.

41–42 Varuṇa:

42 $^{4-6}$ Aśvinau.

43–44 Agni.

45[m]–46 Indra:

46 $^{4.5}$ Mitra, Aryaman, Marutaḥ[n] (B), $^{21-24}$ Dānastuti of Kānīta Pṛthuśravas, $^{25-28.32}$ Vāyu.

47 Ādityāḥ:

^{9} Aditi[l], $^{14-18}$ also Uṣas.

48 Soma.

49–56 Indra:

54 $^{3.4}$ bahudaivata (pragātha)[o].

55–56 Dānastuti of Praskaṇva.

56 ^{5} Agni, ^{5d} Sūrya[p].

57–58[q] [not stated].

59 [mentioned as a khila after i. 73].

60 Agni (A).

61–66 Indra (A):

65 ^{10} Devāḥ (Bhāguri)[r], $^{10-12}$ Viśve devāḥ[s] (Yāska).

67 Ādityāḥ: $^{10-12}$ Aditi[s].

---

[a] No reference to this stanza in Sarv. [b] No reference to this hemistich in Sarv. [c] No mention of these three stanzas in Sarv. [d] Sarv. does not assign these three to the successive pādas of the stanza. [e] Ādityāḥ, Sarv. [f] Sarv.: Dānastuti of Varu Sauṣāmṇa, and no reference to Uṣas. [g] Sarv.: $^{10-12}$ only, $^{13-24}$ Mitra-Varuṇa. [h] No reference in Sarv. to a Dānastuti. [i] No details given in Sarv. [j] Sarv.: $^{1-4}$ *ijyāstavo yajamānapraśaṃsā ca.* [k] Sarv.: $^{10-18}$ *dampatyor āśiṣaḥ*, without further details. [l] No reference to this stanza in Sarv. [m] 45 ^{1} Agni and Indra, Sarv. [n] There is no reference to these two stanzas in Sarv. [o] Viśve devāḥ, Sarv. [p] Sarv.: ^{5} Agni and Sūrya. [q] 58 is not mentioned in Sarv. [r] This stanza is not mentioned in Sarv. [s] These stanzas are not mentioned in Sarv.

68–70 Indra:
 68 ^{14} Ṛtavaḥ, $^{15-19}$ Dānastuti of Ṛkṣa and Aśvamedha [a].
 69 ^{11ab} Indra, Agni, Viśve devāḥ [b], $^{11cd.12}$ Varuna.
71–72 Agni:
 72 haviṣāṃ stutiḥ payaḥpaśvoṣadhīnāṃ ca [c].
73 Aśvinau.
74–75 Agni:
 74 $^{13.14}$ Self-praise of the seer; also Dānastuti of Śrutarvan (B), ^{15} Paruṣṇī [d]
76–78 Indra.
79 Soma.
80–82 Indra:
 80 ^{10} Viśve devāḥ [e].
83 Devāḥ [e].
84 Agni.
85–87 Aśvinau.
88–93 Indra:
 93 ^{34} Ṛbhavaḥ [f] (ārbhavī: B).
94 Marutaḥ.
95–100 Indra:
 96 $^{13-15}$ Indra, Marutaḥ, Bṛhaspati: Indra (Śaunaka), Indra-Bṛhaspati (Aitareya Brāhmaṇa): (B)[g].
 100 $^{4.5}$ Indra ātmānaṃ tuṣṭāva [h], ^{8} Suparṇa [i], ^{9} Vajra [i], $^{10-11}$ Vāc.
101 $^{1-4}$ Mitra-Varuṇa, ^{5abc} also Aryaman [j], $^{5d.6}$ Ādityāḥ, $^{7.8}$ Aśvinau, $^{9.10}$ Vāyu, $^{11.12}$ Sūrya, ^{13} Uṣas or candrasūryayoḥ prabhā [k], ^{14} Pavamāna [l], $^{15.16}$ Go.
102–103 Agni:
 103 ^{14} Agni madhyama, with Marutaḥ and Rudrāḥ [m].

Maṇḍala ix.

Soma Pavamāna is the deity of this Maṇḍala.
5 Āpryaḥ.
66 $^{19-21}$ Agni.
67 $^{10-12}$ Pavamāna and Pūṣan [n], $^{23.24}$ Agni, ^{25} Savitṛ [o], ^{26} Agni and Savitṛ [p], ^{27} Viśve devāḥ [q], ^{29} Agni [r], $^{31.32}$ svādhyāyādhyetṛsaṃstavaḥ.
73 Agni Rakṣohan [s].
83 Gharmasaṃstavaḥ [s].
87 ^{3b} Ṛbhu (B)[s].
112 Indra [s].

---

[a] Sarv.: $^{14-19}$ Dānastuti of Ṛkṣa and Aśvamedha, without any mention of Ṛtavaḥ. [b] Sarv.: Viśve devāḥ only. [c] Agni or haviṣāṃ stuti only, Sarv. [d] Sarv.: $^{13-15}$ Dānastuti of Śrutarvan only. [e] 80 ^{10} Devāḥ, 83 Viśve devāḥ, Sarv. [f] *Aindrārbhavī*, Sarv. [g] ^{14d} Marutaḥ, ^{15} Indra and Bṛhaspati, Sarv. [h] *Indra ātmānam astaut*, Sarv. [i] No reference to this stanza in Sarv. [j] No reference to Aryaman in Sarv. [k] Uṣas or Sūryaprabhā, Sarv. [l] The B MSS. state that according to the Aitareya Āraṇyaka ^{14ab} is addressed to Agni, ^{14c} to the Sun, and ^{14d} to the Middle Agni. [m] Simply *āgnimārutī*, Sarv. [n] Pavamāna or Pūṣan, Sarv. [o] Agni or Savitṛ, Sarv. [p] Or Agni only, Sarv. [q] Or Agni, Sarv. [r] No reference to this stanza in Sarv. [s] No statement in Sarv.

Maṇḍala x.

1–7 Agni.
8 [1–6] Agni, [7–9] Indra.
9 Āpaḥ [a].
10 Dialogue of Yama and Yamī.
11–12 Agni.
13 Havirdhāne.
14 Yama madhyama [b]:
[6] Atharvāṇaḥ, Bhṛgavaḥ, Aṅgirasaḥ, Pitaraḥ [c], [7–9] Pretāśiṣaḥ (B)[d], [10–12] Śvānau.
15 Pitaraḥ.
16 Agni kavyavāhana [e].
17 [1.2] Saraṇyū, [3ab] Pūṣan, [3c] Pūṣan or Agni, [3d] Agni [f], [4–6] Pūṣan, [7–9] Sarasvatī, [10] Āpaḥ, [11–13] Soma [g], [14] Āpaḥ.
18 [1–4] Mṛtyu, [5] Dhātṛ, [6] Tvaṣṭṛ, [7–9] Mṛtyu, [10–13] Pṛthivī [h], [14] Āśiṣaḥ [i].
19 Gāvaḥ; according to some, Āpaḥ: [1cd] Agni-Soma, [2] Indra and Agni incidental [j], [6] Indra [j].
20–21 Agni.
22–24 Indra:
24 [4–6] Aśvinau.
25 Soma.
26 Pūṣan.
27–29 Indra:
27 [15] Marutaḥ, [16] Vajra, [17ab] Agni, Indra, Soma, [17cd] Parjanya and Vāyu, [18] Agni, [19] Sūrya, [20.21] Indra and the bolt, [22] Indra's bow, [23] Parjanya, Anila, Bhāskara, [23d] the last two only, [24] Indra or Sūrya [k].
28 Dialogue of Indra and Seer: Indra is addressed in the odd stanzas.
30 Āpaḥ:
[3.4] Agni madhyama as Apāṃ napāt [l].
31 Viśve devāḥ.
32 Indra.
33 [1] Viśve devāḥ, [2.3] Indra, [4.5] Kuruśravaṇa Trāsadasyava, [6–9] Upamaśravas.
34 [1.7.9.12] Akṣāḥ, [13] Kṛṣi (A); the rest akṣanindā [m].
35–36 Viśve devāḥ:
36 [12–14] Savitṛ (eke), [14] Savitṛ (Śaunaka, Yāska, Gālava) [n].
37 Sūrya:
[6] incidental deities, [11.12] Viśve devāḥ [o].
38 Indra.
39–41 Aśvinau.

---

[a] The pratīka of the hymn, *āpaḥ*, is mentioned, but without a direct statement that it is addressed to the Waters. [b] Simply Yama, Sarv. [c] Liṅgoktadevatāḥ, Sarv. [d] Liṅgoktadevatāḥ or Pitaraḥ, Sarv. [e] Simply Agni, Sarv. [f] Whole of [3] addressed to Pūṣan, Sarv. [g] Āpaḥ or Soma, Sarv. [h] Sarv.: [7-13] Pitṛmedhāḥ. [i] Pitṛmedha or Prajāpati, Sarv. [j] No statement about this stanza in Sarv. [k] None of these details are stated for this hymn in Sarv. [l] There is no statement about these two stanzas in Sarv., the whole hymn being simply described as addressed to Āpaḥ or Aponaptṛ. [m] Sarv. simply states regarding the whole hymn: *akṣakṛṣipraśaṃsā ca akṣakitavanindā ca.* [n] No statement about these three stanzas in the Sarv. [o] No reference to stanzas [6.11.12] in Sarv.

42–44 Indra:

44 ^{11ab} Bṛhaspati [a].

45–46 Agni:

45 ^{12c} Dyāvāpṛthivyau, ^{12d} Viśve devāḥ [a].

47 Indra Vaikuṇṭha.

48–50 Self-praise of Indra Vaikuṇṭha.

51–53 Dialogue of Agni and the Devāḥ [b].

54–55 Indra:

55 ^{5} Sun and Moon [c].

56–57 Viśve devāḥ.

57 ^{1} Indra, ^{2} Agni, $^{3-5}$ Manas, ^{6} Soma [d].

58 Jīvāvṛttiḥ Subandhor manasa stavo vā [e].

59 $^{1-3}$ Nirṛti, ^{4abc} Soma, ^{4d} Nirṛti [f], $^{5.6}$ Asunīti (Yāska: ^{6d} only), ^{7} Bhū, Dyu, Soma, Pūṣan, Kha, Pathyā, Svasti [g], $^{8-10}$ Rodasī (dual), ^{10ab} Indra [h].

60 $^{1-4}$ Aikṣvāku, ^{5} Prayer for Aikṣvāku [i], ^{6} Aikṣvāku, ^{7} Subandhor asum āhvayan [j], $^{8-12}$ asya cetaso dhāraṇāya, ^{12} labdhāsuṃ pāṇibhir aspṛśan [k].

61–66 Viśve devāḥ.

62 Aṅgirasāṃ stutiḥ; $^{8-11}$ Manu Sāvarṇya [l].

63 ^{15} Marutaḥ, ^{16} Pathyā svasti [m].

64 ^{5} Aditi [n].

65 ^{5} Mitra-Varuṇa, ^{6} Vāc madhyamā, ^{12} Aśvinau [o].

66 $^{14.15}$ Vāc madhyamā and Manu (A) [p].

67–68 Bṛhaspati:

67 ^{7cd} Brahmaṇaspati (B) [q].

69 Agni.

70 Āpriyaḥ.

71 Jñāna.

72 Viśve devāḥ (B), ^{2ab} Bṛhaspati (B) [r].

73–74 Indra.

75 Rivers (sravantyaḥ).

76 Grāvāṇaḥ.

77–78 Marutaḥ.

79–80 Agni.

81–82 Viśvakarman.

83–84 Manyu.

Khila 1 (*mama vrate*): Viśve devāḥ.

Khila 2 (*ut*): Agni:

^{4} Mitra-Varuṇa, ^{7} Indra-Agni.

85 ^{1} Sūryā, with Satya, Sūrya, Ṛta, Soma, $^{2-4}$ Soma, ^{5} Candramas [s], $^{6-13}$ Sūryāyai bhāvavṛttam, $^{14.15}$ Aśvinau, ^{16} Sūrya [t], ^{17} Viśve devāḥ [u], ^{18} Sūrya-Candramas [v], ^{19ab} Sūrya, ^{19cd} Candramas [w] ($^{18.19}$ Aśvinau: Aurṇavābha), ^{20} Sūryā, $^{21.22}$ Gan-

---

[a] No reference to this hemistich in Sarv. [b] The Sarv. apportions the speakers in 51–53. [c] No reference to this stanza in Sarv. [d] No details in Sarv. [e] *Mana-āvartanam*, Sarv. [f] Sarv.: ^{4} Nirṛti and Soma. [g] Liṅgoktadevatāḥ, Sarv. [h] Sarv.: ^{10ab} Dyāvāpṛthivyau or Indra. [i] With the stanza *Indra kṣatrā*, but the deity is not expressly stated; Sarv.: Indra. [j] Sarv.: *parābhiḥ* = $^{7-11}$. [k] Sarv.: *labdhasaṃjñam aspṛśan.* [l] Sarv.: $^{1-6}$ Viśve devāḥ or Aṅgirasāṃ stutiḥ, ^{7} Viśve devāḥ, $^{8-11}$ Sāvarṇer dānastutiḥ. [m] Sarv.: $^{15.16}$ Pathyā svasti (no reference to the Maruts). [n] No reference to this stanza in Sarv. [o] In Sarv. 65 is simply *vaiśvadevam.* [p] No reference to these two stanzas in Sarv. [q] No reference to this pāda in Sarv. [r] Sarv. simply states that the whole hymn is addressed to the Devāḥ. [s] Sarv.: $^{1-5}$ Soma. [t] Sarv.: $^{6-16}$ simply Sūryāvivāha. [u] Devāḥ, Sarv. [v] Soma and Arka, Sarv. [w] Sarv.: ^{19} Candramas.

dharva Viśvāvasu, [23] daṃpatī, [24–28] Vadhū [a], [29] Giving away of the bride's garment by the bridegroom, [30] Husband forbidden to take the garment [b], [31] yakṣmanāśinī, [32.33] paripanthinaḥ, [34] Receiver of the bridal dress, [35] Bhāvavṛtti, [36] Dhanāśiṣaḥ (B), [37] Saṃyogāśiṣaḥ (B), [38–47] Prayers for the married couple [c], [43] Prajāpati (B), [45] Indra (B), [48] (=khila) Bṛhaspati (B).

86 Vṛṣākapi [d].

87 Agni [e].

88 The three Agnis (terrestrial, middle, and celestial) [f].

89 Indra, [5] also Soma.

90 Puruṣa.

91 Agni.

92–93 Viśve devāḥ.

93 [14.15] rājñāṃ dānastutiḥ (B) [g].

94 Grāvā [h].

95 Dialogue of Purūravas and Urvaśī [i].

96 Indra [j].

97 Oṣadhīstavaḥ.

98 [1–3] Bṛhaspati [k], [4–7] Devāḥ, [8–12] Agni.

99 Indra.

100 Viśve devāḥ.

101 Ṛtvikstutiḥ [l].

102 Drughaṇa or Indra (Yāska), Viśve devāḥ (Śaunaka) [m].

103 Indra:
[4] Bṛhaspati (B), [12] Apvā, [13] Indra or Marutaḥ.

Khila 1 [n]: [1] Marutaḥ.

Khila 2 [o] (*brahma*): [1] Sūrya, [2] Gharma, [3] Bṛhaspati, [4] Savitṛ, [5–10] Sūrya-Candramas.

104 Indra.

105 Indra.

106 Aśvinau.

107 Prājāpatyā Dakṣiṇā; according to some dakṣiṇādātāraḥ, [8–11] Bhojāḥ [p].

108 [1.3.5.7.9] Saramā, [2.4.6.8.10.11] Paṇayaḥ.

109 Viśve devāḥ.

110 Āpriyaḥ.

111–113 Indra.

114 Viśve devāḥ:
eke: Devāḥ, Indra, Chandāṃsi, Agni madhyama [q].

115 Agni.

116 Indra.

117 Anna [r].

118 Agni Rakṣohan.

---

[a] Sarv.: [20–28] *nṛṇāṃ vivāhamantrā āśiṣaś ca.* [b] Sarv.: [29.30] *vadhuvāsaḥsaṃsparśamocanyau.* [c] The Sarv. gives no details for [32–47], which would therefore be addressed to Sūryā, the whole hymn being described as a self-praise of Sāvitrī Sūryā. [d] Dialogue of Vṛṣākapi, Indrāṇī, and Indra, Sarv. [e] Agni Rakṣohan, Sarv. [f] Sūrya and Vaiśvānara, Sarv. [g] No statement in Sarv. [h] Grāvāṇaḥ, Sarv. [i] The Sarv. apportions the stanzas to the respective speakers. [j] Sarv.: Indra's steeds (*haristutiḥ*). [k] The wording of the BD. here is not explicit, but *ṛgbhiḥ* (viii. 7) I take—*kapiñjalanyāyena*—to mean 'three,' in combination with the contents of the hymn. The Sarv. simply states that the whole hymn is addressed to the Devāḥ. [l] Viśve devāḥ or Ṛtvikstutiḥ, Sarv. [m] Sarv.: Indra or Drughaṇa. [n] This khila of two stanzas, beginning *asau*, is printed in Aufrecht's Rigveda, ii [2], p. 682. [o] The Nākula hymn, to the third stanza of which the pratīka *mahān* refers. [p] Sarv. simply *Dakṣiṇā dakṣiṇādātāro vā.* [q] No reference to this alternative in Sarv. [r] *Dhanānnadānapraśaṃsā*, Sarv.

119 Laba.
120 Indra:
[6] Āptyāḥ incidental [a]
121 Prajāpati [b].
122 Agni.
123 Vena.
124 [1-4] Self-praise of Agni, [5] Varuṇa, [6] Soma, [7,8] Varuṇa, [9abc] Soma, [9d] Indra [c].
125 Vāc [d].
126 Aryaman, Mitra, Varuṇa [e].
127 Rātrī.
128 Viśve devāḥ.
Khila 1 (*namas te*): Vidyut.
Khila 2 (*yām kalpayanti no 'rayaḥ*): kṛtyānāśanam.
Khila 3 (*āyuṣyam*): hiraṇyastutiḥ.
129 Parameṣṭhin: bhāvavṛttam [f].
130 Bhāvavṛttam.
131 Indra:
[4,5] Aśvinau.
132 Mitra-Varuṇa:
[1ab] Dyu, Bhūmi, [1cd] Aśvinau.
133–134 Indra.
135 Dyusthāna Yama [g].
136 Keśinaḥ.
137 [1] Devāḥ, [2-4] Vāta, [5] Viśve devāḥ, [6,7] Āpaḥ [h].
Khila (*bhūmiḥ*): Lākṣā.
138 Indra.
139 [1-3] Savitṛ, [4-6] self-praise of Gandharva, Indra and Sūrya being incidental [i]
140 Agni (B).
141 Agni and Viśve devāḥ [j].
142 Agni.
143 Aśvinau.
144 Indra.
145 Bhāvavṛttam aupaniṣadam sūktam: [1-5] Sapatnyapanodikāḥ, [6] Patisaṃvananī [k].
146 Araṇyānī.
147–148 Indra.
149 Savitṛ.
150 Agni.
151 Śraddhā.
Khila 1: Medhāsūktam.
Khila 2 (*ā sūr etu*): Agni.
152–153 Indra.
154 Bhāvavṛttam.
155 Alakṣmīghnam: [2,3] Brahmaṇaspati, [4] Indra [l], [5] Viśve devāḥ.
156 Agni.
157 Viśve devāḥ (Indra being the chief deity and the Viśve devāḥ, Ādityāḥ, Marutaḥ subordinate) [m].
158 Sūrya.
159 Paulomī praises her own virtues and those of her co-wives [n].
160 Indra.
161 Rājayakṣmaghnam: Indra-Agni (Yāska), liṅgoktadaivatam (eke) [o].

[a] No reference to this stanza in Sarv. [b] Ka, Sarv. [c] Sarv.: [5-8] *yathānipātam*, [9] Indra. [d] *Vāg āmbhṛṇī*, Sarv. [e] Viśve devāḥ, Sarv. [f] *Bhāvavṛttam* only, Sarv. [g] Simply Yama, Sarv. [h] Sarv. describes the whole hymn simply as *vaiśvadevam*. [i] Sarv.: self-praise of Devagandharva Viśvāvasu; no mention of Indra or Sūrya. [j] Viśve devāḥ only, Sarv. [k] Sarv. simply *upaniṣat, sapatnībādhanam*. [l] There is no reference to this stanza in Sarv., the general description of the hymn as *alakṣmīghnam* therefore specifically applying to the first and fourth stanzas. [m] Sarv. simply *vaiśvadevam*. [n] Sarv.: *paulomī śacy ātmānaṃ tuṣṭāva*. [o] The deity not being mentioned in the Sarv. would by the paribhāṣā be Indra. Ṣaḍg., in quoting the BD., remarks that Indra is the deity in the opinion of Śaunaka, who in quoting Yāska

162 Sravatāṃ garbhāṇām anumantraṇam[a]: Agni Rakṣohan[b].
Khila (*venas tat paśyat*): Vena.
163 Yakṣmanāśanam.
164 Duḥsvapnaghnam: Indra and Agni incidental[b].
165 Prāyaścittārtham[c]: Kapota[d].
166 Sapatnaghnam.
Khila (*yenedam*): Manas.
167 Indra:
 [3] Varuṇa, Vidhātṛ, Anumati, Dhātṛ, Soma, Bṛhaspati[e].
168 The father of the seer Anila (i.e. Vāta)[f].
169 Gāvaḥ.
170 Sūrya.
171 Indra.
172 Uṣas.
173–174 Rājñe 'bhiṣiktāyaanumantraṇe[g].
175 Grāvāṇaḥ.
176 Agni:
 [1] Ṛbhavaḥ.
177 Sūrya or Māyābhedam[h]:
 [2] Vāc (Śaunaka: B)[i].
178 Svastyayanam: Tārkṣya[j].
179–180 Indra.
181 Viśve devāḥ.
182 Bṛhaspati.
183 Liṅgoktadevatāḥ:
 [1] Prayer for man desiring a son, [2] prayer for woman desiring a son, [3] self-praise of the seer[k].
184 Prayer for offspring: Viśve devāḥ[l].
Khila (*nejameṣa*): garbhārtham.
185 Śāntyartham pāvanaṃ sūktam[m]: Adityāḥ, Sūrya, Varuṇa, Mitra[n].
186 The father of the seer Ula, i.e. Vāta[o].
187 Agni.
188 Jātavedas.
189 Self-praise of Sārparājñī; Sūrya (eke), Vāc (Mudgala, Śākapūṇi, Śākaṭāyana)[p].
190 Bhāvavṛttam.
191 [1] Agni[q]; [2–4] saṃjñānam[r].
Khila 1 (*saṃjñānam*): [1] Uśanā, Varuṇa, Indra, Agni, Savitṛ, [2] Aśvinau, [3.4.5] Āśiṣaḥ.
Khila 2 (*prādhvarāṇām*): [1] Agni.
Khila 3 (*nairhastyam*): sapatnaghnam: [2] Indra and Pūṣan.
Khila 4 (Mahānāmnya ṛcaḥ): Indra.

---

and others merely means to mention their opinions. [a] *Garbhasaṃsrāve prāyaścittam*, Sarv. [b] No deity mentioned in Sarv. [c] *Kapotopahatau prāyaścittam*, Sarv. [d] Viśve devāḥ, Sarv. [e] Simply *liṅgoktadevatā*, Sarv. [f] Simply *vāyavyam*, Sarv. [g] *Rājñaḥ stutiḥ*, Sarv. [h] Simply *māyābhedam*, Sarv. [i] No reference to this stanza in Sarv. [j] Simply *tārkṣyam*, Sarv.

[k] *Anvṛcaṃ yajamānapatnīhotrāśiṣaḥ*, Sarv. [l] *Garbhārthāśīr liṅgoktadaivatam.* [m] *Svastyayanam*, Sarv. [n] Sarv. simply *ādityam* (= *aditidevatyam*, Ṣaḍg.). [o] Sarv. simply *vāyavyam.* [p] Sarv.: *(sārparājñī) ātmadaivataṃ sauryaṃ vā.* [q] In Sarv. the first stanza to Agni, the remaining three *saṃjñānam.* [r] Cp. BD. viii. 97.

IV. LIST OF STORIES RELATED IN THE BṚHADDEVATĀ.

Agastya, *see* Vasiṣṭha *and* Lopāmudrā.
Agni and his brothers, vii. 61–81.
Atri, *see* Bhṛgu.
Apālā, vi. 99–106.
Abhyāvartin, v. 124–128.

Indra, *see* Gṛtsamada, Trasadasyu, Triśiras, Viṣṇu.
Indra and the seers, vi. 137–141.
Indra's birth and fight with Vāmadeva, iv. 130–135.
Indra as a partridge, iv. 93–94.
Indra and the Maruts, iv. 46–55.
Indra Vaikuṇṭha, vii. 49–60.
Indra and Vyaṃśa's sister, vi. 76–77.

Urvaśī, *see* Purūravas.

Ṛbhus and Tvaṣṭṛ, iii. 83–88.

Kakṣīvat and Svanaya, iii. 142–151.
Kaṇva and Pragātha, vi. 35–39.
Kapota Nairṛta, viii. 67–68.
Kāśyapa Bhūtāṃśa, viii. 18–20.

Gṛtsamada, Indra, and the Daityas, iv. 65–78.
Ghoṣā, vii. 42–48.

Citra, *see* Sobhari.

Trasadasyu, the seer, and Indra, vi. 51–57.
Trita, iii. 132–137.
Triśiras and Indra, vi. 147–153.
Tryaruṇa and Vṛśa Jāna, v. 13–22.
Tvaṣṭṛ, *see* Ṛbhus.

Dadhyañc, iii. 18–24.
Dīrghatamas, iv. 11–15.
Devāpi, vii. 155–viii. 9.
Daityas, *see* Gṛtsamada.

Nāhuṣa and Sarasvatī, vi. 20–24.

Paṇis, *see* Saramā.
Purūravas and Urvaśī, vii. 147–152.
Pragātha, *see* Kaṇva.

Bharadvāja, *see* Bhṛgu.
Bhūtāṃśa, *see* Kāśyapa.
Bhṛgu, Atri, Bharadvāja, birth of, v. 97–103.

Maruts, *see* Indra.

Lopāmudrā and Agastya, iv. 57–61.

Vasiṣṭha and the dog of Varuṇa, vi. 11–15.
Vasiṣṭha and Agastya, birth of, v. 143–159.
Vāmadeva, *see* Indra.
Viśvāmitra, son of Gāthin, iv. 95.
Viśvāmitra and Śakti, iv. 112–120.
Viśvāmitra, Sudās, and the Rivers, iv. 105–108.
Viṣṇu helps Indra, vi. 121–123.

V. LIST OF PASSAGES FROM THE BṚHADDEVATĀ CITED IN OTHER WORKS.

i. 2: Nītimañjarī on RV. i. 1.
ii. 105: Durga on Nirukta ii. 2.
iii. 18–23: Nītimañjarī on RV. i. 116. 12.
iii. 101^{cd}: Ṣaḍguruśiṣya and Sāyaṇa on RV. i. 28.
iii. 140^{cd}, 142–150: Nītimañjarī on RV. i. 126. 7.
iii. 155–156: Nītimañjarī on RV. i. 126. 6, 7.
iv. $1–3^{ab}$: Nītimañjarī on RV. i. 126. 6, 7.
iv. 11–15: Nītimañjarī on RV. i. 147. 3.
iv. 21, 24, 25^{ab}: Nītimañjarī on RV. i. 18. 1.
iv. 22, 23, 24^{ab}: Nītimañjarī on RV. i. 158. 5.
iv. 35: Sāyaṇa on AV. xix. 53. 2.
iv. $49^{cd}–53$: Nītimañjarī on RV. i. 170. 1.
iv. 57–60: Nītimañjarī on RV. i. 179. 1.
{iv. 66–69: Nītimañjarī on RV. ii. 12. 1.
{iv. 66–68: Sāyaṇa on RV. ii. 12.
iv. 93–94: Ṣaḍguruśiṣya on RV. ii. 43.
iv. 96^{bcd}: Ṣaḍguruśiṣya on RV. iii. 5, 6.
iv. $105^{cd}–106^{ab}$: Nītimañjarī on RV. iii. 33. 1.
{iv. $112^{cd}–116^{ab}$: Ṣaḍguruśiṣya on RV. iii. 53.
{iv. $113^{cd}–114$: Sāyaṇa on RV. iii. 53. 15.
iv. 120: Ṣaḍguruśiṣya on RV. iii. 53.
iv. 126: Nītimañjarī on RV. iv. 18. 13.
iv. $130^{cd}–131^{ab}$: Nītimañjarī on RV. iv. 18. 13.
v. 8: Ṣaḍguruśiṣya on RV. iv. 57.
v. 14–21, 22^{cd}, 23: Nītimañjarī on RV. v. 2. 9.
v. $33–36^{ab}$: Nītimañjarī on RV. iv. 30. 15.
{v. 50–79 (excepting 61, 68^{cd}, 71^{cd}): Ṣaḍguruśiṣya on RV. v. 61.
{v. $50–79^{ab}$ (excepting $64^{cd}–67^{ab}$, $69^{cd}–71^{ab}$): Nītimañjarī on RV. v. 61. 17.
v. $72^{cd}–79^{ab}$: Sāyaṇa on RV. v. 61. 17.
{v. 97–101: Ṣaḍguruśiṣya, introduction to RV. v.
{v. 97–102: Nītimañjarī, introduction to RV. v.
v. 106^{ab}: Sāyaṇa on RV. vi. 24. 5.
v. 111^{ab}: Ṣaḍguruśiṣya on RV. vi. 47.
v. 124–128: Nītimañjarī on RV. vi. 27. 4.
v. 129–133: Nītimañjarī on RV. vi. 75. 1.
v. 136–138: Nītimañjarī on RV. vi. 27. 4.
v. 139–140: Nītimañjarī on RV. vi. 47. 22.
{v. 143–155 (excepting 153^{cd}): Nītimañjarī on RV. vii. 104. 16.
{v. $149–155^{ab}$: Sāyaṇa on RV. vii. 33. 11.

vi. 11^{cd}–15^{ab}: Nītimañjarī on RV. vii. 55. 2.
vi. 11^{cd}–13: Sāyaṇa on RV. vii. 55. 3.
vi. 27^{cd}–28: Sāyaṇa, introduction to RV. vii. 104.
vi. 28^{ab}: Nītimañjarī on RV. vii. 104. 16.
vi. 32^{cd}: Sāyaṇa on RV. vii. 104. 22.
vi. 35–38: Nītimañjarī on RV. viii. 1.
vi. 43^{ab}: Ṣaḍguruśiṣya on RV. viii. 4.
vi. 51–57^{ab}: Nītimañjarī on RV. viii. 19. 37.
vi. 58^{cd}–62^{abc}: Nītimañjarī on RV. viii. 21. 18.
vi. 68^{ab}: Ṣaḍguruśiṣya on RV. viii. 27.
vi. 79^{cd}–80^{ab}: Ṣaḍguruśiṣya on RV. viii. 46. Sāyaṇa on RV. viii. 46. 21.
vi. 91^{cd}–92^{ab}: Ṣaḍguruśiṣya on RV. viii. 68.
vi. 99–106: Nītimañjarī on RV. viii. 91. 7.
vi. 99–100, 102^{a-d}, 105–106: Ṣaḍguruśiṣya on RV. viii. 91.
vi. 109^{cd}–113^{ab}, 114–115: Sāyaṇa on RV. viii. 96. 13.
vi. 110: Nītimañjarī on RV. viii. 95. 7.
vi. 121^{cd}–124^{ab}: Sāyaṇa on RV. viii. 100. 12.
vi. 162–163: Nītimañjarī on RV. i. 116. 6. Sāyaṇa on RV. vii. 72. 2 and AV. xviii. 1. 53.
vii. 1–7^{ab}: Nītimañjarī on RV. i. 116. 6.
vii. 1–6: Sāyaṇa on RV. vii. 72. 2 and AV. xviii. 1. 53.
vii. 37^{a-d}: Ṣaḍguruśiṣya on RV. x. 34.
vii. 37^{a-d}: Sāyaṇa on RV. x. 34.
vii. 42–44^{ab}, 45–47: Nītimañjarī on RV. i. 117. 7.
vii. 61–81^{ab}: Old MS. of Ṣaḍguruśiṣya on RV. x. 50.
vii. 61^{cd}–66^{ab}, 74, 75^{ab}, 76^{cd}: Nītimañjarī on RV. x. 51. 8.
vii. 89^{cd}–90^{ab}: Nītimañjarī on RV. v. 60. 12.
vii. 97^{cd}–101: Sāyaṇa on RV. x. 60. 7.
vii. 97–98^{ab}, 99^{cd}–100^{ab}: Nītimañjarī on RV. v. 60. 12.
vii. 109: Ṣaḍguruśiṣya on RV. x. 71. Sāyaṇa on RV. x. 71. 12.
vii. 155–157: Old MS. of Ṣaḍguruśiṣya on RV. x. 98. Nītimañjarī on RV. x. 98. 8.
viii. 1–9: Old MS. of Ṣaḍguruśiṣya on RV. x. 98.
viii. 1^{ab}, 2^{cd}–7^{ab}: Nītimañjarī on RV. x. 98. 8.
viii. 40^{c}: Ṣaḍguruśiṣya on RV. x. 119.
viii. 65^{ab}: Ṣaḍguruśiṣya on RV. x. 161.
viii. 73^{cd}: Ṣaḍguruśiṣya on RV. x. 173.
viii. 98^{cd}: Ṣaḍguruśiṣya on RV. x. 191 (śl. 9^{cd}).
viii. 133: Ṣaḍguruśiṣya on RV. x. 191 (śl. 10^{cd}–11^{ab}).
viii. 135^{a}: Ṣaḍguruśiṣya on RV. x. 191 (śl. 2^{a}).
viii. 136: Ṣaḍguruśiṣya, Introduction i. 2 (p. 57). Sāyaṇa, Introduction, RV. ed. M. M.², vol. i, p. 23.

VI. RELATION OF THE BṚHADDEVATĀ TO OTHER TEXTS.

1. THE NAIGHAṆṬUKA.

[The few deviations of the Bṛhaddevatā from the Naighaṇṭuka are pointed out in the notes.]

Naighaṇṭuka v. 1, 2 (terrestrial deities—forms of Agni and Aprī deities)	is the source of Bṛhaddevatā i. 106–109 [ab].
Naighaṇṭuka v. 3 (other terrestrial deities)	is the source of Bṛhaddevatā i. 109 [cd]–114.
Naighaṇṭuka v. 4, 5 (atmospheric deities)	is the source of Bṛhaddevatā i. 122–129.
Naighaṇṭuka v. 6 (celestial deities)	is the source of Bṛhaddevatā ii. 8–12.
Naighaṇṭuka v. 3 (the part embracing the names Nadyaḥ to Agnāyī)	is the source of Bṛhaddevatā ii. 73–75.
Naighaṇṭuka i. 15 (the steeds of the different gods)	is the source of Bṛhaddevatā iv. 140–144.

2. THE NIRUKTA.

Nirukta.	Bṛhaddevatā.
vii. 3: Evam uccāvacair abhiprāyair ṛṣīṇāṃ mantradṛṣṭayo bhavanti.	i. 3: tadabhiprāyān ṛṣīṇāṃ mantradṛṣṭiṣu.
vii. 1: Yatkāma ṛṣir yasyāṃ devatāyām arthapatyam ichan stutiṃ prayuṅkte, taddaivataḥ sa mantro bhavati.	i. 6: Artham ichann ṛṣir devaṃ yaṃ yam āhāyam astv iti; prādhānyena stuvan bhaktyā mantras taddeva eva saḥ.

Nirukta.	Bṛhaddevatā.
x. 42: Devatānāmadheyāny anukrāntāni, sūktabhāñji ... vii. 13: devatāḥ ... sūktabhājaḥ ... ṛgbhājaś ca ... kāś cin nipātabhājaḥ.	i. 17 (cp. viii. 129): Devatānāmadheyāni mantreṣu trividhāni tu: sūktabhāñjy athavargbhāñji tathā naipātikāni tu.
i. 20: Yad anyadevate mantre nipatati naighaṇṭukaṃ tat.	i. 18: Mantre 'nyadaivate 'nyāni nigadyante 'tra kāni cit.
i. 1: Pūrvāparībhūtaṃ bhāvam ākhyātena‿ācaṣṭe.	i. 44: Yaḥ pūrvāparībhūta ihaika eva ... ākhyātaśabdena tam artham āhuḥ.
vii. 5: Tisra eva devatāḥ ... Agniḥ pṛthivīsthāno, Vāyur vendro vāntarikṣasthānaḥ, Sūryo dyusthānaḥ.	i. 69: Agnir asminn athendras tu madhyato Vāyur eva ca, Sūryo divīti vijñeyās tisra eveha devatāḥ.
vii. 4: Ātmaivaiṣāṃ ratho ... ātmāyudham ... ātmā sarvaṃ devasya.	i. 73: Teṣām ātmaiva tat sarvaṃ yad yad bhaktiḥ prakīrtyate: tejas tv evāyudhaṃ prāhur vāhanaṃ caiva yasya yat.
vii. 18: Yas tu sūktaṃ bhajate, yasmai havir nirupyate, 'yam eva so 'gnir, nipātam eva‿ete uttare jyotiṣī etena nāmadheyena bhajete.	i. 78: Nirupyate havir yasyai sūktaṃ ca bhajate ca yā, saiva tatra pradhānaṃ syān, na nipātena yā stutā.
vii. 19: Jātavedāḥ ... jātāni veda, jātāni vainaṃ vidur, jāte jāte vidyata iti vā, jātavitto vā jātadhano, jātavidyo vā jātaprajñānaḥ.	i. 92: Yad vidyate hi jātaḥ sañ jātair yad vātra vidyate. ii. 30: bhūtāni veda yaj jātaḥ. . . . . . . Yac caiṣa jātavidyo 'bhūd vittaṃ jāto 'dhivetti vā, ii. 31: vidyate sarvabhūtair hi, yad vā jātaḥ punaḥ punaḥ.
vii. 23: Rohāt pratyavarohaś cikīrṣitas tām anukṛtiṃ hotā‿āgnimārute śastre vaiśvānarīyeṇa sūktena pratipadyate ... tata āgachati madhyasthānā devatā Rudraṃ ca Marutaś ca tato 'gnim	i. 102–103: Rohāt pratyavaroheṇa cikīrṣann Āgnimārutaṃ śastraṃ vaiśvānarīyeṇa sūktena pratipadyate. Tatas tu madhyamasthānā devatās tv anuśaṃsati,

Nirukta.	Bṛhaddevatā.
ihasthānam atraiva stotriyaṃ śaṃsati.	Rudraṃ ca Marutaś caiva Stotriye 'gnim imaṃ punaḥ.
vii. 8 : Ayaṃ lokaḥ prātaḥsavanaṃ vasanto gāyatrī trivṛt stomo rathaṃtaraṃ sāma ye ca devagaṇāḥ samāmnātāḥ prathame sthāne vii. 11 : Śarad anuṣṭub ekaviṃśastomo vairājaṃ sāma‿iti pṛthivyāyatanāni.	i. 115–116 : Loko 'yaṃ yac ca prātaḥ savanaṃ kriyate makhe, vasantaśaradau cartū stomo 'nuṣṭub atho trivṛt. gāyatrī caikaviṃśaś ca yac ca sāma rathaṃtaram, Sādhyāḥ sāma ca vairājam Āptyāś ca Vasubhiḥ saha
vii. 8 : Atha‿asya saṃstavikā devā Indraḥ Somo Varuṇaḥ Parjanya Ṛtavaḥ ; Āgnāvaiṣṇavaṃ havir na tv ṛk saṃstavikī daśatayīṣu vidyate ; atha‿api‿āgnāpauṣṇaṃ havir na tu saṃstavaḥ.	i. 117–120[ab]: Indreṇa ca Marudbhiś ca Somena Varuṇena ca Parjanyenartubhiś caiva Viṣṇunā cāsya saṃstavaḥ ; asyaivāgnes tu Pūṣṇā ca sāmrājyaṃ Varuṇena ca. devatām arthatattvajño mantraiḥ saṃyojayed dhaviḥ, asaṃstutasyāpi sato havir ekaṃ nirupyate.
ii. 8 : Atha‿asya karma vahanaṃ ca haviṣām āvāhanaṃ ca devatānām yac ca kiṃ cid dārṣṭiviṣayikam.	devatāvāhanaṃ caiva vahanaṃ haviṣāṃ tathā karma, dṛṣṭe ca yat kiṃ cid viṣaye parivartate.
vii. 10 : Antarikṣaloko mādhyaṃdinaṃ savanaṃ grīṣmas triṣṭup pañcadaśastomo bṛhat sāma. vii. 11 : Hemantaḥ paṅktis triṇavastomaḥ śākvaraṃ sāma‿ity antarikṣāyatanāni.	i. 130–131 : Chandas triṣṭup ca paṅktiś ca lokānāṃ madhyamaś ca yaḥ eteṣv evāśrayo vidyāt savanaṃ madhyamaṃ ca yat ; ṛtū ca grīṣma-hemantau yac ca sāmocyate bṛhat ; śakvarīṣu ca yad gītaṃ nāmnā tat sāma śākvaram.
	ii. 1 : Āha caivāsya dvau stomāv āśrayau Śākaṭāyanaḥ, yaś ca pañcadaśo nāmnā saṅkhyayā triṇavaś ca yaḥ.

Nirukta.	**Bṛhaddevatā.**
vii. 10: Atha‿asya saṃstavikā devā Agniḥ Somo Varuṇaḥ Pūṣā Bṛhaspatir Brahmaṇaspatiḥ Parvataḥ Kutso Viṣṇur Vāyuḥ. x. 11: Bṛhaspatir bṛhataḥ pātā.	ii. 2–3^{ab}: Saṃstutaś caiva Pūṣṇā ca Viṣṇunā Varuṇena ca Soma-vāyv-agni-kutsaiś ca Brahmaṇaspatinaiva ca, Bṛhataspatinā caiva nāmnā yaś cāpi Parvataḥ.
vii. 10: Atha‿api Mitro Varuṇena saṃstūyate, Pūṣṇā Rudreṇa ca Somo, 'gninā [Vāyunā, shorter recension] ca Pūṣā, Vātena ca Parjanyaḥ.	ii. 4–5^{ab}: Mitraś ca śrūyate devo Varuṇena sahāsakṛt, Rudreṇa Somaḥ Pūṣṇā ca, punaḥ Pūṣā ca Vāyunā, Vātenaiva ca Parjanyo; lakṣyate 'nyatra vai kva cit.
vii. 10: Atha‿asya karma rasānupradānam, Vṛtravadho, yā ca kā ca balakṛtiḥ.	ii. 6: Rasādānaṃ tu karmāsya Vṛtrasya ca nibarhaṇam, stuteḥ prabhutvaṃ sarvasya balasya nikhilā kṛtiḥ.
vii. 24: Ādityaraśmayaḥ . . . amuto 'rvāñcaḥ paryāvartante.	ii. 8^{d}–9^{ab}: Sūryasyaiva tu patnayaḥ: amuto 'rvāñ nivartante pratilomās tadāśrayāḥ.
vii. 11: Asau lokas tṛtīyasavanaṃ varṣā jagatī saptadaśastomo vairūpaṃ sāma . . . śiśiro 'tichandās trayastriṃśastomo raivataṃ sāma‿iti dyubhaktīni.	ii. 13: Asau tṛtīyaṃ savanaṃ lokaḥ, sāma ca raivatam; vairūpaṃ caiva, varṣāś ca śiśiro 'tha ṛtus tathā. ii. 14: Trayastriṃśaś ca ya stomaḥ kḷptyā saptadaśaś ca yaḥ; chandaś ca jagatī nāmnā tathātichandasaś ca yāḥ.
vii. 11: Candramasā Vāyunā saṃvatsareṇa‿iti saṃstavaḥ.	ii. 15^{cd}–16^{ab}: Etasyaiva tu vijñeyā devāḥ saṃstavikās trayaḥ: Candramāś caiva Vāyuś ca yaṃ ca saṃvatsaraṃ viduḥ.
vii. 23: Atha‿api vaiśvānarīyo dvādaśakapālo bhavati . . . atha‿api chāndomikaṃ sūktaṃ sauryavaiśvānaraṃ bhavati . . . athāpi haviṣpāntīyaṃ sūktaṃ sauryavaiśvānaraṃ bhavati.	ii. 16^{cd}–17^{ab}: Ke cit tu nirvapanty asya sauryavaiśvānaraṃ haviḥ: sauryavaiśvānarīyaṃ hi tat sūktam iva dṛśyate.

Nirukta.	Bṛhaddevatā.
vii. 14: Agniḥ kasmāt? agraṇīr bhavati, agraṃ yajñeṣu praṇīyate, aṅgaṃ nayati saṃnamamānaḥ.	ii. 24: Jāto yad agre bhūtānām agraṇīr adhvare ca yat, nāmnā saṃnayate vāṅgaṃ stuto 'gnir iti sūribhiḥ.
viii. 1: Draviṇodāḥ kasmāt? dhanaṃ draviṇam ucyate . . . balaṃ vā draviṇam . . . tasya dātā draviṇodāḥ.	ii. 25: Draviṇaṃ dhanaṃ balaṃ vāpi prāyachad yena karmaṇā, tat karma dṛṣṭvā Kutsas tu prāhainaṃ draviṇodasam.
viii. 5: Napād ity anantarāyāḥ prajāyā nāmadheyam.	ii. 27: Anantarāṃ prajām āhur napād iti kṛpaṇyavaḥ.
viii. 6: Narāśaṃso yajña iti Kātthakyaḥ: narā asminn āsīnāḥ śaṃsanti; Agnir iti Śākapūṇiḥ: naraiḥ praśasyo bhavati.	ii. 28: yajñe yac chasyate nṛbhiḥ stuvanty āprīṣu tenemaṃ Narāśaṃsaṃ tu kāravaḥ.
	iii. 2–3: Narāśaṃsam ihaike tu Agnim āhur; athetare Narāḥ śaṃsanti sarve 'sminn āsīnā iti vādhvare. Etam evāhur anye 'gniṃ: Narāśaṃso 'dhvare hy ayam, naraiḥ praśasya āsīnair; āhuś caivartvijo naraḥ.
	ii. 30–31: See under i. 92.
x. 5: Yad arudat tad Rudrasya rudratvam iti Kāṭhakam; yad arodīt tad Rudrasya rudratvam iti Hāridravikam.	ii. 34: Arodīd antarikṣe yad vidyudvṛṣṭiṃ dadan nṛṇām, caturbhir ṛṣibhis tena Rudra ity abhisaṃstutaḥ.
x. 8: Indra irāṃ dṛṇātīti.	ii. 36: Irāṃ dṛṇāti yat kāle Marudbhiḥ sahito 'mbare, raveṇa mahatā yuktas, tenendram ṛṣayo 'bruvan.
x. 10: Parjanyas (tṛper ādyantaviparītasya) tarpayitā janyaḥ, paro jetā vā janayitā vā, prārjayitā vā rasānām.	ii. 37–38: Yad imāṃ prārjayaty eko rasenāmbarajena gāṃ kāle, 'trir Aurvaśaś carṣī tena Parjanyam āhatuḥ. tarpayaty eṣa yal lokāñ janyo janahitaś ca yat,

Nirukta.	**Bṛhaddevatā.**
	paro jetā janayitā yad vāgneyas tato jagau.
x. 12 : Brahmaṇaspatir brahmaṇaḥ pātā.	ii. 40 : Pātāraṃ brahmaṇas tena Śaunahotra stuvañ jagau.
x. 27 : Tārkṣyas : tīrṇe 'ntarikṣe kṣiyati, tūrṇam arthaṃ rakṣaty aśnoter vā.	ii. 58 : Stīrṇe 'ntarikṣe kṣiyati yad vā tūrṇaṃ kṣaraty asau, ... Tārkṣyaṃ tenaivam uktavān.
xi. 6 : Mṛtyur mārayatīti sato mṛtaṃ cyāvayatīti vā.	ii. 60 : Yat tu pracyāvayann eti ghoṣeṇa mahatā mṛtam, tena mṛtyum imaṃ santaṃ stauti Mṛtyur iti svayam.
xii. 16 : Atha yad raśmipoṣaṃ puṣyati tat Pūṣā bhavati.	ii. 63 : Puṣyan kṣitiṃ poṣayati praṇudan raśmibhis tamaḥ, tenainam astaut Pūṣeti.
xii. 25 : Keśī, keśā raśmayas, tais tadvān bhavati, kāśanād vā prakāśanād vā.	ii. 65 : Prakāśaṃ kiraṇaiḥ kurvaṃs tenainaṃ keśinaṃ viduḥ.
xii. 27 : Atha yad raśmibhir abhiprakampayann eti, tad Vṛṣākapir bhavati vṛṣākampanaḥ.	ii. 67 : Vṛṣākapir asau . . . raśmibhiḥ kampayann eti vṛṣā varṣiṣṭha eva saḥ.
xii. 18 : Atha yad viṣito bhavati, tad Viṣṇur bhavati ; Viṣṇur viśater vā vyaśnoter vā.	ii. 69 : Viṣṇāter viśater vā syād, veveṣṭer vyāptikarmaṇaḥ, Viṣṇur nirucyate.
i. 4 : Atha nipātā uccāvaceṣv artheṣu nipatanti : apy upamārthe, 'pi karmopasaṃgrahārthe, 'pi padapūraṇāḥ.	ii. 89 : Uccāvaceṣu cārtheṣu nipātāḥ samudāhṛtāḥ : karmopasaṃgrahārthe ca kva cic caupamyakāraṇāt.
i. 9 : Padapūraṇās te mitākṣareṣv anarthakāḥ kam īm id v iti.	ii. 90 : Mitākṣareṣu grantheṣu pūraṇārthās tv anarthakāḥ : ii. 91 : kam īm id v iti vijñeyāḥ.
i. 4 : Teṣām ete catvāra upamārthe bhavantīti : iveti . . . neti . . . cid iti . . . nu iti.	Iva na cin nu catvāra upamārthā bhavanti te.
ii. 2 : Atha taddhitasamāseṣv ekaparvasu ca . . . pravibhajya nirbrūyād : daṇḍyaḥ puruṣo daṇḍam arhatīti.	ii. 106 : Samāseṣv api taddhite pravibhajyaiva nirbrūyāt : daṇḍārho daṇḍya ity api.

Nirukta.	**Bṛhaddevatā.**
i. 1: Bhāvapradhānam ākhyātam. i. 2: Ṣaḍ bhāvavikārā bhavantīti Vārṣyāyanir: jāyate, 'sti, vipariṇamate, vardhate, 'pakṣīyate, vinaśyatīti.	ii. 121: Bhāvapradhānam ākhyātaṃ; ṣaḍvikārā bhavanti te: janmāstitvaṃ parīṇāmo vṛddhir hānaṃ vināśanam.
xii. 40: Yat tu kiṃ cid bahudaivataṃ, tad vaiśvadevānāṃ sthāne yujyate.	ii. 133: Vaiśvadevaṃ vadet sarvaṃ yat·kiṃ cid bahudaivatam.
ii. 23: Sarasvatīty etasya nadīvad devatāvac ca nigamā bhavanti.	ii. 135^{cd}–136^{c}: Sarasvatīti dvividham ṛkṣu sarvāsu sā stutā: nadīvad devatāvac ca. Tatrācāryas tu Śaunakaḥ: nadīvan nigamāḥ ṣaṭ te.
viii. 22: Tāny etāny ekādaśāprīsūktāni: teṣāṃ vāsiṣṭham ātreyaṃ vādhryaśvaṃ gārtsamadam iti nārāśaṃsavanti; maidhātithaṃ dairghatamasaṃ praiṣikam ity ubhayavanti; ato 'nyāni tanūnapātvanti.	ii. 154^{cd}–157^{ab}: Teṣāṃ praiṣagataṃ sūktaṃ, yac ca Dīrghatamā jagau, Medhātithau yad uktaṃ ca: trīṇy evobhayavanti tu. Ṛṣau Gṛtsamade yac ca Vādhryaśve ca yad ucyate, Narāśaṃsavad Atreś ca dadarśa ca yad Aurvaśaḥ. Tanūnapād Agastyaś ca Jamadagniś ca yaj jagau, Viśvāmitra ṛṣir yac ca jagau vai Kāśyapo 'sitaḥ.
	iii. 2–3: See under ii. 28.
ii. 18: Uṣāḥ kasmād? uchatīti satyā rātrer aparaḥ kālaḥ.	iii. 9: tama uchaty uṣāḥ.
viii. 10: Nakteti rātrināma: anakti bhūtāny avaśyāyena; api vā naktā avyaktavarṇā.	iii. 9: . . . . . . naktānaktīmāṃ himabindubhiḥ; api vāvyaktavarṇeti. nañpūrvāñcer idaṃ bhavet.
viii. 13: Tvaṣṭā tūrṇam aśnuta iti nairuktās; tviṣer vā syād dīptikarmaṇas, tvakṣater vā syāt karotikarmaṇaḥ.	iii. 16: Tviṣitas tvakṣater vā syāt tūrṇam aśnuta eva vā, karmasūttāraṇo veti.
viii. 14: Mādhyamikas Tvaṣṭā ity āhur, madhyame ca sthāne samāmnāto 'gnir iti Śākapūṇiḥ.	iii. 25: Tvaṣṭā rūpavikartā ca yo 'sau mādhyamike gaṇe.

Nirukta.	Bṛhaddevatā.
viii. 3: Eṣa hi vanānāṃ pātā vā pālayitā vā.	iii. 26: Ayaṃ vanānāṃ hi patiḥ pātā pālayatīti vā.
viii. 2: Ko draviṇodāḥ? Indra iti Krauṣṭukiḥ: sa baladhanayor dātṛtamaḥ.	iii. 61: Pārthivo draviṇodo 'gniḥ purastād yas tu kīrtitaḥ, tam āhur Indraṃ dātṛtvād eke tu balavittayoḥ.
viii. 2: balena mathyamāno jāyate.	iii. 62: jāyate ca balenāyaṃ mathyaty ṛṣibhir adhvare.
viii. 2: Ṛtvijo 'tra draviṇodasa ucyante, haviṣo dātāras, te cainaṃ janayanti: 'ṛṣīṇāṃ putraḥ' . . . ity api nigamo bhavati. (balena mathyamāno jāyate) tasmād enam āha sahasas putraṃ, sahasaḥ sūnuṃ, sahaso yahum.	iii. 63–64[ab]: Havīṃṣi draviṇaṃ prāhur haviṣo yatra jāyate: dātāraś cartvijas teṣāṃ, draviṇodās tataḥ svayam. 'ṛṣīṇāṃ putra' ity eṣāṃ dṛśyate 'sahaso yaho.'
viii. 2: Ayam evāgnir draviṇodā iti Śākapūṇir, āgneyeṣv eva hi sūkteṣu drāviṇodasāḥ pravādā bhavanti.	iii. 65: Draviṇodo 'gnir evāyaṃ; draviṇodās-tadocyate: āgneyeṣv eva dṛśyante pravādā draviṇodasaḥ.
xi. 16: Ṛbhur Vibhvā Vāja iti Sudhanvana Āṅgirasasya trayaḥ putrā babhūvuḥ.	iii. 83: Sudhanvana Āṅgirasasy- āsan putrās trayaḥ purā: Ṛbhur Vibhvā ca Vājaś ca, śiṣyās Tvaṣṭuś ca te 'bhavan.
i. 5: Agastya Indrāya havir nirupya Marudbhyaḥ sampraditsāṃ cakāra; sa Indra etya paridevayāṃ cakre.	iv. 48–50: Sa [Agastyas] tān abhijagāmāśu; nirupyaindraṃ havis tadā Marutaś cābhituṣṭāva sūktais tan nv iti ca tribhiḥ. Niruptaṃ tad dhaviś caindraṃ Marudbhyo dātum ichati: vijñāyāvekṣya tadbhāvam Indro neti tam abravīt.
ii. 24: Viśvāmitra ṛṣiḥ Sudāsaḥ Paijavanasya purohito babhūva . . . sa vittaṃ gṛhītvā Vipāṭ-Chutudryoḥ sambhedam āyayāu . . . Sa Viśvāmitro nadīs tuṣṭāva 'gādhā bhavata' iti, api dvivad api bahuvat.	iv. 106: Purohitaḥ sann ījyārthaṃ Sudāsā saha yann ṛṣiḥ Vipāṭ-Chutudryoḥ sambhedaṃ śam ity ete uvāca ha. Pravādās tatra dṛśyante dvivad bahuvad ekavat.

Nirukta.	Bṛhaddevatā.
vi. 31: Karūḷatī . . . Pūṣeti . . . so 'dantakaḥ: adantakaḥ Pūṣeti ca Brāhmaṇam.	iv. 139: Karūḷatīti Pūṣokto: 'dantakaḥ sa iti śruteḥ.
vii. 4: Māhābhāgyād devatāyā eka ātmā bahudhā stūyate: ekasyātmano 'nye devāḥ pratyaṅgāni bhavanti (cp. also vii. 4, under BD. i. 73).	iv. 143: Āyudhaṃ vāhanaṃ cāpi stutau yasyeha dṛśyate, tam eva tu stutaṃ vidyāt: tasyātmā bahudhā hi saḥ.
ix. 40: Śunāsīrau: śuno Vāyuḥ (śu ety antarikṣe), sīra Ādityaḥ saraṇāt.	v. 8: Vāyuḥ śunaḥ Sūrya evātra sīraḥ: śunāsīrau Vāyu-Sūryau vadanti.
iii. 17: Arciṣi Bhṛguḥ sambabhūva... aṅgāreṣv Aṅgirāḥ.	v. 99[cd]: Tato 'rcibhyo Bhṛgur jajñe aṅgāreṣv Aṅgirā ṛṣiḥ.
v. 13: Urvaśy apsarāḥ . . . tasyā darśanān Mitrāvaruṇayo retaś caskanda.	v. 149: Tayor Ādityayoḥ sattre, dṛṣṭvāpsarasam Urvaśīm, retaś caskanda; tat kumbhe nyapatad vāsatīvare.
v. 14: Sarve devāḥ puṣkare tvā adhārayanta.	v. 155: Sarvatra puṣkaraṃ tatra viśve devā adhārayan.
ii. 17: Ahir ayanād: ety antarikṣe; ayam apītaro 'hir etasmād eva nirhrasitopasarga āhantīti. x. 44: Yo 'hiḥ sa budhnyo, budhnam antarikṣaṃ, tannivāsāt.	v. 166: Ahir āhanti meghān, sa eti vā teṣu madhyamaḥ. Yo 'hiḥ sa budhnyo, budhne hi so, 'ntarikṣe, 'bhijāyate.
vi. 5: Śakaṭaṃ śākinī gāvo jālam asyandanaṃ vanam, udadhiḥ parvato rājā: durbhikṣe nava vṛttayaḥ.	vi. 138: Śakaṭaṃ śākinī gāvaḥ kṛṣir asyandanaṃ vanam, samudraḥ parvato rājā: evaṃ jīvāmahe vayam.
xii. 1: Kāv Aśvinau? Dyāvāpṛthivyāv ity eke; ahorātrāv ity eke; Sūryācandramasāv ity eke.	vii. 126: Sūryācandramasau tau hi, prāṇāpānau ca tau smṛtau, ahorātrau ca tāv eva, syātāṃ tāv eva rodasī.
xii. 14: Sūryaḥ sarter vā suvater vā svīryater vā.	vii. 128 (B): Sūryaḥ sarati bhūteṣu su vīrayati tāni vā.
xi. 5: Candramāś cāyan dramati; candro mātā, cāndraṃ mānam asyeti vā;	vii. 129 (B): Cāru dramati vā cāyaṃś cāyanīyo dramaty uta;

Nirukta.	**Bṛhaddevatā.**
candraś candateḥ kāntikarmaṇaḥ … cāru dramati, ciraṃ dramati, camer vā pūrvam.	cameḥ pūrvam ; sametāni nirmimīte 'tha Candramāḥ.
ii. 10 : Devāpiś cārṣṭiṣeṇaḥ Śantanuś ca Kauravyau bhrātarau babhūvatuḥ. Sa Śantanuḥ kanīyān abhiṣecayāṃ cakre.	vii. 155 : Ārṣṭiṣeṇas tu Devāpiḥ Kauravyaś caiva Śantanuḥ bhrātarau Kuruṣu tv etau rājaputrau babhūvatuḥ. Jyeṣṭhas tayos tu Devāpiḥ, kanīyāṃś caiva Śantanuḥ : tvagdoṣī rājaputras tu Ṛṣṭiṣeṇasuto 'bhavat. Rājyena chandayām āsuḥ prajāḥ svargaṃ gate gurau. Sa muhūrtam iva dhyātvā prajās tāḥ pratyabhāṣata.
Devāpis tapaḥ pratipede. Tataḥ Śantano rājye dvādaśa varṣāṇi devo na vavarṣa. Tam ūcur brāhmaṇāḥ : adharmas tvayā carito jyeṣṭhaṃ bhrātaram antarityābhiṣecitam ; tasmāt te devo na varṣatīti. Sa Śantanur Devāpiṃ śiśikṣa rājyena. Tam uvāca Devāpiḥ : purohitas te 'sāni yājayāni ca tveti. Tasyaitad varṣakāmasūktam.	viii. 1 : Na rājyam aham arhāmi, nṛpatir vo 'stu Śantanuḥ. 2 : Tato 'bhiṣikte Kauravye vanaṃ Devāpir āviśat. na vavarṣātha Parjanyo rājye dvādaśa vai samāḥ. 3 : Tato 'bhyagachad Devāpiṃ prajābhiḥ saha Śantanuḥ ; prasādayām āsa cainaṃ tasmin dharmavyatikrame. 4 : Śiśikṣa cainaṃ rājyena prajābhiḥ sahitas tadā. Tam uvācātha Devāpiḥ prahvaṃ tu prāñjalisthitam : na rājyam aham arhāmi tvagdoṣopahatendriyaḥ : yājayiṣyāmi te rājan vṛṣṭikāmejyayā svayam.
ix. 23 : Mudgalo Bhārmyaśva ṛṣir vṛṣabhaṃ ca drughaṇaṃ ca yuktvā saṃgrāme vyavahṛtyājiṃ jigāya.	viii. 12 : Ājāv anena Bhārmyaśva Indrāsomau tu Mudgalaḥ ajayad vṛṣabhaṃ yuktvā aindraṃ ca drughaṇaṃ rathe.

3. ĀRṢĀNUKRAMAṆĪ.

Ārṣānukramaṇī.	**Bṛhaddevatā.**
i. 2: Atrāgnim īḷa ityādi prathamaṃ maṇḍalaṃ prati, Śatarcinas tu vijñeyā ṛṣayaḥ sukhasiddhaye.	iii. 116: Prathame maṇḍale jñeyā ṛṣayas tu śatarcinaḥ; kṣudrasūktamahāsūktā antye, madhyeṣu madhyamāḥ.
ii. 1: madhyameṣv ṛṣayo jñeyā maṇḍaleṣv atha madhyamāḥ. x. 1: . . . . . . daśamaṃ maṇḍalaṃ prati kṣudrasūktā mahāsūktā vijñeyā ṛṣayas tv iti.	(Cp. Sarv. Introduction ii. 2: śatarcina ādye maṇḍale, 'ntye kṣudrasūktamahāsūktā, madhyameṣu mādhyamāḥ.)
x. 45: Ārṣṭiṣeṇas tu Devāpiḥ.	vii. 155: Ārṣṭiṣeṇas tu Devāpiḥ.
x. 95: Prājāpatyasya suktaṃ tad 'apaśyaṃ tvā' Prajāvataḥ.	viii. 80^cd: Prājāpatyasya yat sūktam 'apaśyaṃ tvā' Prajāvataḥ.
x. 100–102: Godhā Ghoṣā Viśvavārā Apālopaniṣan Niṣat; Brahmajāyā Juhūr nāma, Agastyasya svasāditiḥ; Indrāṇī cendramātā ca Saramā Romaśorvaśī; Lopāmudrā ca Nadyaś ca Yamī nārī ca Śaśvatī; Śrīr Lākṣā Sārparājñī Vāk Śraddhā Medhā ca Dakṣiṇā; Rātrī Sūryā ca Sāvitrī brahmavādinya īritāḥ.	ii. 82–84: Ghoṣā Godhā Viśvavārā Apālopaniṣan Niṣat; Brahmajāyā Juhūr nāma, Agastyasya svasāditiḥ; Indrāṇī cendramātā ca Saramā Romaśorvaśī; Lopāmudrā ca Nadyaś ca Yamī nārī ca Śaśvatī Śrīr Lākṣā Sārparājñī Vāk Śraddhā Medhā ca Dakṣiṇā; Rātrī Sūryā ca Sāvitrī brahmavādinya īritāḥ.

4. ANUVĀKĀNUKRAMAṆĪ.

Anuvākānukramaṇī.	**Bṛhaddevatā.**
Anuv. 21: Gautamād Auśijaḥ, Kutsaḥ Paruchepād ṛṣeḥ paraḥ; Kutsād Dīrghatamā ity e- ṣa tu Bāṣkalakaḥ kramaḥ.	iii. 125: Gotamād Auśijaḥ, Kutsaḥ Paruchepād ṛṣeḥ paraḥ; Kutsād Dīrghatamāḥ, śaśvat te dve evam adhīyate.

5. ṚGVIDHĀNA.

Ṛgvidhāna.	**Bṛhaddevatā.**
i. 1. 1 : Namaskṛtvā mantradṛgbhyaḥ.	i. 1 : Mantradṛgbhyo namaskṛtvā
i. 1. 2 : samāmnāyānupūrvaśaḥ.	samāmnāyānupūrvaśaḥ.
iii. 8. 6 : Daśākṣaraṃ tu śāntyartham.	vii. 21 : Daśākṣaraṃ tu śāntyartham.
iii. 22. 3 : Sūryāyai bhāvavṛttaṃ tu.	vii. 123 : Sūryāyai bhāvavṛttaṃ tu.
iv. 1. 5 : Bṛhaspate pratīty etad.	viii. 7 : Bṛhaspate pratīty etad (A). Bṛhaspate pratīty ṛgbhiḥ (B).
iv. 24. 2 : Yathāśvamedhaḥ kraturāṭ sarvapāpāpanodanaḥ, tathāghamarṣaṇaṃ sūktaṃ sarvapāpāpanodanam. (*v. r.* °pāpapraṇoda°)	viii. 92^{cd}–93^{ab} : Yathāśvamedhaḥ kraturāṭ sarvariprapraṇodanaḥ, tathāghamarṣaṇaṃ brahma sarvariprapraṇodanam.

6. SARVĀNUKRAMAṆĪ.

Sarvānukramaṇī.	**Bṛhaddevatā.**
i. 3 : etāḥ praügadevatāḥ.	ii. 135 : etāḥ praügadevatāḥ.
i. 4 : surūpakṛtnuṃ (daśa) aindram.	ii. 139 : surūpakṛtnum ity aindram.
i. 12 : Pādo dvyagnidaivato nirmathyāhavanīyau.	ii. 145 : pādas tatra dvidevataḥ : nirmathyāhavanīyārthau.
i. 13 : iti pratyṛcaṃ devatāḥ.	ii. 146 : pratyṛcaṃ yās tu devatāḥ.
i. 14 : Aibhir vaiśvadevam.	iii. 33 : āgneyaṃ sūktam aibhir yad vaiśvadevam.
i. 18 : caturthyām Indraś ca Somaś ca pañcamyāṃ Dakṣiṇā ca.	iii. 68 : caturthyāṃ Soma Indraś ca pañcamyāṃ Dakṣiṇādhikā.
i. 23 : antyā adhyardhā āgneyī.	iii. 97 : adhyardhā antyā agnidevatā.

Sarvānukramaṇī	Bṛhaddevatā.
i. 24: ādau kāyyāgneyyau sāvitras tṛcaḥ . . . asyāntyā bhāgī vā.	iii. 98: kāyy ādyā, āgneyy ṛk, Savitus tṛcaḥ: 'bhagabhaktasya' bhāgī vā.
i. 40: ut tiṣṭha . . brāhmaṇaspatyam. i. 41: yaṃ rakṣanti nava Varuṇa-mitra͜aryamṇāṃ: madhye tṛca Ādityebhyaḥ.	iii. 107: ut tiṣṭha brāhmaṇaspatyaṃ, yaṃ rakṣanti trayas tṛcāḥ Varuṇa͜aryama-mitrāṇāṃ: madhya Ādityadaivataḥ.
i. 50: antyas tṛco rogaghnaḥ.	iii. 113: rogaghnas tṛca uttamaḥ.
i. 91: tvaṃ Soma . . . saumyam i. 92: etā u tyāḥ . . . uṣasyaṃ . . . tṛco 'ntya āśvinaḥ.	iii. 124: tvaṃ Soma saumyam, auṣasam etā u tyās, tṛco 'śvinoḥ.
i. 94: pūrvo devās trayaḥ pādā daivāḥ.	iii. 126 (A): pūrvo devā ity ṛco devadevās trayaḥ pādāḥ.
i. 95: dve . . . auṣasāya vāgnaye. i. 96: sa pratnathā . . . draviṇodase. i. 98: vaiśvānarasya . . . vaiśvānarīyam. i. 97: apa no . . . śucaye.	iii. 129: dve virūpe sūktam auṣasāgnaye sa pratnatheti draviṇodase 'gnaye. vaiśvānarasyeti vaiśvānarīyam; asmāt pūrvaṃ śucaye 'gnaye punaḥ.
i. 99: jātavedase . . . jātavedasyam; etadādīny ekabhūyāṃsi: sūktasahasram etat Kaśyapārṣam.	iii. 130 (B): jātavedasyaṃ sūktasahasram eke aindrāt pūrvaṃ Kaśyapārṣaṃ vadanti. jātavedase sūktam ādyaṃ tu teṣām: ekabhūyastvaṃ manyate Śākapūṇiḥ.
i. 108: Ya Indrāgnī . . . aindrāgnaṃ tu.	iii. 131: trīṇy, aindrāgne ya indrāgnī:
i. 110: tataṃ . . . ārbhavaṃ tu.	tatam ity ārbhave pare.
i. 114–115: imā . . . raudraṃ, citraṃ . . . sauryam.	iii. 139[a]: imā raudraṃ, paraṃ sauryaṃ citram.
i. 120: antyā duḥsvapnanāśinī.	iii. 139[d]: antyā duḥsvapnanāśinī.
i. 142: samiddha āpriyaḥ . . . antyaindrī.	iv. 16: samiddha āpriyo 'ntyaindrī.

Sarvānukramaṇī.	**Bṛhaddevatā.**
i. 164: alpastavaṃ tv etat.	iv. 43 (A): sūktam alpastavaṃ tv etat.
i. 164: gaurīr iti ... etadantaṃ vaiśvadevam.	iv. 42^{ab}(B): gaurīrantaṃ vaiśvadevam.
i. 164: Indraṃ Mitraṃ sauryau vāntyā Sarasvate Sūryāya vā.	iv. 42^{cd}(B): Indraṃ Mitram ime sauryau; saurī vāntyā Sarasvate.
i. 165: ayujo Marutām.	iv. 44: Marutām ayujaḥ.
i. 179: brahmacāry antye ... apaśyat.	iv. 59: brahmacāry uttame jagau.
i. 190: anarvāṇaṃ bārhaspatyam.	iv. 63: Bṛhaspater anarvāṇam.
ii. 29: dhṛtavratāḥ ... vaiśvadevam.	iv. 84: dhṛtavratā vaiśvadevam.
ii. 32: dve dve Rākā-Sinīvālyoḥ.	iv. 87: dve dve Rākā-Sinīvālyoḥ.
iii. 2, 4: vaiśvānarīyaṃ tu ... samit-samid āpriyaḥ.	iv. 96: vaiśvānarīye samit-samid āpryaḥ.
iii. 20: Agnim uṣasam (ādyāntye) vaiśvadevyau.	iv. 102: agnim uṣasaṃ vaiśvadevī.
iii. 53: abhiśāpās tā Vasiṣṭhadveṣiṇyaḥ, na Vasiṣṭhāḥ śṛṇvanti.	iv. 117^{d}, 118^{b}, 119^{a}: Vasiṣṭhadveṣiṇyaḥ smṛtāḥ, abhiśāpā iti smṛtāḥ, Vasiṣṭhās tā na śṛṇvanti.
iii. 58, 59, 60: Dhenur ... Mitraḥ ... iheha vaḥ.	iv. 122: dhenur mitra iheha vaḥ.
iv. 13: liṅgoktadaivataṃ tv eke.	iv. 129^{a}: liṅgoktadaivate sūkte, eke.
iv. 15: ṛṣir bodhad ity ābhyāṃ [*v.r.* dvābhyām] Somakaṃ Sāhadevyam abhyavadat.	iv. 129^{cd}: ṛṣir bodhad iti dvābhyāṃ stauti Somakam eva tu.
iv. 15: parābhyām asyāśvinau.	iv. 130^{b}: parābhyām Aśvinau stutau.
iv. 53, 55–57: tat ... sāvitraṃ tu ... ko vaiśvadevam ... mahī ... dyāvāpṛthivīyaṃ, kṣetrasya ... tisraḥ kṣaitrapatyāḥ.	v. 7^{a}: Tat sāvitre dve tu, ko vaiśvadevam; v. 7^{b}: mahī dyāvāpṛthivīyaṃ paraṃ tu yat, v. 7^{c}(B): kṣetrasyeti tisras tu kṣaitrapatyāḥ.

Sarvānukramaṇī.	Bṛhaddevatā.
iv. 58: sauryaṃ vāpaṃ vā gavyaṃ vā ghṛtastutir vā.	v. 11 [cd] Apāṃ stutiṃ vā yadi vā ghṛtastutiṃ gavyam eke sauryam etad vadanti.
v. 27: nātmātmane dadyāt.	v. 32[c] (B): ātmā hi nātmane dadyāt.
v. 61: Vaidadaśvī Taranta-Purumīḷhau.	v. 62[ab]: Taranta-Purumīḷhau tu rājānau Vaidadaśvī ṛṣī.
v. 85: pra samrāje . . . vāruṇam.	v. 89[cd]: vāruṇaṃ tu pra samrāje
v. 86: Indrāgnī . . . aindrāgnam.	indrāgnī aindrāgnam uttaram.
v. 87: pra vo . . . mārutam	v. 90[a]: Viṣṇunyaṅgaṃ paraṃ preti mārutam.
vi. 48: antyā Dyāvābhūmyor vā Pṛśner vā.	v. 114[d]: antyā Dyubhvoḥ kīrtanā Pṛśnaye vā.
vi. 68: śruṣṭī vām aindrāvaruṇam.	v. 121[c]: śruṣṭīti caindrāvaruṇam.
vi. 69: saṃ vām . . . aindrāvaiṣṇavam.	v. 121[d]: sam aindrāvaiṣṇavaṃ param.
i. 166: Mitrāvaruṇayor dīkṣitayor Urvaśīm apsarasaṃ dṛṣṭvā vāsatīvare kumbhe reto 'patat.	v. 149: tayor Ādityayoḥ sattre dṛṣṭvāpsarasam Urvaśīṃ retaś caskanda; tat kumbhe nyapatad vāsatīvare.
vii. 60: yad adya . . . saury ādyā.	vi. 5[ab]: yad adyaikot sūryas tisra
vii. 62: ut Sūryaḥ . . . tisraḥ sauryaḥ.	ud vetīty ardhapañcamāḥ
vii. 63: ud vetīti cārdhapañcamāḥ.	sauryaḥ.
vii. 66: caturthyādyā daśādityās, tisraḥ sauryaḥ.	vi. 8[ab] (B): yad adya sūra ity ādyā daśādityā ṛcaḥ smṛtāḥ.
	vi. 9[ab] (B): stutā ud u tyad ity etās tisra sauryas tataḥ parāḥ.
vii. 99: urum ity aindryaś ca tisraḥ.	vi. 25[c]: urum aindryaś ca tisraḥ syuḥ.
vii. 97: yajñe . . . aindryādi . . . anty aindrī ca,	vi. 26[cd] (B): yajña ādyendram evāstaut, antyā tv Indrābṛhaspatī;
tṛtīyānavamyāv aindrābrāhmaṇaspatye.	vi. 27[ab]: tṛtīyā navamī caiva stautīndrābrahmaṇaspatī.
vii. 104: aindrāsomaṃ rākṣoghnam.	vi. 27[d]: aindrāsomaṃ paraṃ tu yat;
	vi. 28[a]: ṛṣir dadarśa rākṣoghnam.

Sarvānukramaṇī.	**Bṛhaddevatā.**
vii. 104 : pra vartayeti pañcaindryaḥ ; mā no rakṣa ity ṛṣer ātmana āśīḥ.	vi. 31^{a} : pra vartayeti pañcaindryaḥ. vi. 31^{c} : ṛṣis tv āśiṣam āśāste vi. 31^{d} : mā no rakṣa iti tv ṛci.
viii. 5 : antyāḥ pañcārdharcāś Caidyasya Kaśor dānastutiḥ.	vi. 45^{cd} : ity ardharco dvṛcaś cāntyaḥ Kaśor dānastutiḥ smṛtā.
viii. 46 : pragāthau ca vāyavyau.	vi. 80^{c} : ā naḥ pragāthau vāyavyau.
viii. 47 : antyāḥ pañcoṣase 'pi.	vi. 83^{c} : antyāḥ pañcoṣase 'pi syuḥ.
viii. 68 : Ṛkṣāśvamedhayor dānastutiḥ.	vi. 92^{ab} : Ṛkṣāśvamedhayor atra pañca dānastutiḥ parāḥ.
viii. 72 : havīṣāṃ stutir vā.	vi. 93^{cd} : athavā sūktam uttaraṃ haviṣāṃ stutiḥ.
viii. 100 : ayaṃ te . . . Nemo Bhārgavaḥ.	vi. 117^{d} : Nemo 'yam iti Bhārgavaḥ.
viii. 101 : vāyavye sauryau . . . uṣasyā.	vi. 126^{c} : vāyavye saurye uṣasyā.
ix. 67 : sāvitry āgnisāvitrī vaiśvadevī.	vi. 132^{cd} : ubhābhyām iti sāvitrī āgnisāvitry ṛg uttarā, vi. 133^{a} : punantu māṃ vaiśvadevī.
x. 17 : dve Saraṇyūdevate.	vii. 7 : Saraṇyūdevate dvṛce.
x. 19 : agnīṣomīyo dvitīyo 'rdharcaḥ.	vii. 20^{cd} : ardharcaḥ prathamāyās tu agnīṣomīya uttaraḥ.
x. 25, 26 : bhadram . . . saumyam, pra hi . . . pauṣṇam.	vii. 23^{ab} : bhadraṃ saumyaṃ, pra hi pauṣṇam.
x. 33 : dve Kuruśravaṇasya Trāsadasyavasya dānastutiḥ . . . mṛte Mitrātithau rājñi tatsnehād ṛṣir Upamaśravasaṃ putram asya vyaśokayat.	vii. 35 : Kuruśravaṇam arcataḥ pare dve Trāsadasyavam. mṛte Mitrātithau rājñi tannapātam ṛṣiḥ paraiḥ vii. 36 : Upamaśravasaṃ 'yasya' caturbhiḥ sa vyaśokayat.
x. 47 : Vikuṇṭhā nāmāsurī, Indratulyaṃ putram ichantī, mahat tapas tepe ; tasyāḥ svayam evendraḥ putro jajñe. Sa Saptagustutisaṃhṛṣṭa ātmānam uttarais tribhis tuṣṭāva.	vii. 49 : Prājāpatyāsurī tv āsīd Vikuṇṭhā nāma nāmataḥ ; sechantīndrasamaṃ putraṃ tepe 'tha sumahat tapaḥ. vii. 50^{c} : tasyaṃ cendraḥ svayaṃ jajñe.

Sarvānukramaṇī.	Bṛhaddevatā.
	vii. 57 bcd: Saptagustutiharṣitaḥ, ātmānam eva tuṣṭāva aham bhuvam iti tribhiḥ.
x. 50: vaṣaṭkāreṇa vṛkṇeṣu bhrātṛṣu Saucīko 'gnir apaḥ praviśya.	vii. 61 cd: vaṣaṭkāreṇa vṛkṇeṣu bhrātṛṣu,
	vii. 62 b: Saucīko 'gnir iti śrutiḥ,
	vii. 62 c: sa prāviśad apakramya
	vii. 62 d: ṛtūn apo vanaspatīn.
x. 56: dvaipade tv Atrimaṇḍale.	vii. 86 b: dvaipadā ye 'trimaṇḍale.
x. 56: Aikṣvāko rājāsamātiḥ.	vii. 85 c: rājāsamātir Aikṣvākuḥ,
x. 56: Bandhvādīn purohitāṃs tyaktvā,	vii. 85 d: purohitān
	vii. 86 a: vyudasya Bandhuprabhṛtīn,
x. 56: anyau māyāvinau śreṣṭhatamau matvā purodadhe . . .	vii. 86 d: tato māyāvinau dvijau
	vii. 87 ab: Asamātiḥ puro 'dhatta: variṣṭhau tau hi manyate.
x. 56: . . bhrātaras trayaḥ	vii. 89 d: bhrātaras trayaḥ
mā pra gāmeti . . . svastyayanaṃ japtvā yat te yamam iti . . . mana-āvartanaṃ jepuḥ.	vii. 90: jepuḥ svastyayanaṃ sarve meti Gaupāyanāḥ saha; mana-āvartanaṃ tasya sūktaṃ yad iti te 'bhyayuḥ.
x. 60: ā janam iti . . . catasṛbhir Asamātim astuvan.	vii. 96: ṛgbhir eti catasṛbhis tata Aikṣvākum astuvan.
x. 60: Agastyasya svasā mātaiṣāṃ rājānam astaut (cp. Ārṣ. x. 24).	vii. 97 ab: Agastyasyeti mātā ca teṣāṃ tuṣṭāva taṃ nṛpam.
x. 60: Subandhor jīvam āhvayan.	vii. 100 d: Subandhor asum āhvayan.
x. 60: tam antyayā labdhasaṃjñam aspṛśan.	vii. 102 ab: labdhāsuṃ cāyam ity asyāṃ pṛthak pāṇibhir aspṛśan.
x. 62: ṣaḷ aṅgirasāṃ stutiḥ.	vii. 102 cd: ṣaḷ . . . aṅgirasāṃ stutiḥ.
x. 71: Bṛhaspatir jñānaṃ tuṣṭāva.	vii. 109 cd: taj jñānam abhituṣṭāva sūktenātha Bṛhaspatiḥ.
x. 81: Ya imāḥ . . . vaiśvakarmaṇam.	vii. 117 b: ya imā vaiśvakarmaṇe.
x. 98: Ārṣṭiṣeṇo Devāpiḥ (cp. Ārṣ. x. 45).	vii. 155 a: Ārṣṭiṣeṇas tu Devāpiḥ.

Sarvānukramaṇī.	Bṛhaddevatā.
x. 101: ud budhyadhvaṃ . . . ṛtvikstutiḥ.	viii. 10^{b}: ud ity ṛtvikstutiḥ param.
x. 103: āśuḥ . . . Aindro 'pratirathaś, caturthī bārhaspatyā.	viii. 13^{b} (B): Aindro 'pratiratho jagau. viii. 14^{a} (B): caturthī bārhaspatyā syāt.
x. 107: Dakṣiṇā vā Prājāpatyā.	viii. 22^{d}· Prājāpatyātha Dakṣiṇā. (Ārṣ. x. 50^{a}: Prājāpatyā Dakṣiṇā vā.)
x. 109: te 'vadan . . . Juhūr Brahmajāyā . . . vaiśvadevam.	viii. 36: te 'vadan vaiśvadevaṃ tu Brahmajāyā Juhūr jagau.
x. 124: Agnivaruṇasomānām.	viii. 41^{c}: Varuṇendrāgnisomānām.
x. 132: Ījānaṃ maitrāvaruṇam.	viii. 47^{a}: maitrāvaruṇam Ījānam.
x. 155: arāyi . . . alakṣmīghnam.	viii. 60^{a}: yad arāyīty alakṣmīghnam.
x. 157: imā nu kaṃ vaiśvadevam.	viii. 61^{d}: vaiśvadevam imā nu kam.
x. 164: apehi duḥsvapnaghnam.	viii. 67^{a}: duḥsvapnaghnam apehīti.
x. 166: ṛṣabham . . . sapatnagham.	viii. 69^{c}: ṛṣabhaṃ mā sapatnaghnam.
x. 170, 171: vibhrāṭ . . . sauryaṃ . . . tvaṃ tyam.	viii. 73^{a}: vibhrāṭ sauryaṃ tvaṃ tyam.
Sarv. Intr. ii. 7: arthepsava ṛṣayo devatāś chandobhir abhyadhāvan.	viii. 137^{abc} (A): arthepsavaḥ khalv ṛṣayaś chandobhir devatāḥ purā abhyadhāvan.

7. KĀTYĀYANA'S SARVĀNUKRAMAṆĪ OF THE VĀJASANEYI-SAṂHITĀ.

The passage in iv. 10 beginning athātaś chandodevatāḥ (Weber's ed. of the VS., p. lv) is based on BD. viii. 105–107^{ab}, 108^{cd}–111. The whole of one śloka, and parts of others, are metrically recognizable:

Sarvānukramaṇī.	Bṛhaddevatā.
iv. 10: sarvā ṛca āgneyyaḥ . . . . sāmāni saurāṇi sarvāṇi brāhmaṇāni ca.	viii. 110: samastā ṛca āgneyyo vāyavyāni yajūṃṣi ca; sauryāṇi caiva sāmāni sarvāṇi brāhmaṇāni ca.

VS. Sarvānukramaṇī.	Bṛhaddevatā.
Devatām avijñāya yo juhoti devatās tasya havir na juṣante.	viii. 131^{cd}: juṣante devatās tasya havir nādevatāvidaḥ.
saṃnyasya manasi devatāṃ havir hūyate.	viii. 132: avijñānapradiṣṭaṃ hi havir neheta daivatam. tasmān manasi saṃnyasya devatāṃ juhuyād dhaviḥ.
svādhyāyam api yo 'dhīte mantradaivatajñaḥ, so 'muṣmin loke devair apīḍyate.	viii. 133: svādhyāyam api yo 'dhīte mantradaivatavic chuciḥ, sa sattrasad iva svarge sattrasadbhir apīḍyate.
Tasmāc ca devatā vedyā mantre mantre prayatnataḥ: mantrāṇāṃ devatājñānān mantrārtham adhigachati.	i. 2: Veditavyaṃ daivataṃ hi mantre mantre prayatnataḥ: daivatajño hi mantrāṇāṃ tadartham avagachati.
na hi kaścid avijñāya yāthātathyena devatāḥ śrautānāṃ karmaṇāṃ vipraḥ smārtānāṃ cāśnute phalam.	i. 4: na hi kaścid avijñāya yāthātathyena daivataṃ laukyānāṃ vaidikānāṃ vā karmaṇāṃ phalam aśnute.

8. BHAGAVADGĪTĀ.

Bhagavadgītā.	Bṛhaddevatā.
viii. 17^{ab}: sahasrayugaparyantam ahar yad brahmaṇo viduḥ.	viii. 98^{cd}: sahasrayugaparyantam ahar brāhmaṃ sa rādhyate.
Ṣaḍguruśiṣya, p. 167, 9^{cd}: sahasrayugaparyantam ahar yad brāhmam ucyate.	

9. HEMACANDRA'S ABHIDHĀNACINTĀMAṆI.

Abhidhānacintāmaṇi.	Bṛhaddevatā.
Last śloka, p. 443, ed. Böhtlingk: Iyanta iti saṃkhyānaṃ nipātānāṃ na vidyate: prayojanavaśād ete nipātyante pade pade.	ii. 93: Iyanta iti saṃkhyānaṃ nipātānāṃ na vidyate: vaśāt prakaraṇasyaite nipātyante pade pade.

VII. INDEX OF SANSKRIT WORDS AND NAMES.

[N.B.—Finite Verbal Forms, simple and compound, are given under the root; participles, gerunds, infinitives, simple and compound, in their alphabetical order.]